Barbed-Wire Surgeon

Barbed-Wire Surgeon

By Alfred A. Weinstein, M.D.

Deeds Publishing | Atlanta

Published by Deeds Publishing
Marietta, GA
www.deedspublishing.com
www.alfredweinstein.com

Printed in The United States of America

Library of Congress Cataloging-in-Publications Data is available upon request.

ISBN 978-1-937565-96-1

Books are available in quantity for promotional or premium use. For information,
write Deeds Publishing, PO Box 682212, Marietta, GA 30068 or
info@deedspublishing.com

Third Edition, 2014

First Edition, 1948, The Macmillan Company
Second Edition, 1965, Lancer

10 9 8 7 6 5 4 3 2 1

To Hanna

WHOSE LOVE KEPT A SPARK
OF LIFE FLICKERING IN A
DYING BODY

CONTENTS

FOREWORD

BARBED-WIRE SURGEON **WAS ORIGINALLY PUBLISHED** in hardcover in 1948 and paperback in 1965. During that time, my grandfather Alfred's best-selling book enjoyed eight printings and was a selection of the popular Book-of-the-Month Club. It is unique in that Al began writing it almost immediately after arriving home from his release as a POW in the Philippines and Japan. Due to this, the level of detail is remarkable. I also find it quite interesting that while his body was beginning to heal itself from the physical deprivation and abuse it suffered, he felt compelled to relive these experiences so soon after his release as a prisoner. I suppose that by doing so, he also began the long journey of emotional healing that one might desperately need in order to cope with such unimaginable trauma.

Unfortunately, Al passed away in 1964, a full six years before I was born. Since we never met, I consider myself extremely lucky to have his writings to bring me closer to him. Not many people have that opportunity. Luckily, my grandmother, Hanna, lived until 1999. I was able to spend time with her throughout my life and have numerous interesting conversations. She didn't talk much about her past, but she was always interested in discussing current events. As an Austrian refugee, she escaped Europe and survived the war in Manila, then lived a long life in Atlanta, Georgia. They both not only live on in the memories of my family, but in the lives of the people they touched.

Initially, my family and I had discomfort with some of the terms that Al used when referring to the Japanese in the book such as "Jap" and "Nip." We thought about changing these. However, they are a reflection of the time in which *Barbed-Wire Surgeon* was written as well as being one more representation of the relationship between prisoners and those who captured and abused them. We also feel that making such wholesale changes to the book would affect the integrity of the story as told by Al. Personally, I didn't feel like I had the right to make these changes. We are most proud of the fact that later in his life, Al returned to Japan on a trip of reconciliation. Additionally, he spent his life standing up for equality and speaking out against prejudice.

Briefly, I would like to acknowledge my father, Ron; aunt Elsa; and uncle Mack for allowing me the privilege of republishing *Barbed-Wire Surgeon*. I also want to thank Professor Sharon Delmendo for planting the seed and encouraging me to take on the project. Her interest and research in Al and Hanna's life story has not only cemented her role as the de facto Weinstein family historian, but has exposed me to many facts that I had previously not known. Lastly, I greatly appreciate Nelson Logan, a one-time patient of Al's, for his assistance and persistence through the years in wanting to see this book republished.

In honor of my grandparents, Dr. Alfred and Hanna Weinstein, we are grateful for the opportunity to share *Barbed-Wire Surgeon* once again.

- Brian Weinstein

INTRODUCTION

I WROTE A STORY. I had to write it. Every fiber of a brain and body which had survived forty months in Japanese prison camps cried out for it. It had to be written from memory. I had written four diaries. They were all destroyed. The first I buried under the lonesome pine towering over Little Baguio, Bataan, in the Philippines, the night before we surrendered to the Japs in April, 1942. I returned to that encampment, overgrown by jungle, three and a half years later. Tropical rains had mildewed the diary and red ants had eaten it.

Before I was packed into a Jap prison ship in March, 1944, I gave a second diary to Lieutenant Dick Hedrick, operator of our secret radio at Cabanatuan Prison, north of Manila. I have never heard from him. I don't know if he is still alive. The third diary I tore up when the Nip secret police, the Kempei Tai, raided Shinagawa prisoner-of-war hospital in Tokyo, searching for a short-wave radio set with which they were convinced we were sending news of Jap ship movements to the States. The last one I destroyed before I was sent to Omori Punishment Camp in Tokyo in the summer of 1944. But the experiences of these forty months were indelibly seared into my brain. I needed no diary.

This is the story of a group of doctors, dentists, nurses, and medics who continued to fight the Japs after the surrender of Bataan and Corregidor. They were fighting battles in which flattery, knavery, infinite patience, and a painfully acquired knowledge of Jap psychology were their only weapons in their struggle to keep a spark of life flickering in their fellow prisoners. They fought for more medicine and food for the sick and less body-bruising work for the well. The fight went on month after month, year after year, while we waited ever so impatiently for Uncle Sam to take us home alive. It is a story of tiny gains and many losses, heartbreaking and body-crushing rebuffs, while prisoners died who could have been saved. Many of these doctors and medics died fighting their battle; others were beaten and tortured by the Japs for their devotion to their ideals; still others, riddled with tuberculosis and beriberi, survived to be liberated.

This is a story of G.I. Joe in prison: how he lived, how he adjusted himself to life under the Nips, what he thought about and what he dreamed about. They were a motley, ragged, hungry throng. Under an ugly patina of filth and starvation, their basic individualities continued to glow feebly and occasionally to break forth into flame. Some were rugged, some were weak. As the months faded into years, the feeble faded out of the picture. In the witch's caldron of a Jap prison, G.I. Joe fought for his life with all the breaks against him.

Against a somber tapestry of chronic hunger, starvation, and disease, a thin golden thread of the love of a man and woman weaves back and forth. It disappears for months and years, but is ever present. It snaps and breaks, but reappears more vibrant and glowing. Can a woman's love for her man be responsible for the survival of individuality in the face of pestilence and torture?

In its broader aspects this is a tale of mankind with his veneer of civilization stripped away.

In this story an attempt is made to portray the behavior of thousands of men who were faced with the acute danger of disintegration of body, mind, personality, and spirit in a Jap prison camp. Does man continue to love his brother when steeped in disease, chronic starvation, and death? Why did the Japs behave like Japs? How much punishment can man take before he loses his divine spark of humaneness? What role did the minister and the priest play in keeping that spark flickering? How low in animal-like behavior can man sink and still revert to manliness?

These were the questions imposed upon twenty-two thousand American soldiers captured in Bataan and Corregidor. This book, in so far as I have been able to do so, contains some of the answers offered by one of the four thousand fortunate survivors.

PROLOGUE

Down the last hundred yards of winding street Captain Kaufman and I trudged, soaked with perspiration and streaked with dirt. We turned the last corner and could see a stretch of canal separating the low-lying manmade island on which Omori Headquarters Camp rested. We stopped at the foot of a rickety, humpbacked, wooden footbridge which spanned this canal.

"Yasume Ka?" we asked the guard. (May we rest?)

"Ush," he said, flashing a gaping mouth full of gold-plated teeth at us.

It was a placid scene, far removed from prison life and war. On the right in the distance was a forest of chimneys belching black clouds of smoke which floated lazily upward. Interspersed were clusters of flat squat oil reservoirs and larger gas tanks. Behind was a gently swelling hill covered with deeply tinted, green towering pine trees through whose spreading branches we could see the sun reflecting from the white walls of a great mansion, the home of one of the members of the royal house. Far off to the left were the huge, rambling two-story barracks of the naval training station filled with thousands of would-be admirals. In the canal, about as wide as a football field, were several small skiffs drifting idly with the tide. One of them near us was filled with four Nip versions of the American Huckleberry Finn. Grasping their poles, they watched their lines to detect the first evidence of a bite. A sudden jerk and up came a flashing silver-gray fingerling. Triumphantly, young Huckleberry Moto rebaited his hook and slouched back on his haunches.

"Owari!" barked the guard. (Finished!) Shouldering our packs again, we shuffled over the footbridge past several acres of garden where pumpkin vines, peanuts, soybeans and eggplants were eking out a stunted, miserable living from the barren, sandy, shell-covered soil. We entered the acre-large compound which housed six hundred Allied prisoners, some of whom passed us silently without a glance of welcome or recognition. We were led to the administration building. There we dropped our luggage in front of the office, more commonly called the "cage," which housed the official disciplinarian, Corporal Watanabi. We learned later to refer to him as the "Bird," "Wily Bird," "Mr. Adam" or the "Animal."

A question we were to hear repeated time and time again among the prisoners in this prison was: "What's the position?"

The reply would be either: "The Animal is in his cage," in which case we all relaxed and breathed easily for a short respite, or: "The Animal is on the prowl," whereupon we buckled down to our work and waited tensely for the Animal to strike.

In the office, ready to greet us, were Cato Chui (Lieutenant Cato), Watanabi, and Nishino San (Mr. Nishino). Lieutenant Cato was camp commandant, a wizened, dark-faced Nip with thick glasses, closely set, shifty eyes, pudgy nose, and loose slobbering lips. Watanabi was a well-built Nip about five foot seven, with sturdily built shoulders surmounted by a well modeled head and features almost Occidental in type. His face was marred only by a slight cast to the eyes which became intensified when he flew into a rage. Dressed in a white jacket and trousers like an ice-cream salesman, he gazed at us, a wry, sardonic smile on his handsome face. I made a mental note that he didn't look as bad as his reputation. The most obsequious Nishino looked more like the prewar Hollywood version of a Westernized Nip. Slim, slant-eyed, thin-lipped, with long hair well pomaded, he started off the proceedings by interpreting Lieutenant Cato's speech.

"You two have been sent to this camp because you have a bad attitude and are arrogant. Our reports say you have refused to cooperate with the Nipponese authorities and have disobeyed the orders of officers of the Imperial Nipponese Army. You are on our official black list."

Grinning, he added: "It is our duty to teach you discipline and impress upon you that you are prisoners and must obey all orders of the Nipponese even should they emanate from a third class private. We forgive you for your past offenses and hope you will be obedient here. Unfortunately, we have enough doctors in this camp and so you will not do professional work. You will not be treated as doctors. You will do physical labor similar to that done by other prisoner officers. Do you understand?"

"Hai (Yes)!" we both shouted in the best Japanese style.

"You will now stand at attention until Corporal Watanabi is ready to inspect your luggage."

We stood at the Nip version of attention, head erect, eyes staring, body stiff, all fingers of hands extended and pressed hard toward the thighs. This began at ten o'clock. The Bird sat in his office in front of us, sneaking a look at us out of his slant eyes from time to time. At noon, a guard approached, leading Private First Class McDermit, one of our medics who had come with us from Manila and was working at Shinagawa prisoner-of-war hospital. Laboring in the supply department as he did, he often made trips to Omori under guard to haul necessities back to the hospital.

The guard had words with the Bird. His face tightened and darkened with anger. Flinging himself out of his chair he dashed out of the building to McDermit.

In pidgin English he demanded: "Why did you leave our supply room to go to the latrine?"

"I wanted to give some pepper and salt to one of my friends here," McDermit answered, stiffening his bony, five-foot-three frame to attention.

"Ah, so ka?" the Bird answered softening. "It is kind and noble of you to share your food with your friend. I admire you, but," face darkening again, "it is against my orders for you to communicate with anyone in this camp."

Lifting a haymaker from the ground, he knocked McDermit cold with his clenched fist, turned on his heel and reentered his office.

After a few minutes, eyes still glazed, McDermit picked himself up and staggered away.

Life was vastly different two and a half years earlier…

CHAPTER 1.
Flight from Manila

THE WAR STARTED FOR US at Fort Mckinley, Manila, on December 8, 1941, with a sickening roar of exploding bombs as Nip planes droned overhead, leveling our air installations at adjacent Nichols Field. In the hysteria that flooded the fort, two Filipino infantry regiments, camped on the golf course in front of our quarters, opened up with everything from machine guns to forty-fives against enemy planes fifteen thousand feet overhead. Green and red tracer bullets squirted through the air in cascades that were picturesque until they tore their way through the roof of our own quarters with an ugly ripping sound. We flattened out on the floor of the veranda and lay there watching the show until the last wave of bombers had dropped its load and disappeared. Then, with helmets bobbing and gas masks flopping, we made a dash for the hospital several blocks away.

This was a two-story stucco building surrounded by graceful verandas and protected by a deep, red-tile roof with a lazy Spanish pitch. Shaded by flame trees, covered by winding, flowering ivy, and fronting the green of the golf course, it served as a temporary home for three hundred Filipino and American patients from the fort and the post of Manila. Half of them had succumbed to the fleshy lure of the Orient and were under treatment for contributions made to them by long black-haired, gentle-voiced, soft-skinned little brown sisters.

As we scrambled toward the operating pavilion, we heard the wail of ambulance sirens in the direction of Carabao Gate.

The medics carried the first load of wounded into stifling operating rooms flooded with glaring lights. They were rapidly sorted into two groups: those who could wait, and the acute emergencies who were still bleeding. Silence hung heavy. No bellowing, whimpering or shrieks of pain.

I didn't know how to explain the quiet. It may have been because the wounded were all slugged with a heavy dose of morphine before they arrived in a rear installation where definitive surgery was done, or because they were too exhausted by a long ambulance ride to voice their agony. It may have been that after the first sharp, searing pain, their nervous system was dulled; that they experienced overpowering relief on finally arriving alive at a hospital. It may have been because of release of nervous tension following the realization that they were wounded and need no longer expose themselves to sudden death from further enemy action. It may have been a combination of all these factors and others I couldn't visualize.

Nurses administered morphine. Medics deftly cut away clothing from the casualties. They scrubbed dirt and grease from the depths of jagged wounds with gauze soaked in diluted green-soap solution. They rinsed the wounds with liters of saline. Steady-handed anesthetists drove long, glistening needles into the naked backs of the wounded. Pints of rich, red, life-giving blood followed by blood plasma poured into exsanguinated patients.

A young Filipino soldier was on the operating table. He had been hit in the abdomen by a bomb fragment. Through a jagged wound below the belly button a loop of glistening intestine, covered with oozing blood, peeped out.

"How do you feel, Joe?"

"I do not understand very well English, sir," he whispered like a child phrasing a sentence which has no meaning.

"Mazakeet, Joe?" (Painful?)

He smiled wanly at the familiar phrase. *"Au-Au,"* he replied. (Yes, sir.)

"You'll be O.K. Want to see the priest?"

"Mabuti po," he whispered, his long eyelashes fluttering. (Thank you, sir.)

While ruddy-faced Father Dugan of Boston administered last rites, a lifesaving procedure was attempted. Contused skin and muscle about an ugly wound were rapidly trimmed away with scissors and scalpel. The wound was enlarged quickly upward and downward to expose more adequately the interior of the abdomen, which was filled with clotted and liquid blood and feces. This was sponged and scooped out rapidly, revealing a spurting blood vessel where the small bowel joins the large near the appendix. We all breathed easier after a clamp was placed on it. In a deliberate and methodical manner we studied all organs in the lower abdomen, including each loop of small and large bowel, to determine the extent of the injury. A chunk of bomb fragment about the size of a half dollar had made four perforations in the small gut and was found imbedded in the muscles of the posterior abdominal cavity. Through one of the perforations a round worm about the size of an American earthworm could be seen crawling.

We were later to find that worm infestation among Americans and Filipinos was widespread. We learned to conduct a worm hunt in all abdominal surgery. I once found six wriggling free in the abdominal cavity. I haven't any idea of the number I missed. It must have been large.

We sutured the holes with a double layer of atraumatic intestinal catgut, packed the belly with twenty grams of sulfathiazole powder, put a rubber drain in place, and closed the belly wound. A quick change of gloves and gown and Colonel Adamo and I went to work again. All operating tables remained loaded until about 3:00 A.M., when the last operation was completed. Physically weary and mentally unstrung, I went to the toilet and puked up everything I had eaten.

During the next few days we operated constantly. One of our patients was an aviator whose observation plane was shot down by our own troops, who thought he was a Jap. He parachuted near the hospital. Working his rope controls wildly, he pendu-

lumed back and forth to avoid being hit by our own men whose
nerves were so wracked by constant bombing that they fired at
anything in the air.

"I'll never go duck hunting again," he muttered mournfully
as we dressed the flesh wound on his shoulder.

On December 13, our commanding officer, Colonel Duckworth, said grimly: "We are taking over a number of large buildings in Manila to accommodate ten thousand anticipated casualties. A small group of medics will remain here at Fort McKinley.
The others will be distributed between the Philippine Women's
University, the Normal School, La Salle College, Holy Cross,
Sternberg, Jai Alai, and Santa Escolástica. You will report to your
destination today. That is all."

Genial Lieutenant Gus Laudicina of St. Louis and I drew
the last assignment, a cloistered Catholic girls' school in Pasay, a
southern suburb of Manila near the bayside. It was an L-shaped
two-story building recently constructed of concrete and red-
dish-tinted limestone. Of Spanish design with barred windows,
red-tiled floor and roof, its sweeping colonnaded verandas faced
inward toward a huge flowering patio.

The sisters greeted us warmly. They worked with us through
the long hours of tropical nights, transforming their teaching
institution into a hospital. I shall long remember the soothing
rustle of their garments and the cool sweetness of their voices
as they went about their duties. Many of them were destined
to be raped and slaughtered by the Nips before the recapture of
Manila. Under tightlipped Colonel Fields of the dental corps we
worked furiously, setting up an operating pavilion and general
hospital for a thousand patients. Our chaplain, a reservist, was
Father Cummings, a Mariposan brother who had taught philosophy and history in Manila for eleven years. Tall, ruddy and cor-
pulent, cheerful and worldly, he loved mankind and was beloved
by those who came under the magic of his warm, pulsating kind-
liness. We organized the detachment and patients' mess, the admission setup for casualties, the operating pavilions. We loaded
classrooms, halls, and hallways with row upon row of new metal

cots covered with gleaming white linen. We had just breathed a sigh of relief and settled down comfortably in our quarters when new orders arrived.

"A small medical detachment will remain at Santa Escolástica. All others will be distributed to help set up other hospital units."

Growling, grumbling, cussing and stewing, Gus and I loaded our personal effects in my Chrysler coupe. Away we went to our next station, the Women's Normal School near the new sky-scraping City Hall on Dewey Boulevard. We drove past the rusting hulks of Spanish warships sunk in the Spanish-American War to a three-story, dirty white-brick building that smelled of chalk, turpentine floors, and dried urine. Dozens of graceful, soft-voiced Filipino nurses were busily engaged in scrubbing walls, floors, and furniture. Captain Jimmy Bruce was in charge, a tiny, chirping, fighting cock of a man who made up in spirit and initiative what he lacked in size. The next few days were a confusion of dirt, bedbugs that raised hell with our sleep, and masses of hospital equipment that had to be lugged and sorted. As usual, help was short, but everyone pitched in regardless of rank.

Then we were on the move once more, this time to Jai Alai, the exquisite modernistic building nearby, which I had visited frequently before the war. Its Keg Room and restaurant were no longer filled with tipplers. In their place we feverishly installed an extensive X-ray setup and operating pavilion. The Fronton Pavilion no longer resounded with the sharp crack of a hard rubber ball against the wall and the roar of the crowds. On its highly polished floor rested hundreds of surgical beds waiting to receive their loads of wounded. Only the weaving ghosts of brilliantly dressed men and women danced to the strains of the tango in the air-conditioned ballroom where we set up our cots and wearily dropped into deep slumber at the end of the day.

After a backbreaking day of labor, life at Jai Alai had its compensations.

"What will it be, Gus," I asked Laudicina as we looked from the third floor over the serried rows of empty spectators' seats that sloped down to the Fronton Pavilion, "turkey or filet mignon?"

He gravely laid his finger against his temple, "Make mine a filet."

"You know, the cold storage plant which was a part of Jai Alai has been turned over to the army with the building itself," I told him. "I've got it right from the horse's mouth that there's a ton of Stateside steak, a half ton of turkey and five hundred pounds of Maine lobster stored there. What about that?"

"Make mine a double filet."

It was really a swell deal, a soldier's dream come true. We got permission to organize an officers' mess, retaining the same swank cook and waiters natty in their green and white uniforms. They were only too glad to stay, for they had no place to go. For several days we gorged ourselves on onion and mushroom soups, Kansas City steaks, broiled lobster and dainty Viennese pastry, all served on snowy linen gleaming with silver.

It was too good to last. Rumor had it that the chief of the combined Manila hospital units put the kibosh on it. The order came two days later that we had to eat field rations. There was an explosion in the kitchen when our temperamental chef refused to cook corned willy, baked beans, meat and vegetable stew, and canned soup.

"I have trained in the art of cooking too long to degenerate into a hash slinger," he shouted.

He was replaced, but even the Filipino waiters were apologetic as they dished out the lowly army viands on the splendid service.

"What does that dumb bastard expect to do with this cold-storage chow when we retreat into Bataan?" he raged.

I don't know who was responsible for the order, but we had our suspicions. When we pulled up stakes on December 23rd, this Heaven-sent food was abandoned to the Nips. I was especially miserable about the loss of the lobster, which I can eat three times a day. In the dismal years to come, my most devastating nightmares concerned themselves with trying to scale a high wall which enclosed mountains of this food.

We waited for the storm to break over us, whiling away the little spare time we had playing bridge for huge stakes. We listened tensely to the radio.

"Help is on the way," was the constant refrain.

All we had to do was hold the enemy in Lingayen Bay where they had made their initial landing, and we would be reinforced. The Nips were bombing continuously, concentrating on the airfields in the vicinity of Manila and the shipping installations in the port area. Casualties, which were light, were being routed to Sternberg Hospital for the present. Our quarters were good, chow plentiful, and spirits high, but nerves were violin-string taut.

The telephone rang. "We're sending you a patient with acute appendicitis."

An ambulance rolled up a few minutes later. A Filipino soldier, strapped to the litter and apparently writhing in pain, was unloaded on the operating table. We couldn't get a straight story out of him. Either he understood no English or was wildly incoherent with the toxemia of his disease. A hasty examination was made. A nurse administered morphine. After it took effect he received a spinal anesthesia. His belly was painted with iodine and draped with sterile linen. As the surgeons completed their "scrub" and prepared to don operating gowns, the phone rang again.

A medical orderly dashed into the room. "That guy is a nut," he said breathlessly, pointing to the linen-swathed body. "The ambulance brought him here by mistake. He's supposed to be delivered to the La Salle Psychopathic Hospital."

We never received or found out what happened to our patient with the inflamed appendix. As a matter of fact, the only patient we treated in this most elaborate receiving and evacuation center was not a war casualty. A G.I. fell off a truck just outside Jai Alai and suffered an anterior dislocation of the hip.

On the same day the ominous news broke that we were to move again, this time to jungle-bound Bataan. I had only one consolation: as part of the forward echelon I'd miss the heart-breaking, back-bruising task of ripping up and transporting the equipment we had installed at Jai Alai.

That evening I went to say good-bye to Herr and Frau Kaunitz, their son Fred and daughter Hanna, Viennese refugees who had arrived in Manila in 1938. Gentle, worldly, and hospitable, they were one of the few contacts with normal living I had in prewar, lustful, hurly-burly Manila. I unloaded my old-style tin helmet, gas mask, and pistol with a sigh of relief. I was especially glad to get rid of the forty-five. In fact I was scared stiff of it and always carried it empty with the clip of cartridges in my pocket.

After dinner Hanna and I drove slowly through blacked-out Manila. The streets were deserted except for army vehicles moving slowly with their hooded blue lights. Through the heart of the city we crawled until the broad expanse of Manila Bay lay before us shimmering in the light of a full tropical moon. In the distance we watched a pillar of fire ascending from the burning oil depots of Cavite Navy Yard, wrecked by the Japanese bombers earlier in the day. The crackle of small-arms fire echoed through the still air as fifth columnists took potshots at patrolling G.I.'s.

Along the silver-spun south road bordering the Laguna de Bai we rolled through the coconut country toward wind-swept Tagaytay Ridge twenty miles away. Stopped repeatedly by patrols and slowed down by roadblocks, it was midnight before we arrived and parked at the summit of the ridge overlooking volcanic Lake Taal.

We talked quietly of many things: our first meeting, the last dance we had been to, and all the other things in between. It had been fun, and now, I knew, much more than that. There was a sudden pause in our reminiscent chatter, as though we both knew we had been trying to stall for time, to hang on to the past, desperately.

But the present had to be acknowledged. I told Hanna that the army was pulling out of Manila and heading for Bataan.

Her only answer was a tightening of her arms around my neck. We said nothing: there was nothing more to say, in words. The Southern Cross rose high in the starlit sky and tilted back into the ocean again. The first rays of the sun tinted the China Sea before Hanna and I drifted back into Manila. I wondered when and if I would see her again.

CHAPTER 2.
Limay : On The Shores
of Manila Bay

LIEUTENANT GUS LAUDICINA AND I drove slowly in the Chrysler through the ever thickening traffic. We eased down Dewey Boulevard toward the center of town. Trucks, staff cars, pot-bellied Pambusco busses and jeeps honked irritably at slower moving vehicles. Cocheros perched precariously on two-wheeled, gaily-striped red and green caratelas (wagons), lashed their silver-spangled, frothing miniature ponies. Stolid, heavy-shouldered carabaos with wide-spreading curved horns plodded along, dragging low-slung carts supported by huge rumbling wooden wheels. Tiny yellow Austin-like taxis darted back and forth through the tangled mess. Jangling streetcars loaded with a teaming mass of brown-faced people crawled by. Vehicles were heaped with household goods, trunks, pet fighting cocks, raucous lamp shades, and fat-bellied babies. The inhabitants of Manila fled from a doomed city.

We finally broke loose on Rizal Avenue and scooted north, leaving behind huge movie palaces, department stores, and novelty shops, empty, silent, and boarded. Past the confines of the Chinese cemetery, with its temples for the dead and its Buddha-like statues, we drove to the Balintawak Monument which commemorated the Filipino struggle against Spanish rule. We emerged into the flat, dry rice country with its meandering Pampanga River in which herds of carabao were blissfully soaking their huge carcasses, and went on to San Fernando City, where we bought a hastily prepared lunch and the store's supply of Coca Cola. At this most important rail and road junction, we turned sharply west and entered the forbidding realm of the Bataan Peninsula, which we had come to know by name only, as the home of man-killing, estivo-autumnal malaria. We rattled down the narrow, rocky coastal road bordering the eastern confines of Bataan through bamboo thickets and coconut groves. The jungle on our right grew thicker and more confining with its huge vine-covered, spreading trees and matted underbrush. Through the heart of the peninsula reared a serrated, heavily foliaged range, similar to the North Georgia Mountains, that terminated in towering Mount Sumat, from which the landscape dwindled to flat country at the tip of the peninsula.

The road sign at a collection of tiny bamboo shacks mounted on high stilts read "Limay." Round-eyed children stared at us as we turned the car sharply down a winding dirt road, heading toward the beach and our new home.

It was a striking contrast to the air-conditioned, gracefully constructed beauty of Jai Alai. Formerly used to house Filipino Scouts on maneuvers, these single-story, clapboard, tin-roofed buildings, accommodating eighty cots apiece, were laid out in a spacious quadrangle, eight on each side. On the far side, adjacent to a native barrio (village), we would establish the mess and nurses' quarters. At the near end, completing the square, we would erect the operating pavilion. Fronting the beach was a huge, tin covered warehouse, stuffed with war-reserve medical supplies. The enclosure itself was dotted with lofty, shiny, green-leafed mango trees loaded with fruit not yet ripe.

I thought it was a lousy-looking setup and said as much to Gus.

"Not too bad, Al. Flush toilets, plenty of water, tons of medical equipment, a cool breeze blowing in from the beach, and a village close by where we ought to be able to do a little trading."

Gus was always like this, optimistic and determinedly cheerful, even during the imprisonment that was to come —even to his final day of anguish on a Jap prison ship.

Later that afternoon the rest of the medical complement rumbled in on busses and trucks. To avoid any misconception on the part of the Nip observation plane, "Photo Joe," buzzing overhead, we hoisted a Red Cross flag and painted a huge red cross on bed sheets spread in the center of the compound. We spent a busy eighteen hours unloading trucks and emptying the warehouse. We counted noses and found we had about a hundred medics, fifty American and Filipino nurses, and forty doctors. A hell of a lot of people, I thought. We were to learn differently in the near future.

I had been with our commanding officer Colonel James Duckworth, or the "Duck" as we called him, since I arrived in the Philippines in July, 1941. More than six feet tall, with square head, powerful jaw, piercing eyes, and massive body, he was not a man to be monkeyed with. Throughout a lifetime spent in the army, he was known as a determined, positive character who called a spade a spade regardless of the consequences to himself. Never a soft-soap artist, he was not loved by his men, but he was respected and obeyed. I myself was fond of him and admired his clear-thinking, administrative ability. He didn't mince words. He gave you a job to do and expected it to be done. Neither did he fuddy-duddy about and get in your hair while you were working. He took it for granted that his men had brains and let them solve their problems in their own manner.

Second in command was Colonel Adamo, M.C., chief of all professional services. He was slender and delicately built, with gentle eyes and flecks of white about his temples. After working his way through medical school by rolling cigars with his deft, supple fingers in a Tampa factory, he had spent years in post-graduate work studying brain surgery. Put in charge of the limited surgical facilities of the Tampa City Hospital, he trained himself to be a one-man operating team. This training was soon to save hundreds of American lives on Bataan.

A new acquisition, Commander Smith, a surgeon from Cavite Navy Yard, was Chief of Surgery. He was a solemn, thin-faced man with inexhaustible stamina and courage. I was to see him operate quietly and efficiently twenty-four hours at a time without a break. He was high-strung, but he never cracked up. He never pushed his subordinates around. He was an especially steadying influence on me, and I needed plenty of steadying.

I used many means of staying on an even keel. I had given up smoking several years before the war because of a chronic cough, and missed it terribly as the war progressed. Foraging for a sub-stitute up and down the Bataan Peninsula, I bought up stacks of chewing gum at fabulous prices. This cud-chewing helped con-siderably. I also learned that swearing was a good way to let off steam while Nip planes were dropping eggs in the vicinity. With the many nationalities represented in camp, I learned to cuss flu-ently in English, Tagalog, Spanish, Italian, and Yiddish. Wear-ing a baker's hat (for some reason we found very few operating caps in the warehouse), sporting a long mustache, chewing gum steadily, letting fly with an incessant stream of invectives against the Nips, I made a sorry professional figure. I believe many of my corpsmen thought I was nuts. I didn't give a damn because it was one way I could keep my mental equilibrium when the going got rough.

Life was placid during those first days. The fighting was still north of Manila and casualties were still being routed to Stern-berg Hospital in that city. But the war clouds could be seen roll-ing closer. Day after day we saw flights of Nip bombers making their run over Allied shipping in the harbor. There was an aban-doned five-thousand-ton Norwegian freighter anchored about a mile off shore that seemed to have a charmed life. Although rid-ing high and obviously empty, the Nips dropped load after load, trying to sink it. We could see huge geysers spouting fore and aft as she rocked crazily back and forth. A bomb finally landed amidships and up she went in a blaze of fire. But she didn't sink.

Across the bay one night, the horizon was illuminated by a dull red glare. Thirty miles away we saw columns of fire and smoke leaping skyward as the oil and gasoline dumps in Manila were destroyed. This flaming picture of destruction, more than any other, impressed us with the fact that we were in the soup. The city was being abandoned and we were locked up tight on Bataan.

I went foraging, buying as much food as I could in the provincial capital of Balanga north of us, and stored as much as I could in my car. Canned meat, fish, vegetables, and fruits made the basis of many a midnight party when we again retreated southward to Little Baguio. The day before Christmas, weary of enforced inactivity, Gus and I bounced northward again in my car to kill some time.

There was little traffic on the road except for an occasional truck and carabao cart plodding down the narrow rocky road. Thoughts of my last Christmas in Atlanta, spiced with the taste of Southern-fried chicken, candied yams and marshmallow and Brunswick stew, flitted through my mind when we saw a sign, "Chickens for Sale."

As we dismounted a sad-faced, middle-aged Filipino dressed in white shirt and trousers greeted us.

"Good morning," we responded. "We want to buy some chickens."

He nodded politely. "How many do you want?"

I had visions of scrawny, worm-infested native chickens scratching in a dung heap.

"How many do we want, Gus?"

"Let's see 'em first."

On the outskirts of the jungle we were shown a model chicken farm. Hundreds of plump Plymouth Rocks and Rhode Island Reds in wire coops elevated from the ground lined a yard that was immaculately clean. Sitting on their perches, the hens cocked a wary eye at us, milling their feathers.

"I am Jose Guerrerra. I am a graduate of an agricultural school, sir," the Filipino said proudly, "and as a pensionado of the government I have studied the science of chicken-raising in the States. I brought back these breeds from the States. I have raised them for years."

He went into a long harangue on raising chickens, how their illnesses were treated, and how their diet was balanced and fortified with vitamin foods. We listened politely but were bored stiff.

"And now," he concluded sadly, "my fat birds will be killed by bombs or eaten by Japs."

As he spoke I visualized the officers' and nurses' mess groaning with mountains of fried chicken on this, our first Christmas in the jungle.

The price was right—a dollar a bird, a half buck for a fryer.

The sky was tinted with the blazing colors of a tropical sunset when we finished cleaning the chickens and turned southward back to Limay.

The day before New Year's we made another haul, not as savory as the chickens, but more enduring. Our chief of X-ray was a man whom we had inherited from Sternberg Hospital. He was a quiet, harmless lightweight without personality. He had spent many years in his specialty and knew his business well. I believe he had an invalid mother whom he supported, but no wife. As a matter of fact, we knew nothing definite about his private life, if he had any. Hanging on the outskirts of a bull session he occasionally interjected remarks which, surprisingly enough, had a hint of wit and humor. For the most part, he engaged in two phobias: dirt-chasing and fly-killing. Rag in hand, he polished his X-ray equipment by the hour until it sparkled. Bent over the floor, using a tiny Filipino hand broom, he swept and swept and swept. He stalked flies as though they were his personal enemies. Face drawn and tense, he maneuvered toward his prey which was circling for a landing on the table. We all beat a hasty retreat. It was against the rules of his private warfare to smack them with a swatter. Arm outstretched, body poised, his hand swooped toward his victim like a sea gull diving at a fish. Carefully he inserted the fingers of one hand into the clenched fist of the other and drew forth his struggling captive. Then, with fiendish glee, face twitching and eyes rolling wildly, he deliberately pulled off both wings and watched the fly crawl about helplessly. Surfeited, he brushed it to the floor and ground it under his heel.

At other times, filled with mounting nervous tension, he dashed away from the outskirts of a baloney session and ran about in ever-narrowing circles, in short hops, wildly slapping his heels. We never could figure out this performance. He made our evenings hideous with his eternal rat hunts. We didn't know when he slept. We often found him, at all hours of the night, crouched in a corner with a long bamboo pole in his hand waiting for the evening rat race to begin in our quarters. Before the war the army was interested in retiring him, but they were not able to prove he was psychopathic—just queer. We agreed. We all expected him to crack up completely when the war began, and were worried about a good replacement.

The good Lord provided. While hunting for fun and food in Balanga City, we spotted a truck and trailer drawn up near a sleepy, sun-swept plaza. There were three Filipinos squatting on their heels like birds on a pole while a fourth, an alert, slim-waisted, anxious-looking fellow, was pacing back and forth.

"What's the trouble, Joe?" I asked.

"I have very much trouble, sir. I do not know what to do, sir," he said worriedly. "My name is Dr. Medina. I worked for the Philippine Department of Health when the war began, sir. I was conducting a malaria and tuberculosis survey in this province. This trailer is the X-ray unit."

I perked up my ears. Wheels began revolving in my brain.

"What are you going to do?"

"I do not know, sir. My wife and family are yet in Manila, sir, but the Japs are now in San Fernando City. I am afraid to try to go through their lines. Also, sir, my truck no longer wishes to work."

"Do you have any friends in Balanga?"

"Oh, no, sir, I am not from this poor province," he said proudly. "I am from Manila."

"What about your companions?" I nodded toward the trio sitting passively with long brown dhobie cigarettes hanging limply from their lips.

"Ah, yes. Those are my helpers, Lamotin, Lagnitin, and Ladingin. One takes X-rays very well, sir. The second makes the laboratory work. And Lagnitin drives the truck when it wants to run. They are hungry. I am also hungry, sir, but we do not have many pesos. Food is very high, sir."

"Dr. Medina," I said cautiously. "How would you and your companions like to join the army?"

"But, sir," he protested, "I do not know yet how to shoot the gun."

"Don't worry about that. All you'll have to do is shoot the X-ray plate. You'll have plenty of chow," I added encouragingly. "After the Japs are driven back you can again find your family in Manila."

He turned to his helpers. They jabbered back and forth interminably in Tagalog. Round and round they went with much headshaking and shrugging of shoulders. Finally Medina turned with a smile on his face and said cheerily, "We are happy to join the American Hospital, sir."

Before they could change their minds I hurriedly hailed a passing wrecker which towed us to Limay, thirty kilometers south. I explained the situation to Colonel Duckworth, who consented to make the deal official without going through a lot of red tape. Dr. Medina and the three "L's" served with us throughout the hectic days of the cane-field fighting on the Abucay Hacienda Line when casualties by the thousands were evacuated to our field hospital for treatment. They were well trained, devoted, courageous members of our staff, and worked uncomplainingly for days without respite. When we moved south to Little Baguio they were ordered to Field Hospital No. 2, which had no X-ray unit.

To our pleased amazement our X-ray man didn't go haywire during the Bataan campaign. Although he came close to it, he continued to work and work well in spite of his peculiarities.

After New Year's it was evident that the honeymoon was over. We squared away for action, sterilizing huge piles of operating gowns, linen, gauze, towels, and swabs in the utility room of the operating pavilion. Having no electric sterilizer, we used multi-jet, pressure-pumped Bunsen burners placed under steel-jacketed pressure cookers. The utility and operating room remained suffocatingly hot in spite of the wide-open windows. Because we still hoped the Nips wouldn't bomb Red Cross installations, we were not blacked out. Miss Frances Nash and Miss Easterling, two of our nurses, drove themselves as if beset by devils until their neatly starched uniforms were crumpled, sweat-soaked rags. Frances especially was a dynamo, driving the medics with her lashing tongue until they cussed her sullenly under their breaths—not openly, because they were sure they'd get the back of her hand. A strapping, brown-haired, comely girl, raised on Georgia-grown pork, black-eyed peas, hominy and grits, she packed a mean wallop.

We set up eight operating tables with their gleaming spotlights standing at attention beside them. We had no fixed overhead lights. These "spots" were of inestimable value to me with my minus-three-and-a-half-diopter, nearsighted eyes. Trying to work in the depths of a blood-filled belly, I'd rant and rage until some long-suffering medic would focus a "spot" more sharply on the operative field.

Between the operating tables we placed wooden saw-horses of unequal height on which litters loaded with patients suffering from shock would be placed. This position—feet higher than head—permitted blood to drain more rapidly from the body to the heart, which pumped it to a brain anemic from loss of blood. We placed stacks of blankets and hot-water bottles near the saw-horses so that they could be instantly used to swathe and keep warm the shock casualties. We sterilized gleaming nickel-plated instruments by the hundreds of pounds: hand and Gigli (woven-wire) saws, chisels, elevators, bone rongeurs, nibblers, drills, scalpel handles, Stinman pins (like tenpenny nails), and Kirshner wire drills (for bone work), hemostats of many sizes and shapes, retractors, intestinal clamps, and needles. To save time the utility nurses sorted them out on a huge table covered with sterile sheets. From here they were transferred when needed to smaller stands near the operating tables.

In an adjacent building Lieutenant Willie Perilman of West Virginia, and tiny Lieutenant Jack Gordon of Sioux City, Iowa, set up a receiving station where ambulances loaded with sick and wounded made their first stop. Here these doctors sorted out medical cases and sent those obviously seriously wounded to us. They worked on so-called minor casualties themselves, many of which would be considered major casualties in civilian practice: jagged flesh wounds of the arms and body, amputations of fingers and toes, lacerations of the face—in fact everything they could handle with novocaine anesthesia and without a trained anesthetist. Willie and Jack were an inseparable pair, both of them industrious, kindly, soft-spoken, well trained and courageous. And of a courage that knew the nature of fear. Some men, like Captain Paul Ashton, apparently had no fear reaction in their make-up. I've seen Paul walk steadily through the hospital compound at Little Baguio while it was being bombed and not flicker a muscle of his face. Although Willie and Jack felt the horror of fear keenly and bitterly, it never interfered with the performance of their duty. They would work during a bombing, their faces drawn and gray and with stomachs twitching until, unable to control themselves any longer, they would dash outside the building, vomit, and return to their work. In spite of their fear reaction we thought they were the bravest men in our unit. They worked day and night, treating four patients to our one.

We divided ourselves into operating teams. The leader of each team had another doctor, a nurse, and a medic as assistants and helpers. Commander Charles Smith worked on the more serious fractures; Captain Paul Roland, a handsome, meticulous surgeon from New York, handled the belly cases; Captain Joe Bulfamonte of Pennsylvania did the arm and leg wounds; Colonel Schock, regular army dentist, and Lieutenant Chamberlain did face and jaw plastic work. There was plenty of it to do. Colonel Adamo and I teamed up, operating on brain, bladder, chest, and belly wounds.

We had only two trained anesthetists: Lieutenant Armstrong, a cheery-faced, tow-headed youngster whose wry, crooked-toothed grin never left his face, and a short, loud-mouthed, cocky, cigar-smoking wise guy from the East who shall be nameless. He was one of the very few doctors in our hospital to turn into a washout. A really topflight anesthetist, he resented being used as such, and wanted to become a surgeon in eight easy lessons. He was repeatedly reprimanded by Commander Smith for attempting to operate on serious surgical cases. Finally we had to get rid of him. He was sent out in the field with a medical detachment. Six weeks later he hobbled into the hospital after we had moved to Little Baguio, disheveled, gray faced, trembling, all the fight whipped out of him.

I asked him what his trouble was.

"Al, my heel's killing me. I'm afraid I've got a tumor on it," he said, his face twitching. "I had a small tumor removed from it eight years ago and it looks like it's coming back."

I examined him. He had a bone bruise caused by a fall over an embankment. There was also a small, hard, some-what tender scar from a previous operation, but no evidence of a recurrence of a tumor.

"What do you want me to do?' I asked, as though I didn't know.

"Al, I want you to operate on my foot and cut that tumor out," he begged.

"There's nothing in that foot that I'd cut out," I said, and turning on my heel, walked off. He finally sold another surgeon a bill of goods and was operated on. For weeks he hobbled about pitifully on crutches, but when the hospital was bombed for the first time he threw them away and scampered like a fleet-footed rabbit.

For three weeks the big guns roared in the not-so-distant north, making day and night hideous with their interminable grumbling, while American blood trickled into the camps, cane fields and jungle thickets. We were about thirteen miles south, too far to see the exploding shells or hear the crackle of machine-gun and rifle fire, but we did see the effects of the fighting on those who survived the inferno. By the many hundreds they poured back, transported on ambulance, bus, truck and mule-pack train from the flat country and the mountains. Exhausted by days of combat, racked with malaria, dehydrated by the tropical heat, blood oozing from massive wounds, they flooded the operating tables and littered the floor.

"All hands on deck!" rang through the hospital, a call to arms that our benumbed, sleepless brains were later to resent bitterly.

"Take that belly case first, Roland," said Commander Smith, who was checking the medical tags on patients as they were littered in. "No, no, not that one; he can wait. What about this brain, Frank?" he asked Colonel Adamo, who quickly unwrapped a massive bandage from a comatose patient.

"Hopeless," Adamo muttered. A bomb fragment had sheared away the posterior half of the skull, exposing a mess of soggy mush. "Don't know why he's still alive."

"O.K.," Smith snapped to a corpsman. "Take him to ward four and take this officer to the morgue," pointing to a silent form lying on a litter, cheeks sunken and mottled, mouth open and flecked with bloody froth.

"I'll handle this fellow with a bullet wound in the spine," said Adamo.

"Bulfamonte, take this soldier with the fractured femur. Colonel Schock, what about this Filipino with the jaw wound?" A machine-gun burst had blown away the upper jaw, leaving a gaping hole in his face.

"I'll take the corporal," Colonel Smith said to Miss Bernatitus, pointing to a two-striper whose dog tag read, "Multiple shrapnel wounds of the chest and abdomen."

The tables were all loaded. We went to work. Short as we were of doctors, we often used medical corpsmen for assistants. Mine was Private First Class Liebert of Virginia, ex-boxer and semipro football player before he joined the army. A well trained technician, his very size, as well as his mental stability, helped steady me while Nip planes zoomed overhead. He had laughing blue eyes and clean-cut features marred only by a scar on his cheek from a haymaker. He didn't mind my cussedness and irritability under fire.

Sounds familiar to the operating pavilion vibrated through the air: the zzz-zzz-zzz of a saw as it cut through bone, the rasp of a file as the freshly cut end, dripping red marrow, was ground smooth; the plop of an amputated leg dropping into a bucket, the grind of a rounded burr drill eating its way through a skull, the tap, tap, tap, of a mallet on a chisel gouging out a shell fragment deeply imbedded in bone, the hiss of the sterilizer blowing off steam, the soft patter of nurses' feet scurrying back and forth, the snip of scissors cutting through muscle, the swish of the mop on the floor cleaning up blood, the strangling, gasping, irregular respiration of soldiers with chest wounds; the shallow, soft, faint breathing of those under a smooth anesthesia; the snap of rubber gloves on outstretched hands, the rustle of operating gowns being changed, the shuffle of feet as weary surgeons and nurses shifted their weight from one leg to another.

Hours passed into days. Eyes burned and smarted from constant strain under the glaring spotlights. Streaked with blood and feces, operating drapes piled in the corner of the utility room until they reached the rafters. Scalpels dulled as they cut through tough skin fascia and muscle. Rivulets of sweat washed away the nurses' rouge and powder, leaving only lipstick to match the ruby-red blood. Dirt-begrimed faces were seen in a blur as they passed before our vision. Ears automatically registered sounds coming through a stethoscope and eyes mechanically took blood-pressure readings. Fingers almost of their own accord examined fractured legs and board-like bellies filled with infection. Back-weary medics shuffled in with strangely silent casualties and out again with the men on whom we had finished. Chaplains moved quietly about, giving last rites to those sinking fast, saying their Hail Mary's in soft, humble voices. The dark of the night melted under the heat of the sunrise and flowed away. The hot noonday sun was displaced by the cool light of the rising moon as the streams of living and dying continued to pour into the operating room. My mind functioned through a haze, making decisions almost automatically:

What's the use of trying to save that leg? He'll be a cripple all his life. The bone's smashed all to hell. Take it off.

How would you like to be one-legged at twenty? Give him a chance. Put it in traction.

That pulse is damn fast and feeble. You'll kill him if you operate now. Give him some blood and heat and rest. He may snap out of it.

Look at those God damn worms crawling out of the gut.

I wish I were fishing in the Chattahoochee, that's what I wish. I'm sick of this.

That loop of gut is dead. How are you going to hook up the cut ends? Side to side would work best.

For Christ's sake, do you think you've got all day to finish? End to end is faster and will serve well enough. Hurry—hurry—hurry! You've got dozens waiting to be patched up.

This skull is as thick as a gorilla's. I wish we had some electric drills. Jesus, my hands are tired.

I think this bastard blew a hole through his own hand. I'll bet a million bucks that's a powder burn around it. What a mess.

Quit stalling. Are you going to take it off or leave it on? You killed that last guy fumbling around in his chest.

He was on his way out before he got on the table.

Why didn't you leave him alone?

He was bleeding.

Why didn't you stop it?

I couldn't find the God damn bleeding vessel.

That's what I thought. You killed him! You killed him! You killed him!

From time to time our spike-mustachioed, orchid-growing Mess Sergeant Gaston sent over coffee, doughnuts, and sandwiches which we gulped down. Then back to work we went. Days stretched into weeks as the heavy fighting continued and the wounded poured into the hospital. In a thirty-six-hour stretch in

January our tiny group of surgeons did four hundred and twenty operations. Strained to the breaking point by constant tension, we became irritable, crabby and hypercritical of each other and our assistants. I don't know why the medics, who were under the same tension, didn't knock us on our butts for our childish petulance.

Sleep was irregular, brief but profound. I dreamed I was at a dance at the Manila Hotel.

The vaulted ceiling reflected the strains of the waltz. Immaculately dressed men in formal evening attire and women in flashing low-cut gowns dipped and swayed past the lofty colonnades, leaving a trail of entrancing perfume in their wake. Pleasantly crocked, I danced with Hanna in my arms, her warm bosom pressed against mine. The orchestra suddenly broke into a throbbing beat: faster and faster went the music, louder and louder—

I awakened with a start. Our barracks were filled with doctors tearing out of the building in their pajamas. Outside I heard the clanging of the bell and shouts of "Everybody out—gas attack!"

Since the war started, we had argued about whether the Nips would use gas. Rumor had it that they had brought huge supplies of gas bombs and shells with them when they landed in the Philippines. We had been issued gas masks which we kept constantly on our persons, under the operating table or beside our beds. Our gas signal was the clanging of the bell, thus far used only in practice runs.

I struggled out of bed, stupid with sleep. Frantic with fear, I fumbled about in the dim light of the quarter-moon for my mask. I took a deep breath and flopped it on my face, forgetting to take out the molded cardboard form which maintained the shape of the rubber face when not in use. Opening my eyes, I couldn't see through the right one.

Jesus Christ, I thought to myself. I've gone blind in one eye.

I ran my finger around the edge of the rubber face and found a huge leak. Petrified, purple with air hunger but still holding my breath, I pulled the mask off and readjusted it. In doing so, the cardboard form inside flopped back, covering both eyes.

Good God! I thought as I again opened my eyes. Now I'm blind in *both* eyes. This is the end.

The alarm had sounded just before my nightly run to the latrine. My bladder was full and fear had made its walls contract. The deep breath I had taken had increased the pressure on it to such an extent that only by inordinate will power had I avoided wetting myself while fumbling with the gas mask.

If I'm going to die, I might as well die comfortable, I thought, pawing my way blindly toward an open window.

There I stood in the light of the moon, mask on, stark naked, a steady stream curving to the ground below. This last maneuver was greeted with a roar of laughter. I ripped the mask off and saw a cluster of nurses and doctors standing by, clapping and cheering.

Another evening we were awakened by the earsplitting roar of heavy guns that seemed to come from the beach itself. The Nips had mounted 105's on barges, had hauled them by water past our lines and were blasting our troops from the rear near the beach of our hospital. They had escaped notice because our soldiers had been using barges to bring supplies from the rear areas to forward installations. The Japs were driven off—this time. Beach patrols were strengthened and instructed to fire on any waterborne units if the proper password was not given immediately. Several nights later we heard the *woom* of mortars and crackling bursts of machine-gun fire several hundred yards from the hospital. We dashed out on the beach. There were three barges drawn by a motorboat. In the distance an unmistakably Filipino voice floated in—"Don't fire, Joe!" This plea was followed by the frantic off-key rendering of "God Bless America." They had forgotten the password.

It was evident that our lines could not continue to hold. The Nips hammered them with tens of thousands of fresh troops while our own battle-weary units held on doggedly without replacements. Loss of manpower by malaria, dysentery, and battle casualties were mounting alarmingly. Our hospital with its thousand patients was filled and overflowing. It was necessary to set up a convalescent hospital in the jungle if we were to accept more casualties.

We got the word that the hospital had to pull back. We spent two frantic days slapping plaster on the fracture cases to make them transportable. We packed equipment, trucked patients to Hospital No. 2, ripped up water pipe and wire which we could not replace: We said good-bye to the sixty-four white crosses in our little cemetery and rode south to Little Baguio. The next day the buildings that had housed us were destroyed by Jap shellfire and bombs.

CHAPTER 3.
Little Baguio:
Under The Lonesome Pine

THERE ARE MANY FACTORS THAT go into the selection of a site for a hospital in the field. Among them are the following: an adequate water supply, shelter for patients against torrential downpours and the blazing tropical sun, and finally, easy availability to adequate roads so that battle casualties would not be shaken into irreversible shock in transport. Little Baguio met all of these requirements. It was about two acres in size, situated on the east road of Bataan about a mile inland from the coast down toward the tip of the peninsula. Before the war its sheds had housed a motor-repair shop for troops on maneuvers. On a hill overlooking it, a half-mile away, was an artesian well and concrete pool for chlorinating our water supply. It was simple to run water by gravity from it to the hospital itself. The cool, wind-swept, shaded compound several thousand feet above sea level, fringed with towering hardwood trees with their huge buttressing "skirts," was free of the dreaded estivo-autumnal malaria which abounded throughout Bataan. That was why it was named after Baguio, healthful summer capital of the Philippines in the mountain province of North Luzon.

On a curving graveled path leading to the quadrangle, Lieutenant Claude Fraley, U.S.N. Dental Corps, and his gang of hustlers built a flimsy-walled admitting office with operating rooms for minor surgery. This housed Lieutenant Willie Perilman and

Jack Gordon. They lived and worked there day and night without relief throughout the whole campaign. When it was shattered by bombs they rebuilt it themselves, with the help of their medics. It wasn't the Mayo Clinic in design or construction, but it served its purpose. A graveled road led up a grade past six concrete-floored, tin-roofed sheds that had formerly served as garages. Similar sheds were constructed behind and above this area, expanding the hospital's bed capacity to a thousand. How and where Fraley and his gang got the necessary wood, nails, bolts, and tools to finish the job I'm not quite sure. I believe he employed a combination of barter, soft soap, hospital alcohol, and outright thievery, more politely known as "moonlight requisitioning."

In the center of the compound stood a wooden frame building similar in size and shape to the operating pavilion in Limay. Frances Nash and her operating crew transformed it into another efficient unit. Colonel Schock and Captain Brewer, a tall blond from the Middle West, had a fine dental setup which hummed continuously. It was humming one night in March, 1942, during the heavy fighting when a pregnant Chinese woman arrived. She was married to a civilian engineer on Bataan. His name was Sullivan, I believe. A disgusted truck driver dumped her off at the admitting office.

"Of all the God damn times to have a baby," he grumbled.

The mother was young, plump and good-looking, with only a faint Oriental cast to her modest eyes. Breasts swelling ripely, rotund abdomen covered by a thin pink slip, she announced in a softly slurred voice, "My baby soon wants to leave me."

While men bled and died next door in the operating pavilion, the wail of a newborn babe could be heard in the dental room as Captain Osborne finished the delivery. It was a godsend to the nurses to have the infant to play with and fondle. In a few days they knitted and sewed enough baby clothes to outfit a kindergarten. Into the long hours of the night arguments raged as to what to call the kid. The grateful mother was willing to accept any moniker. The more formal names—Susan, Eleanor Grace, Helen—were out. It had to be something special and fancy. We finally compromised optimistically and prematurely on Victoria Bataan Sullivan, a curious combination for any kid to carry around for the rest of her life.

In the rear of the quadrangle were two rambling wooden structures: one was the officers' quarters; the other housed the nurses' and combined officers' mess. Electric light and plumbing were installed. We were quite comfortable, but it was a comedown from Jai Alai with its air-conditioned rooms and gaily uniformed waiters. Still, it turned out to be a Waldorf-Astoria compared with what awaited us in Japan.

Our mess attendants were retired Filipino Scouts who became increasingly mournful and solicitous as the food situation became worse. My attendant, Sergeant Moreno, had been a member of the Twenty-seventh Philippine Scout Cavalry. Less than a month ago, when the same unit had been shot to pieces by Nip tanks near Lingayan Bay, the remnants of the troop retreated into Bataan. The horses were used at first for pack trains and reconnaissance duty.

One day we were served a meat stew which had an especially strong flavor and unchewable quality.

"Is this beef, Sergeant Moreno?" I asked.

"No, sir."

"It doesn't taste like carabao. Is it?"

"No, sir."

"What the hell is it?"

"Twenty-seventh Cavalry, sir," he said sadly.

Beside the officers' quarters was a two story, double-decker building. Floors made of strips of bamboo nailed side by side with a space between the strips permitted continuous ventilation. As time passed, new wards of this shanty-type construction were created so that we housed about seventeen hundred battle casualties before the surrender took place.

When our forces retired southward from Limay to lick their wounds, the Nips decided to take a break themselves. A ten-mile-wide strip of no man's land across the southern third of Bataan followed the course of the Pilar-Bigaac Road which was dominated by our artillery positions on towering, tree-clothed Mount Sumat. During this lull, with only daily patrol skirmishes occurring, casualties were light. We had a chance to relax and catch our breaths before the next wave of fighting.

Procuring the necessary consent, Gus Laudicina and I took off in my car for the mountains. We traveled over a twisting trail recently cut by the engineers, just wide enough for an automobile. We bounced and writhed over roots and rocks, shaded by the overhanging branches of mango, papaya, and hardwood trees which interlaced above us. Not the best treatment for a new Chrysler, but I had decided to smash it, if necessary, rather than let it fall into the hands of a potbellied Nip war lord. It was cool and peaceful as we ground upward steadily into the heart of the jungle. Occasionally the road curved past a clearing with a few single-roomed bamboo shacks on stilts surrounded by clumps of banana trees with their wide-slatted, deep green leaves. It crawled along the brink of a precipice from which we could hear the rapidly rushing waters of a mountain stream in a hidden valley far below. The fresh-cut road ended in a tangle of underbrush through which a well defined footpath twisted its way around huge tree trunks. Perspiring freely, we followed it on foot into the deep gloom of the mountain forest accompanied only by the grunting squeak of a wild pig frightened by our approach. The forest thinned out as the sun poured a brilliant white blast into a tiny clearing in which three doll-like bamboo shacks stood, their walls leaning crazily.

"Gus," I whispered. "We're in luck. It's a Negrito settlement. You know, the tiny pigmies. The Filipinos in Manila call them Baloogas (dirty ones)."

"Yeah?" he replied, interested. "I've heard of 'em."

We crawled to the edge of the clearing. There were two gray, frizzly-haired elders wrapped in red-and-black striped loincloths, squatting on their heels. With a chunk of limestone they were busily polishing a wooden dart about eight inches long. On the ground was a long blowgun. One of them got up, stretched to his full height of four feet, and walked over to the other elder who was stringing a bow longer than himself. Several tiny women with skirts of loosely woven fiber material were suckling infants from their miniature pear-shaped breasts. Coal black, with kinky hair, they all had sharply defined Western features. A cluster of bare-bottomed kids were playing with a mangy dog, cuffing him about.

"Watch this," Gus said as he tossed a pack of Camels at the feet of the bow maker. He looked at it, startled, let out a yelp and scampered into the forest. The others vanished, even the hound dog. We waited silently for several minutes and tossed another pack, and then a third. Temptation was too great. The elders warily drifted toward the cigarettes. We stretched, brushed our clothes, and walked into the open. I offered the kids some of my precious hoard of chewing gum. Soon we were all happily smoking, chewing, and eating bananas.

They knew Americans, but spoke very little English. By sign language they explained the use of the blowgun and poisoned dart, and they let us try their bow and arrow. They had several types of arrows: one was American Indian style with a metal tip instead of an arrowhead; a second had for its tip a circular crown of slivers of bamboo and was used for bird shooting; a third, built like the first, had a long piece of bamboo tied loosely to its shaft by fine grass and attached firmly to its bow end by a hemplike string. They used this arrow for hunting wild pig, the bamboo strut acting as a drag to slow the runaway animal as it thrashed through the thickets. They killed the exhausted pig with their tiny bolos. After this demonstration we swapped cigarettes, combs, and handkerchiefs for coconut, papaya, and bananas. Well loaded down, we retraced our steps and wove our way back to the hospital.

The lull still continuing, we arranged for a swimming party at Seseman Cove on the bay facing Corregidor. The nurses packed our sandwiches. Laughing, giggling, and kidding each other as if we were safe in the States eight thousand miles away, we piled into cars and hospital trucks for the trip over the new dirt road. On a bluff overlooking the dazzling white sandy strip, we could see Corregidor doggedly hunched in the sea while a flight of Nip planes made a run over it well out of the reach of antiaircraft guns. A footpath zigzagged down to the beach. It was a mass of barbed-wire entanglement and razor-edged bamboo poles sunk in the sand, their ends pointing seaward. Several hundred yards off shore floated four PT boats with their torpedo tubes painted black, two forward and two aft, dully reflecting the brilliant sun. Changing our clothes in the underbrush, we gingerly made our way through the barricades, guided by smiling members of a Filipino Army detachment. We whooped and galloped happily down the gently sloping beach and dove into the calm blue tropical waters. Forgetful of the war and the shark-infested bay beyond us, we swam or floated, lazily spouting water through our teeth. One of our girls, her beautiful curves etched by a scanty bathing suit, didn't know how to swim. A bald-headed captain gallantly offered to teach her. To the innocent bystander it looked more like a Swedish massage than a swimming lesson. She didn't seem to object.

We swam leisurely to one of the PT boats and were helped aboard by a Filipino.

"Hello, Joe," said Gus to the machinist mate. "What's new?"

"I do not know yet, sir," Joe replied, wiping the grease off his hands with an oily rag. "Maybe soon we will be very busy, sir," he said. "We have worked very hard to make the engines run happy. These two are good mechanics," he added, pointing to his grinning companions, "but the small one, he is very stupid. He is from the provinces." These boats, officered by Americans, were soon to make a wild dash one moonlit night, crashing over the log booms guarding Subic Bay, to sink three Nip vessels in the harbor and make their getaway.

We swam ashore, lolled about the beach, and washed down some carabao sandwiches with a lemonade made from calamanse juice, a concentrate of native lime. We drove back to the hospital refreshed and invigorated.

With the fighting at a standstill, romances begun in Manila again blossomed and bloomed. A total of fifty nurses attracted swarms of young fliers with their crush hats and assured manners. When food was adequate, they were welcomed and fed at our mess. When food dwindled, they were pointedly advised to visit the hospital after evening chow. Courting still continued more and more feverishly. Romantic wedding ceremonies took place in concealed jungle chapels while the guns roared and the sky was speckled with Nip bombers. Romance under these circumstances had an intensity and overpowering quality never experienced in leisurely peacetime life. Men who had never uttered the words, "I love you", without flinching, did so with a naturalness and sincerity that was touching. Confirmed bachelors, who had coolly resisted love's refrain, found themselves uttering the words, "Will you marry me?" with an intensity born of desperation. They knew they were to die or be captured by the Nips, yet they dreamed and planned for the future during the long tropical nights.

We got permission to have a dance in the officers' mess, a masquerade, no less. While death was closing in on all sides, we clung frantically to life. With his usual hocus-pocus Lieutenant Claude Fraley was able to dig up an old hand-winding portable phonograph and a handful of records, vintage 1920. All of the nurses dressed in their finery and depleted their cache of make-up and perfume. It was exciting to see them transformed into gay and colorful personalities after months of khaki shirts and baggy pants. Colonel Schock came dressed as an old, unshaven bum, ragged trousers supported by a knotted rope, gnarled walking cane in one hand, tin cup in the other. One of the medics thumped out dance music on a broken-down upright piano, procured God only knows where. Two of our corpsmen of Mexican descent lazily strummed and sang "South of the Border." Gus Laudicina obliged with Italian songs. A couple of our Filipino nurses did native dances.

One of the medic truck drivers brought the news. The Nips were on the march again. Fresh troops from Manila were pounding the center of the Pilar-Bigaac Line. They were not only pounding but pouring through a soft spot. They steam-rolled several Philippine Army divisions, developing a wedge which we later referred to as "the Pocket." Simultaneously, they landed by the thousands in barges at night at the western tip of Bataan. The Nip strategy called for these two groups to fight their way toward each other, dividing the lower third of the peninsula into isolated western and eastern halves, each of which then could be handily mopped up. It looked like the beginning of the end for us.

This was fighting of the worst type, deep in the heart of dense jungle or on cliffs and beachheads well removed from even a vestige of a road. Our soldiers showed the strain of their ordeal when they were transported to the hospital. Haggard, hungry, dehydrated, bled out, they had lain in their foxholes and first-aid stations for days until they were carried by hand litter or mule pack over mountains and through swamps to where ambulances could navigate. Their wounds stank to high heaven and crawled with fat maggots. On admission to the hospital, it was dangerous to do more than give them a transfusion and load them up with fluids and food to ward off impending shock and death. Their first request was always for food.

An undersized Filipino had a mortar-shell fragment in a compound fracture of the thigh. We questioned him before he was put under a general anesthesia.

"Joe, how many days has it been since you have eaten?"

"Three days, sir," was the prompt reply. "Yesterday, today, and tomorrow." He knew postoperative treatment.

At Limay we had seen a few patients with gas gangrene, but none as far gone as most of these lads. Gas gangrene of the extremities is caused by a host of germs that flourish and multiply in contused, destroyed muscle tissue. One of these is the Bacillus Welchii, named after its discoverer. It is a black-staining germ that looks like a domino under the microscope. This germ and many others like it are capable of producing a highly toxic poison which travels up the extremities along the nerve trunks. It can also be absorbed by the small blood vessels directly and carried to the brain. Within as brief a period as one to three days, it can produce coma and death. These germs or their spores (precursors) are anaerobic and can grow only in deep perforating wounds away from the oxygen in the air. There they produce their toxic poison and tiny bubbles of gas. These accumulate within the covering sheath of the muscle which has been contused and partially destroyed by shrapnel. By actual mechanical pressure these bubbles interfere with the blood supply to and from the muscle. The extremity swells and balloons out to twice its normal size in several days so that massive death of muscle tissue takes place. This dead muscle serves as more nourishment for the germs which in turn produce more gas. A vicious circle is thus established, inevitably leading to death if its course is not interrupted.

We had seen a few of these patients at Limay, where Colonel Adamo and Captain Wilson, doctor and ex-breeder of mink and beaver from the Far West, had handled them. They had tried and used up our tiny stock of mixed gas-bacillus antitoxin without much evident luck. Possibly large enough doses were not used, or possibly the antitoxin had deteriorated from exposure to tropical temperatures in transit during our flight from Manila. Penicillin had not yet been discovered, but even if it had, it would have been eight thousand miles away. We had to fall back on the drastic mutilating technique devised during the First World War.

Willie Perilman and Jack Gordon in the admitting office examined all deep, contused or perforating wounds, feeling the tissue carefully for gas bubbles and smelling the foul mess for a faint, cloying, sickeningly sweet odor which is characteristic of this inflection. They sent patients with evidence of the disease immediately to the isolation gas-gangrene ward because the infection is highly contagious. Willie, with his long nose and delicate nostrils, became a past master at the sniffing maneuver. They took swabs deep in the tissues of suspected cases for examination under the microscope. Those that showed organisms with physical characteristics similar to the Bacillus Welchii were also isolated. We were not equipped to identify all other organisms which could produce the same clinical picture.

Under a small dose of spinal anesthesia or light gas-oxygen general anesthesia, these patients were operated on. In a patient with gas gangrene of the thigh, for example, long multiple parallel incisions were made from the knee to the hip bone, cutting through skin, soggy swollen tissue and the tough facia which envelopes each muscle mass. By doing so, gas in the tissue could escape, preventing further mechanical strangulation of muscle. Air entering the wound prevented growth of gas-forming, poison-producing germs. Grayish-yellow dead and dying muscle bundles were removed. We then irrigated the surgical wounds with copious amounts of hydrogen peroxide and packed them with gauze impregnated with azochloramide, a chlorine-producing chemical which acts like oxygen on the oxygen-hating germs.

The response to this treatment was dramatic. In many instances the soldiers lost their toxicity in twelve to twenty-four hours. Their pulses slowed, their blood pressure rose, they lost their mental confusion, and they took nourishment with gusto. If they were worse after twenty-four hours it became necessary, in an attempt to save life, to consider amputating the leg, leaving the cut exposed to the air.

Under spinal anesthesia we had finished operating on a young aviator with a massive mortar-shell wound on the buttock and thigh. With no planes to fly, these boys who had had no training in ground fighting had been formed into provisional infantry units and thrown against the oncoming Japs. This officer had been in transit two days from his foxhole over rough mountain terrain.

"Well, Doc," he whispered weakly, "am I going to make it?"

On the basis of our experience, his chances were damn slim. In fact, nonexistent, because at operation gas bubbles had been found riding as high as his loins.

"Yeah, Johnny," we replied. "You've got a fighting chance. You'll be O.K. We've seen worse cases make the grade."

He fell into a sleep and was soon dead.

Among ourselves, we often argued the morality of telling a badly wounded, dying soldier that he would live. "Tell him the truth. He's askin' for it."

"Hell, no. Who wants to be told flat-footedly that he's goin' to kick off?"

"Give him a chance to compose his soul. Some soldiers have one."

"Forget it. They want to be reassured they're gonna live when they ask."

"He may want to write a last letter to his folks."

"Let 'em die in peace. Why make their last few hours or days miserable waitin' to die. Slug 'em hard with morphine and let 'em drift off painlessly."

The arguments raged back and forth with nobody knowing the correct answer. Most of us followed a middle course, ducking the question or avoiding a direct answer. If a patient looked as if he might kick the bucket, we called in the chaplain to give him last rites, collect personal mementos, and write last messages. These men were trained to give religious consolation and comfort in a calm, tender manner. Their appearance meant to the wounded that they were seriously ill, yet it did not have the same disastrous mental effect of a flat, "Yes, you're gonna die," coming from a medical officer. We had seen too many apparently hopelessly shocked casualties make the grade to tell any man that death was inevitable. More often than not, they didn't have to be told. As days wore on and they steadily became weaker, they adjusted themselves to the fact that they were not going to live.

They carried a twenty-year-old aviator into the operating room. He was tall and his blue eyes were shaded by a tangle of curly blond hair. He looked like a young college kid. He had gas gangrene of the thigh and a nasty extensive shrapnel wound that had ripped his foot to pieces.

Face greenish-white, bled out and semi hysterical, he kept groaning: "Jesus Christ, Doc, don't take it off. Don't. Please don't."

We assured him we wouldn't. We treated him for shock, operated on his thigh, and put his foot in plaster. The toxicity from the gas-bacillus infection subsided. The thigh healed well. But the foot got nowhere fast. Day after day we picked pieces of bone out of the stinking mess while he gripped the bed during the excruciatingly painful dressing. Dripping perspiration, he watched our facial expressions to see if he could find therein what he dreaded to learn.

"How about it, Doc?" he would ask eagerly, face half smiling, forehead filled with fear. "Am I gonna keep it?"

We thought it would be brutal to tell him the truth when he wasn't prepared for it and didn't want it.

For ten days we nursed that foot along without any progress until one day he said somberly: "You know, Doc, I don't think that foot's gonna be any use to me even if it does heal. How about taking it off?"

We did. He was not unhappy. We had given him time to learn the truth and make his adjustment to it without breaking him up mentally.

Hospital construction continued. To replace surgical beds taken from other wards, Fraley rounded up a hundred nondescript Filipino men from a nearby civilian camp sometimes visited at night by the corpsmen. They came in droves, glad to work for army chow and the American dollar. Each carried a short bolo, an all-weather tool that served as plane, chisel, knife, rasp, and screw driver. They were incredibly clever with it. Work details went out to bamboo thickets and came back loaded with twenty-five-foot-long trees. Their trimmed branches were sorted out and made into brooms; the leaves served as sawdust for the damp earth floor of the wards; the poles themselves were split into thin laths by driving them against the sharp edge of an upright length of iron planted in the ground. Heavier bamboo trees were notched to fit snugly and served as beams for double-decker wards with a long center aisle. Our Filipinos laced these beams together with strips of wet rattan and precious wire and floored them with strips of bamboo laid side by side. The finished product housed a hundred and fifty patients. In other wards, three-decker beds of a similar nature were constructed. When we ran out of crutches for our convalescent patients, we set up a crutch-and-cane factory operated by dozens of these natives. All this work took place while the medical and surgical work of the hospital was going full blast. It was a beehive.

After heartbreakingly bitter fighting, the Jap assault troops pounding the Pocket were cut off, surrounded, and finally wiped out. Much of the action took place at night as the Nips in the north attempted to rescue their regiments surrounded by Americans and Filipinos.

Lieutenant Basil Dulan, M.C., and Captain Walter Kostecki, M.C., were wearily trudging down a mountain trail one night during this period.

"Walter," said Basil, deep lines of fatigue etched on his face, "we're lost and you know it."

"Like hell we are," Kostecki answered, his slight, wiry frame bristling with resentment. "Just follow me. I'll lead you back to mama."

They plodded along the winding trail and rounded a huge tree, almost falling over a soldier squatting half asleep, elbows resting on his machine gun, head drooping on his arms.

"Just a minute, Basil," Walter said with complete assurance. "This Filipino can give us the right dope."

"Say, Joe," tapping him on the shoulder briskly, "wake up. Where are we? Where's the Forty-fifth Philippine Scout Regiment?"

The head lifted itself slowly and blinked in the murky gloom.

"Beat it, Basil, it's a Nip!" bellowed Walter, making a mad dive into the underbrush. Dulan legged it up the path again, crouching low. He made his getaway, but Walter didn't come back.

Our troops isolated multiple Nip landings on the west coast. Repeated attempts by the Japs to reinforce these regiments by sea were unsuccessful. Our few P-40's strafed their barges from the air, light coast artillery manned by the marines smashed them from the shores, while the infantry and tank units mopped up more than two thousand enemy troops on land. We breathed more freely again. Maybe we would hold until the promised help from the States arrived.

During this scrap we received some forty-two Nip casualties. Exsanguinated, begrimed, with massive wounds covered with dirt and maggots, most of them were too weak to resist our attempts to clean, feed, and operate on them. Fraley and his gang constructed a ward for them and filled it with cots and surgical beds. A high barbed-wire fence surrounded the compound to keep revengeful Filipinos out rather than prevent the Nips from escaping. After the first few days of sullen terror they finally got it through their thick skulls that we were trying to heal them. They received the same linen and towel issue, the same chow, cigarettes, and candy that our men got, no more, no less.

A powerfully built, short-legged Nip with a bullet wound through his upper arm was brought into the operating room, a walking-wounded in good shape. Wild-eyed with terror, he struggled with us as we tried to strap him to the table before starting the anesthesia. With a shriek and a howl he broke loose and tore about the pavilion with all of us in wild pursuit until he was cornered and put to sleep.

Later that day we got hold of a tiny half-Filipino, half-Jap civilian whom we used as an interpreter. "Ask the Jap why he's so scared."

They jabbered back and forth for a while. Finally Felix said in his lisping English, "His officers have told him that the Americans torture and kill all prisoners."

This in part is one of the explanations of Bushido, or fighting spirit, that the Nips boast about; a desperation, when cornered, born of fear rather than courage. There were other explanations. The Nip soldiers told us that if they permitted themselves to be captured, they or their families would be severely punished after Japan won the war. They would never be permitted to return to their relatives. Not only would their families be permanently disgraced but their food ration would be cut or discontinued. These Nip soldiers wanted to live as desperately as American soldiers, but with the cards stacked against them there was nothing to do but fight and die. Some of them believed that if they were killed in action they would become gods. Many of them didn't. Trained from infancy to follow blindly the orders of their superiors or suffer the consequences (immediate physical punishment and imprisonment), their inculcated reflex action of obedience often overshadowed the basic instinct of self-preservation. There is no one explanation of the will to fight in the Jap soldier.

We were hungry and getting hungrier. As a result of constant physical and mental exertion, loss of sleep and short rations, I had lost twenty-five pounds in three months. This was about the average loss for hospital personnel. From the baggy droop of the trousers of some of our plumper nurses—Misses Lewey, Hogan, and Cassiani it was evident that they had lost a good deal more.

In January, 1942, everybody on Bataan went on two-thirds rations in an attempt to stretch out a dwindling food supply. In the delaying action that our forces in southern Luzon had fought to prevent the Nips from cutting off our northern units retreating from Lingayen Bay early in the campaign, it was necessary to burn and blow up huge food stores. Similarly, when we scrambled out of Manila around the curve of the bay to reach San Fernando and drew back into Bataan, many supplies could not be transported for lack of trucks. This included the mountains of steaks, turkey, and Maine lobster in Jai Alai.

There were sixty-five thousand Filipino troops, fifteen thousand Americans and about ten thousand civilian Filipinos to feed behind our lines. A lot of open mouths and hungry bellies. A jungle bakery was set up that turned out twenty thousand small loaves a day until, before long, it ran through our meager flour supply. The Quartermaster Corps impounded the limited rice supplies grown in jungle-bound Bataan, set up rice mills and husked it. They set up fish traps along the coast and netted several thousand pounds a day until the traps were destroyed by dive bombers. They distilled sea water to make salt. They made rendezvous with small inter-island boats that ran the gauntlet of Nip destroyers to bring thousands of sacks of rice from the Central Philippine Islands to Bataan. The last of these ships was sunk in February, 1942.

The troops went on rice twice a day as their basic food in January, 1942. They learned to cook and eat it and were glad to get it. We at the hospital were more fortunate. Our canned-food allowance was greater. We could serve some canned meat, beans or vegetable stew with our two rice meals. We received one doughnut and tea for lunch until the beginning of March, when we ran out of flour. We set up a special diet kitchen under red-haired Miss Juanita Redmond, later to escape from Corregidor and return to the States. The more seriously sick and wounded continued to receive some milk, meat, liver (when available), and extra vitamins until the surrender. The veterinarians set up a corral for carabao, horses, and mules in the mountains and went into the butchering business. We learned to eat, enjoy, and anticipate this meat when and as it came in.

Our setup in the hospital was infinitely better than G.I. Joe's in his foxhole out in the hills. In addition to a greater food allowance, we had plenty of water for our homemade showers and all the water we wanted to drink. We were on a main road and could go after our rations by truck if they did not arrive. He, on the other hand, was out in the middle of nowhere fighting in his foxhole and sleeping near it. His chow arrived cold twice a day, if it arrived at all: in the early hours of the morning and late at night. Brought by truck on newly hacked jungle trails, it was then carried by litter and mule pack to his isolated position. To supplement his meager ration, he hunted, killed, and ate anything that walked, crawled or flew: wild carabao, pig, monkey, lizard, and snake. He got lean, haggard, and wild-eyed. He was constantly hammered by dive and high-level bombers, battered by massed tanks and artillery, and pounded by tens of thousands of fresh, well-fed Jap shock troops, seasoned fighters from the China campaigns. Why didn't they quit and desert in droves? The answer can be found only in their basic self-respect, love of country, and hatred for the Nips. They limped back to the hospital with foot drop (paralysis of the outer muscles of the lower leg), their faces puffy from beriberi, gums bleeding from scurvy, tongues raw and mouths ulcerated from pellagra.

Sleeping in mosquito-infested Bataan without nets, without prophylactic quinine, they came down with racking chills and fever. Before the fall of Bataan, as high as 80 per cent of a typical regiment had malaria.

A man can go a long time without food in the tropics, but he goes raving mad in a couple of days without water. The few watering points and water trucks were totally inadequate. The Lister bags issued to each company were not plentiful enough when the outfit was deployed to cover a half-mile of line. The chlorine for them soon ran out. It was not possible at all times to boil water because of the danger of campfires attracting dive bombers and enemy artillery. Thirst-crazed men drank water they knew to be polluted, from carabao wallows and stagnant mountain pools. At least 30 per cent of the troops had bacillary dysentery, 10 per cent amoebic dysentery, and the rest some variety of worm infestation of the bowel.

They were carried to the hospital. We washed, shaved, and clothed them. We fed the sickest extra chow; the rest ate what we ate. We treated them as best we could with our dwindling supply of medicine, replenished occasionally from stocks in Corregidor and brought over by boat at night. There was never enough to cure them. We could hope only to control their disease. After a rest of a week or two, they went back to fight and die.

We entered the final hectic days as free men in the hospital oppressed by impending disaster and flooded with work. The long-expected all-out frontal attack by the Nips had begun. For weeks our G-2 had received reports of thousands of fresh Jap troops being brought to advanced positions along the Bigaac-Pilar Road. Our Filipino informants brought news of hundreds of tanks, huge dumps of ammunition and supplies rumbling southward out of Manila. Wild rumors floated through the hospital:

Chiang Kai-shek had sent troops to reinforce us—some men actually claimed to have seen them.

Negroes on white horses had landed on Batangas across the bay, American cavalry Negro divisions, and the long-expected reinforcements from the States were offshore, ready to land and catch the Nips from the rear.

It was all scuttlebutt of the rankest kind.

In the meantime Nip planes bombarded us with propaganda pamphlets urging the Filipino troops to desert, instructing them how to turn in and offering them amnesty.

Large flights of Nip bombers were in the air constantly dropping their loads on all roads, bridges, and installations. Surrounded as our hospital was by a huge ammunition dump of high explosives and artillery shells on our left, a motor pool on our right, a unit of the Two Hundredth Antiaircraft on a hill behind us, and a quartermaster dump on the road in front, we heard the deafening crash of falling bombs day after day. We were petrified that on some of their runs loads of bombs aimed at these installations might be short or long and land in our tiny area, plainly marked as it was by Red Cross flags and signs painted on the roofs of the wards. We had had a close miss in Limay when the Nips, while bombing a bridge nearby, dropped a load two hundred yards from our buildings. Working indoors, we could hear the Nip planes droning overhead but couldn't tell when we were within bombing range. Although I didn't particularly enjoy the prospect of being killed by high explosives, I was especially horrified by the vision of being crushed to death by falling timber.

To make matters worse for us, the road swung in a wide curve behind the hospital to climb a slope we called the Zigzag. From within the operating rooms, heavily laden trucks grinding up this steep grade sounded exactly like Nip bombers high overhead. Standing tense at the operating tables, faces drawn and hands trembling, we paused in our work, listening to the grind of the motor, praying for the change in the sound when the truck driver shifted his gears into second. If the gears didn't shift, we waited even more intently for the scream of a falling bomb. It was a noise we had to hear only once to remember for life. To me it sounded like a giant locomotive blowing off steam, first faintly and distantly, then with a maddening increasing crescendo that filled the whole world with its horrible rasping hissing. When we heard that awesome sound, sterile gown and gloves notwith-standing, we made a hasty dive for the floor. Flattened out, we waited for the tearing crash of the explosion. Storybook writers talk about men in danger seeing their lives pass in review in their minds' eye. I was conscious only of an overwhelming desire to live.

On March 27 the Nips dropped some incendiaries in our rear area. The enlisted men's barracks caught on fire and was par-tially burned. Private First Class Burks, M.C., had his upper jaw blown off. Although we didn't believe the raid was aimed at the hospital, that didn't put Burks's jaw back on his face.

We had been working all night. I had reached the point where, bombs or no bombs, I had to get some sleep if I was to refrain from going completely whacky.

"Joe," I said to Captain Bulfamonte, who was resting on a cot near me, "wake me up if anything happens." I plopped on my cot and fell immediately into a profound slumber. I dreamed of my trip cross-country before the war.

I had left El Paso and the flat dry mesquite country of the Mex-ican border. The brilliant sun flooded the landscape. The motor purred happily, devouring the miles. Images floated by my eyes of a week end at the Grand Canyon: the pleasant lodge, the spectacular vista of purples and reds, the exciting trip down the face of the gorge to the bed of the Colorado. I relived my visit to Boulder Dam. A guide was taking us through the intricacies of various levels on the downstream face.

"Looks like you have a leak," I said, pointing to a crack in the concrete wall.

"Oh, yes," he said blandly. "This dam is going to bust wide open in a few minutes."

While we watched, the tiny crack grew larger. The drip of water coalesced into a trickle, a stream, a torrent until, with a roar and a crash, the walls of the dam tumbled over upon us.

Panic-stricken, I awakened suddenly. The air was filled with the roar of exploding bombs and a pungent odor of smoke. Walls and floor heaved and tossed. Beams groaned, creaked, and fell apart. There was a trickle of blood coming from a wound on my forehead.

Confused by the blast, I stumbled out. One bomb had dropped on the left wing of the officers' quarters and demolished it. The right wing, where I had been sleeping, was still intact but riddled with shrapnel. Bombs were still dropping throughout the hospital area, sending up showers of dirt, pebbles, and clods of earth. Clouds of smoke filled the air as small incendiary bombs exploded and sent their burning, spluttering contents in all directions. Lying flat in a drainage ditch, chest heaving with terror, I waited for the ear-shattering explosions to subside. Then I made a dash for the operating rooms. The compound was empty except for a solitary figure that I could see through the haze. There was Colonel Duckworth with a fire extinguisher nestled in his huge arms like a toy, playing its stream on a burning building. The silent bodies of fourteen of our native hospital bedmakers were strewn about. A truck loaded with dead, charred bodies lay on its side in the road. The litter bearers brought in our Private First Class Fred Lang, M.C., dead with a hole through his heart. Master Sergeant Spielhoffer, M.C., was carried in with his foot torn off. He died later of uncontrollable infection.

The same day the Nip radio sent over a "So-sorry" broadcast in English. "We regret the unfortunate bombing of Hospital No. 1. It was a mistake."

We knew it was deliberate. We knew we were living on borrowed time. On April 5 we got it again. As the bomb bays opened and the bombs came whistling down, Private First Class McNulty, M.C., made a dash for a dugout near the kitchen. It was filled with Filipino mess attendants. Trying to wedge in, he thought angrily: To hell with this joint; it's too God damn crowded, and threw himself into a near-by drainage ditch. In the blinding crash that followed, the Filipinos were all crushed to death.

The next day I was leaving the wrecked officers' quarters with Father Cummings of San Francisco, our beloved and respected Mariposan brother whom I had first met at Santa Escolastica in Manila. We were crossing the bare plaza in the center of the compound when we heard the screech of Nip dive bombers coming over the mountains and bearing down directly at the hospital. There was no shelter available, no time to run. We hit the dirt and waited, but not long. The world exploded. I don't know how long we were knocked out. Bleeding from the nose and ears, drums shattered, concussed, holding on to each other, we stumbled toward the wards through the dusty, smoky murk. I saw him enter a ward filled with several hundred fear-maddened patients whose fractured legs and arms were tied down in traction so that they were unable to move. I mounted the veranda of the operating pavilion from which post I could see and hear him.

"O.K., boys, O.K. Take it easy," he shouted in a dry husky voice. "You're all right. It's all over. Calm down. The planes have gone."

He mounted a little wooden box. With arms outstretched, hands and fingers trembling, he entreated: "O.K., men. Let's say a prayer together. You know the Lord's Prayer. I'll start in and you follow."

The words cut clear through the weeping and groans of the wounded:

"Forgive us our trespasses, As we forgive those who trespass against us. And lead us not into temptation, But deliver us from evil..."

The ever increasing crescendo of a ghastly whistle and screech drowned him out. A half-ton bomb landed in the center of the ward. A heavy pall of dust settled slowly over the compound.

Through the portals of the operating room the medics carried in unrecognizable masses of human wreckage still pulsating with life. A hundred were killed in a flash, a hundred and fifty wounded, including nurses Easterling, Palmer, and Hogan. Corporal McFee, M.C., had a back cut to shreds. Private First Class Hale had a hole in his belly. I saw Father Cummings being littered in, face gray, eyes open, lips moving. I nodded to the litter bearers to carry him to my table and I checked him over hastily.

"Not bad, not bad, Father," I said, my voice full of relief. "Your left forearm is torn up a little but everything else is O.K."

He attempted a feeble smile, whispering, "Guess the Devil wasn't ready for me, Al," and closed his eyes.

While Captain Al Poweleit, M.C., decorated for bravery many times in General Weaver's tank outfit, and sweet-faced Benilda Castaneda and I attempted to reconstruct the muscles of his forearm, a curious religious service took place. Father Cummings, fingering his rosary, his eyes still shut, said a Hail, Mary and Benilda Castaneda made the response.

"Hail, Mary, full of Grace, the Lord is with thee, blessed art thou amongst women and blessed is the fruit of thy womb, Jesus. Holy Mary, mother of God, pray for us sinners now and at the hour of our death."

While they were praying Al and I swore steadily: "The yellow bastards... The slit-eyed lice... The mother-loving sonsabitches..."

Prayers and imprecations wove themselves in an odd refrain of point and counterpoint. They were praying and we were cursing, but we were all addressing the same listener.

Hours later, Liebert and I finished a head case together. It had been a long and tedious job of removing a fragmented, depressed piece of skull over the back of the head about two inches in diameter. Liebert had been unusually slow and I was irritable, as usual.

I snapped: "For God's sake, Liebert, what the hell's the matter with you? Have you been hitting the hospital alcohol again?"

He shook his head confusedly, "I don't know, Doc. I've had a pounding headache ever since I got hit on the helmet with some shrapnel a couple of hours ago." He bent his head so that I could see a ragged hole in the crown of his helmet.

"You damn fool," I stormed, "why didn't you tell somebody about it? Take it off."

I ran a gloved hand through his thick brown hair. A finger slipped into a depression with rough bony edges about two inches above and behind his right ear.

"Everything O.K., Doc?" he asked.

"Yeah, everything is O.K.," I muttered. "Climb on that table."

With Al Poweleit's help we shaved the head, anesthetized the scalp, clipped away the fragmented bone of the skull, and removed an ugly chunk of shrapnel buried deep in the brain.

When we were finished bandaging his head, I noticed he was grinning through his pain. I asked him wearily what the hell was so funny.

He said: "As long as I could hear you cussing I knew everything was all right."

Waves of bombers were still making their runs near the hospital area. For safety's sake, we carried Liebert into a near-by bamboo thicket that had a long slit trench and gently lowered him into it. One of the surgical nurses, black-haired Miss Easterling, offered to stay up with him all night, despite her wounds. We wrapped our patient in blankets and put him to sleep under the canopy of a star-filled night. I returned the next morning to check his dressing.

"How did he spend the night, Easty?" She was bleary-eyed with fatigue.

"Oh, he tumbled and tossed, but not too bad."

"How's about it, Liebert?"

"O.K. Ready to go to work," was the forced, thick response.

Made uneasy by the drone of approaching bombers, I stood up in the trench. There was a flight of six, two-motored jobs heading our way. I watched intently trying to estimate their course, eyes dazzled by the sunlit sky. The motors throbbed in deafening crescendo as they approached. People scurried for shelter and the compound was suddenly deserted. Shading my eyes, I caught the glint of the sun on the bombs as they dropped through the air.

"Jesus Christ, hold on to everything!" I bellowed, squatting down, chin resting on knees, arms doubled against the belly, face jammed in the farthest corner of the trench. The bombs landed with a tremendous blast. We were showered with the usual pebbles and dirt, but nothing worse.

I opened my eyes. While I had cowered in the corner, East-erling had thrown her body over Liebert's, spread-eagle fashion.

To Sergeant Joe Robertson, medic and ex-trapper of Rock Springs, Wyoming, I am grateful for giving me back a whole day that had been blown out of my life. The Nips had bombed the hospital again on April 7, 1942. A close hit had creased my scalp and blown me over. This was about ten A.M. Thereafter I remember doing only two operations. According to Joe, who was "circulating nurse," I operated all day and all night until after sunrise the next morning. The only peculiar behavior he noticed on my part was that I swore more than usual and in several lan-guages, one of which, Yiddish, was strange to him. Also, every time he offered me a new operating gown in exchange for the bloody one I was wearing, I pushed it impatiently away.

For twenty hours I had operated steadily with brief respites for coffee and sandwiches. A steady stream of patients passed be-fore me on the operating table. My mind functioned automat-ically, my fingers worked mechanically with a scalpel in living tissue, my dull lips uttered instructions to assistants. I have no recollection of whom I operated on or what I did. Did these pa-tients live? Did they die? To this day I have no idea.

CHAPTER 4.
Surrender At
Little Baguio

DURING THE NEXT DAY THE camp was flooded with more rumors and counter rumors:

The line across the Bataan peninsula at Limay had been broken. A new line ten miles north of us, with Mount Sumat as its center, was being formed. Our artillery positions on the mountain were decimating Nip columns attempting to advance along the eastern coastal road. The Thirty-first and Fifty-seventh Shock Regiments were moving forward to plug gaps in the new line.

From ambulance drivers and wounded pouring into the wrecked hospital, no clear picture could be pieced together. They knew only of heavy fighting going on in their limited sectors. Covered with mud, hungry and bleeding, it was with the greatest of difficulty that patients could do more than identify themselves and answer simple medical questions.

After a lean supper the news broke and reverberated hollowly through the hospital. The Nips were flooding down the road; our troops had been ordered to drag their weary bodies southward of us to Mariveles at the tip of the peninsula and there ground arms. The official surrender would take place on April 9. We accepted this news with mixed feelings. The sick were too ill to give a damn one way or the other. My assistant, Sergeant Robertson, and some of the other corpsmen who had sworn they would never be captured drifted off into the jungle to hide out. After several days in the mountains unsuccessfully attempting to work his way north through the Nip lines, Robertson swam eight kilometers of shark-infested waters to be washed up alive and kicking at Corregidor.

Most of us stayed for various reasons. We had eighteen hundred helpless casualties to treat and feed. We were afraid that if we were found by isolated bands of Nips trying to escape through the jungle we would be knocked off. Where reason and duty were wedded so harmoniously, it was not difficult to make a decision. We stayed.

The strength-sapping tropical sun had set. The early evening breeze rustled through the giant hardwood trees, making the vine-bedecked branches sway gently. The crickets were out in swarms, filling the air with their rasping music. Mysterious jungle grunts and whispers drifted into our compound.

This tropical noisy silence was broken by the grinding of gears as two swollen-bellied Pambusco trucks creaked their way slowly up the grade outside. They stopped in front of the nurses' quarters.

"O.K. girls," bellowed a burly transportation officer. "Orders are for all of you to go to Corregidor on the double. The tug is waiting at Mariveles. Take only what you can grab. No more than a suitcase apiece. Make it snappy. Don't know when the Nips are coming down the road."

To a group sitting dazed on the porch he shouted: "For Chri'sake, hurry up! I've got to get you out in five minutes. The road south is jam-packed."

Shaken out of their lethargy, the nurses scurried into their quarters, reappearing almost instantly with a pitiful handful of personal effects. Farewells were hasty and tearful, kisses sweet and salty. In the blackout, pierced by the beams of blue-paper-covered flashlights, we waved farewell to a courageous, lovable group of girls.

We got the word later in the day that the huge ammunition dumps on the hill overlooking the hospital a half-mile away were to be set off at eleven P.M. Hurriedly, we stationed fire guards throughout the hospital area to deal with stray exploding shells. We gently unloaded the medically ill from our homemade, triple-decker bamboo beds and placed them on the floor. Even more gently did we take our fracture cases out of their "Rube Goldberg" traction beds and laid them on the ground in Thomas splints where they would be less likely to be hit by shell fragments. Those who could walk crowded into air-raid shelters or huddled between the protecting skirts of the giant hardwood trees. Having seen too many men buried alive in air-raid shelters, I preferred the protection of a shallow foxhole and the company of two of my patients.

At the appointed hour, the sky line behind the hospital was illuminated with an eye-searing glare as the first warehouse filled with dynamite and high explosives was detonated. The earth trembled as if shaken by a giant fist. The trees creaked their complaints bitterly while the air was filled with the roar of released energy. Blast followed blast interminably until it seemed as if the shreds of my already ruptured eardrums would be ripped from their moorings. It would be a hell of a note, I thought, to get knocked off by one of our own shells. The hours passed, marked by the whine of tracer bullets through the sky and the shrill whistle of shells lobbing their way overhead. At three P.M. it was evident that the major portion of the demolition had been completed. We set to work putting the camp to rest and the fracture patients in their harnesses again.

Early the next morning Colonel Duckworth assembled the full complement of the hospital staff. Decked out as usual in freshly starched and pressed khaki, square jaw set grimly, face filled with pent-up emotion, he said almost harshly:

"The fighting is over, but our show still goes on. We've got a load of eighteen hundred sick and wounded to take care of. That's my job. That's your job. Don't forget that. We've stuck together well during the fighting. Let's continue to do so. The Japs ought to be here sometime this morning. I want every one of you to continue working in the wards and in the operating pavilion as usual. I don't know what's going to happen. I'll do the best I can to protect all of you." With a drawn, gray expression, he ordered the Red Cross flag to be lowered and a white bedsheet substituted. It hung listlessly from the top of its makeshift pole.

It wasn't long before we heard the sound of distant firing muffled by the clanking of iron treads. A line of Nip medium tanks rounded the curve and came pounding down the road toward the hospital, machine guns blazing, spraying the underbrush.

Flanked by Captain Lemke, M.A.C., and Claude Fraley, Colonel Duckworth marched quickly down the road to meet the enemy. The leading tank stopped. Machine guns swiveled to cover the tiny group. The turret opened and a much bebraided Nip poked his head out and expectorated a long string of Japanese. When this brought no response the Nip barked into the tank and clambered down, followed by a subordinate who was apparently an interpreter.

"This is the general of the tank unit," he said curtly.

Colonel Duckworth saluted sharply. "I am the commander of this hospital. It is my duty to surrender it to you."

"You have Japanese wounded soldiers in your custody?" the general asked.

"Yes, forty-two."

"Send them here immediately."

A line of straggling, walking wounded came limping out of the Nip ward. There was much bowing, scraping, saluting, and questioning back and forth between them and the Nip general.

He turned to Colonel Duckworth at length and said: "These soldiers say you have treated them well and kindly. You have fed and clothed them and given them good surgical care. How many have you killed?"

"None have died although there are many who are still seriously ill after operation. Some of these may die."

"Show them to me."

Led by our C.O., the general strutted into the Nip ward where Captain Dan Golenternick, M.C., was busy dressing a leg case. The Jap motioned to him to continue his work. Of all the wards in the hospital, fate had destined that the Nip ward was to suffer least from the bombings the hospital had undergone during the past ten days. The showers were functioning; the latrines were working; the roof was intact. The slopeheads, wearing clean pajamas, were lying on surgical beds covered with clean linen. Candy and cigarettes were on their side tables. An interchange of rapid-fire questions and answers took place, apparently to the satisfaction of the Nip general who gradually relaxed and became less formal. He was then taken on a tour of inspection of the hospital grounds. He pointed to the huge bomb crater in the heart of the hospital and asked what had happened.

"A Japanese bomb," Colonel Duckworth said briefly. "This area housed a ward of two hundred and fifty patients when the bomb exploded. A hundred died and the others were wounded. The ward disappeared."

Sucking through his teeth, he muttered to himself. The interpreter translated. "That's too bad. That is unfortunate."

Then turning, he said: "You have treated my soldiers well. I shall make the hospital my headquarters for the next few days. I shall bivouac my tanks here. I shall instruct my men to refrain from interfering with you or your duties. Carry on with your work." Saluting briskly, he departed.

I counted sixteen tanks as they lumbered in. They maneuvered into position covered-wagon style, a circle with guns pointing outward. The compound was suddenly filled with a swarm of Nips climbing out of their tanks and quickly going about their business of refueling, replacing treads, and oiling. As dusk fell the gloom was splintered by gleaming sparks from many campfires as each tank crew sat about on their haunches cooking their rice and soybean mix in individual pots.

"What a break," I whispered to Jack Gordon as we returned to our quarters after the last case was finished.

"Yeah," said Jack grimly. "You certainly can't predict what these yellow bastards will do. I figured this was the end. Maybe it's just the beginning." He was prophetic—horribly so.

CHAPTER 5.
Prison Life Begins
At Little Baguio

AN IMMENSE SILENCE HUNG OVER the hospital, stifling, heavy, and oppressive. Doctors and corpsmen went about their work quietly and grimly. They gave orders in subdued voices, examined and treated their patients without banter. The patients themselves had little to say and less desire to say it. We felt an overwhelming sense of relief now that the bombings had ended and a surge of happiness that we had come out of it alive. Yet we still had a wild, unshakable premonition of impending disaster whenever Nip planes zoomed overhead on their course to Corregidor. Our relief was overshadowed by the sickening realization that we had surrendered and were prisoners of Japan. The more optimistic still kidded themselves with the idea that as long as Corregidor held we had hopes of recapture. Most of us felt that the show was over and that we were in the soup for God knew how long. We were seven thousand miles away from home and safety; we had thousands of sick and wounded to house, feed, and treat; we had a tiny food supply and less medicine. Worst of all, we were at the mercy of an arrogant, brutal enemy who had a deeply inculcated hatred for us. And we were still punchy from the bombings.

Our stupor, lethargy, and depression was evident to Colonel Duckworth who assembled us again at the foot of the white flag.

"Men," he said grimly, "we're in a mess. I know it as well as you. But we're not going to get out of it by moping, whining or asking for sympathy. I know the Japs better than you do and I can assure you, you won't get sympathy from them. If you become a disheveled, slovenly mob, they will treat you as such. This will not happen as long as I am alive. Although you are prisoners, you are still members of the United States Army. We must impress the Japs that we are a well-disciplined, smart-looking, smoothly functioning outfit. Their god is discipline. They begrudgingly admire it in others as much as in themselves. You must maintain your own self-respect. You must shave every day, keep your clothes washed and pressed and shoes shined. We've got plenty of soap and water. Use it. Salute your arms off, smart and snappy, especially when Nip inspection parties come through.

"I can't begin to control them unless I can prove to them I can control you. I must impress the Japs that I take it for granted the sick and wounded will get what they need. I must flatter them, let them feel that Japan is a humane nation and as its representatives I expect them to act humanely.

"We've had a lucky break. We've made a good start. We are temporarily under the protection of the Jap tank general who is pleased with the treatment we gave the Jap wounded. I'll push that luck as far as it will go, but I need your cooperation. I've given you my orders. They must be followed out. We still have our own M.P.'s and our own brig. And by God I'll use it if I have to. [And he did.] That is all." His jaw closed with a snap.

Ashamed of our own weakness, angered by his reproach and steadied by his rocklike character, we rolled up our sleeves and went to work. There was plenty to do. Every building and ward in the compound was completely or partially wrecked except for the one that had housed the Nip wounded. Foraging through the engineer dumps several miles behind the hospital, Fraley and his construction gang found piles of timber, kegs of nails, sheet metal and wire which they loaded on our trucks and furtively brought back to the hospital. Doctors and medics alike who could be released from professional work piled into the task of clearing away wreckage and debris, pulling down irreparable shacks, filling in bomb craters, salvaging clothing, shoes, cots, and medical equipment.

Huge trees uprooted by bombs were sawed into lengths and chopped into kindling. The thud of picks digging post holes, the tapping of hammers and the clang of sheet metal being fitted on the roof of reconstructed wards could be heard from dawn to twilight.

There was a lofty pine tree in front of the surgical pavilion that looked like the fade-out of an old Mack Sennett comedy. Soaring a hundred feet in the air, its branches were draped with blankets, pajamas, linen, sheets, shattered arms, legs, and tin roofing metal deposited there when a bomb had blown an adjacent ward sky high. Private Ivy, a guitar-strumming, good-natured hillbilly from Arkansas, and lantern-jawed Corporal Nygaard of Montana scaled its dizzy heights and cleared its branches. We all felt better when the carnage could no longer be seen. While working on it they built a crow's nest from which we could watch local Nip troop movements and the fighting on Corregidor later on.

Chaplain Tiffany and Father McDonnell, tall, emaciated, genial young padre from New York, rebuilt the officers' quarters, sweating in the broiling sun for days on end. The lives these men led during the fighting and after the surrender were sermons in themselves. Father McDonnell had been in the front lines with the Forty-fifth Philippine Scouts, working more often as a first-aid man under fire than as a psalmist in the rear. Chaplain Tiffany had been with us throughout the show as a litter bearer day and night, substituting for the medics when they were ready to cave in with exhaustion.

Our personnel had changed. We had gained new faces and lost old ones. Colonel Adamo, Commander Smith, and Lieutenant Nelson, our three best surgeons, had left for Corregidor with the nurses before the fall of Bataan. Al Poweleit had gone up the road with General Weaver the night before the surrender. Personnel from the Twelfth Medical Regiment and a few medical officers of various infantry units had been absorbed into the hospital on the day of surrender. Captain Andy Rader, a little spark plug with sharp brown eyes and close-clipped mustache, became executive officer. He carried out Colonel Duckworth's policies smoothly and well. Officers and men liked him for the sensible, man-to-man approach he used. He gave us credit for having brains and let us use them. In all contacts with subordinate Jap officers he served as a buffer for Colonel Duckworth, who refused to deal with any Nip unless he was a high-ranking officer. By preventing himself from being pushed around, the Duck gained face in the Jap's eyes.

It was a fascinating game of psychology we watched unfold, with our lives and the lives of our patients at stake. Colonel Duckworth maintained a formal, formidable front, respectful but dignified. Andy helped him by doing the necessary dirty work cleverly, willingly, and well. The Duck awed the Jap brass; Andy soft-soaped the young Japs. Supported by his professional staff and tough, disciplined medics, the Colonel deliberately and cautiously wove his way back and forth through the intricacies of the Nip mind. There could be no blunder.

Whenever he learned of a bigwig coming in to inspect, he had us put on a big show. We scrubbed and cleansed the entire area. We delayed procedures on patients who needed operations of choice until just before their arrival. Then, with all the tables loaded, we went to work, stopped when the inspecting party entered, saluted, and went back to work again. It was obvious that they were impressed and, incidentally, convinced of the necessity of letting us keep our equipment and supplies. We put out our cleanest linen for the ward beds, scoured the concrete floors and raked the earthen ones. We made fly traps by the hundreds to keep the area insect-free. Kitchens were immaculate and utensils gleaming. The officers and medics bellowed "Attention!" and almost tore their arms out saluting the Duck every time they saw him with the Nips. Standing rigidly, they waited until the salute was returned. It was almost like a comic opera, but we played it in dead earnest.

Slim, dark-haired Lieutenant Tarzan Tucker of New Orleans was a newcomer to the hospital. Drawling, soft-spoken and tolerant, he was the peace maker of our group in the endless, argumentative bull sessions we held nightly.

"You know God damn well that the War Department never planned to reinforce us in Bataan. They're a bunch of stinkin' liars. We're all suckers."

"The hell you say! They were all set to send us help. We laid down too soon."

"Laid down too soon? Why you stupid bastard, who are you to talk? All you've done since the war started is lay on your fat butt and sleep all day."

And Tarzan would pipe up: "All right, all right. Take it easy. We're all hungry now. That's all. It won't make things any easier if we start taking it out on each other."

Lieutenant Al Mohnac of New Jersey, dentist and plastic surgeon, had joined us. He had had a rough time in the field and was grateful to be in the security of the hospital. The athletic type, he rigged up a chinning bar and got us interested in keeping fit when the work in the hospital slowed down. Although I got nothing out of the chinning bar except a strained back, he did teach me how to patch and sew clothes. We slept on adjoining cots. I had one jar of sweet mixed pickles left from my foraging before the surrender. Nightly we went through the solemn ceremony of eating one sliver apiece before we went to bed. We made that jar last a month.

Reinforced by these newcomers, we piled into the backlog of work. After the bombing of April 7, we had evacuated about a thousand patients to Hospital No. 2. Dazed and concussed, many had wandered off into the jungle and up the road in their hospital pajamas and slippers. Some started on the Death March in this costume. I don't know if they ever finished, but the chances were against it. Since all our nurses had gone to Corregidor, the new medics who took over some nursing functions were a godsend to our overworked corpsmen. They already had their hands full on many different work details: wrecking, construction, wood chopping, latrine digging, sanitation control, burials, and mess.

Things settled down after a fashion. We set up a routine of sorts even though we had the uneasy feeling that we might be ordered to pack up and move at any moment. The Nip tanks rumbled out of our compound after a few days. We drew a deep sigh of relief. The Japs had shaken down a few of the medics but nobody had been seriously maltreated. Before he departed, the tank general posted "Keep Off—Out of Bounds" signs about the area. Apparently he was a man of much importance because very few Nip soldiers straggled through the hospital even though the road was clogged with them.

The Jap general assured us that we would receive enough rice in weekly installments to keep us going. He implied that we would have to hump ourselves for any extras. After much haranguing, the Duck and Andy were able to wangle passes from him authorizing us to forage anywhere south of Balanga City, about two thirds of the way down the peninsula. We had plenty of gasoline buried throughout the area and had unearthed gasoline dumps in the motor pool a mile away. Andy Rader, Fraley, Lieutenant MacAndler, Tarzan Tucker, and Charley Keltz took off into the jungle day after day with their medics to see what they could find. Disheveled, sweat-soaked and begrimed, they came back empty handed.

Tarzan said: "We walked down to the old quartermaster dump. What do you think we found? Hundreds of cases of fruit juice, canned milk, and fruit. Think of it. Hundreds."

We all stirred happily.

"And each one had a hole punched in it," he added, "a tiny little ole hole."

Then our luck turned. MacAndler bumped into a Nip soldier who could speak a little English. He was off duty and was looking for excitement.

"And so we went hunting wild carabao in the hills and brought down two," he announced triumphantly. After that, hunting expeditions went out daily. Sometimes we bagged carabao, horses, mules, and calesa ponies—sometimes nothing. It was evident that this hit-or-miss system would not adequately fill the bellies of a thousand men. Rader rode boldly into the Nip headquarters in Balanga and requested permission to buy carabao from the natives. And, surprisingly enough, he got it.

We set up a corral near the hospital. For the remainder of our stay at Little Baguio we were assured of a fairly adequate meat supply in the form of a carabao stew to add to our rice twice a day. It wasn't much, yet it made the steamed rice, which was nauseatingly unattractive to our sick patients, more savory and palatable. We still had a small stock of condensed milk and fruit juices which we dished out only to the postoperative patients and to the very seriously ill. They also got whatever liver, tongue, and sweetbreads were left after these items had passed through the hands of the galley crew.

Try as we might, there was a certain inevitable shrinkage of food in the galley which in some prison camps became quite serious. At Little Baguio, however, with a group of well-disciplined officers and medics, it was minimal. Every part of the animal was used from the brain to the tail. The guts, after cleansing, made a palatable soup. The bones were boiled and reboiled to get every ounce of marrow out of them. At this stage in the game we did not try eating the hide. That came later.

Other foraging details reported increasing success. Tarzan Tucker located several large banana and plantain groves. The line we followed was this: officers and men going out to gather fruit were entitled to eat as much of it as they liked while they picked. Everything loaded on the truck became the property of the hospital and was deposited in the food stores. This ruling was necessary to prevent accusations of food hoarding and nasty recriminations. Hungry men are suspicious of their fellow sufferers. Tarzan's detail returned with the complacent look that comes with a belly distended with food. The truck, loaded high with banana stems, drove into the compound, cheered on by convalescent patients assembled en masse. Everybody had a half-dozen ripe yellow bananas that night. For days thereafter we had a handout as the green ones turned mellow.

Our luck continued. Andy Rader located a small pineapple plantation in the heart of the jungle. With considerable difficulty we were able to drive our truck near it. We humped sack after sack of the juicy fruit. At midday we gorged ourselves on pineapple out in the field until our mouths were literally sore from the tart juices. That night when a handout of pineapple, chilled in our dozen refrigerators, was issued, we were ready for more. We had the "trots" all night, but it was worth it. Other windfalls came along; mango and coconut groves were spotted and plucked of their delicious sustenance. Mangoes were especially delicious with their tender, sweet, brilliant orange-colored meat wrapped in a thin yellow skin that peeled away easily. When green, the coconuts were especially good for the convalescents. Keltz was appointed salad specialist. Aided by several Filipinos who knew jungle plants, he came back daily loaded with bamboo sprouts, the flowers of banana trees, the hearts of young native trees, edible roots and vines. Chopped up, seasoned with a little coconut oil and acetic acid, they made a very palatable side dish. By his usual sleight of hand, Fraley dug up a huge fish net from one of his mysterious sources. For days his detail of navy corpsmen patiently tarred and repaired it. We never had a chance to use it, but it was a swell idea.

We had a scare when Colonel Duckworth came down with acute appendicitis. Captain Charley Osborne operated on him after holding off several days, hoping the inflammation would subside. The appendix was difficult technically to remove, being tied down behind the large bowel by adhesions. He finally got it out. The Duck was violently ill for days thereafter with nonfunctioning, distended bowels. The wound ruptured. After a stormy course he made the grade. He had a huge incisional hernia which grew steadily larger until I could have put two fists into the abdominal defect. Tough turkey that he was, though, he had an abdominal support made and was soon stomping about as chipper as ever. If he had kicked off, we really would have been in a mess.

The Nips collected all but one of our radios. At this period we were permitted to listen to the local and long-distance stations. The newscasts were so depressing that it was with dread that we tuned in. Singapore fell; the Nips stormed through Burma. In the West, the Germans marched triumphantly through the Ukraine. From the States we got nothing but production figures and words of encouragement for those embattled on Corregidor. Perched on our crow's-nest in the lonesome pine, we could see the bombs bursting on that sullen island and shells landing from hundreds of Nip batteries that lined the Bataan coast.

Fraley, the super-optimist, once came scrambling down from the perch with binoculars slung about his neck, bursting with excitement. "Fellers," he said, "I just counted a flight of two hundred planes heading this way and they're not Jap!"

He was right; they weren't Jap planes. They were sea gulls.

He was about as good a military strategist as he was a spotter. One day when we were arguing about the military situation he said: "The crux of the campaign against Japan will be the Burma Road. We must retake it, fight the Japs in China, establish air bases there, and destroy Japan by bombing."

"How about a naval fight across the Pacific first, with the recapture of the Philippines cutting the Japs off from their southern positions?" I wanted to know.

"It's possible," he said in his self-assured manner, "but I'll bet you twenty-five bucks that no American soldier sets foot on the Philippines before the surrender of Japan."

I'm still waiting to get paid.

For weeks the Nip batteries, many of which were in the hills overlooking the hospital, pounded Corregidor. To the question often posed: Why doesn't Corregidor return fire? We got an answer one afternoon when the air vibrated with the thunder of ten-inch shells passing overhead toward the Nip guns. They were low enough so that the vibration they set up made the trees shed their leaves. To me they sounded like the roar of a subway train— only worse. The shells flew all night, exploding with crashes that reverberated through the mountains. Disgusted with myself for not being able to sleep, I dragged into a foxhole and sweated it out there. None landed in our compound, but several socked Hospital No. 2. Throughout that night we heard the continuous crackle of small-arms fire on Corregidor. The next day we got word that the Nips had landed and that surrender was inevitable. The news crackled through the wards like electricity. We had been whipped. The future lay before us dark and dismal. Soldiers who had kept a stiff upper lip broke down, wept, cursed or stomped about in deep black depression.

It didn't last. Human nature has a great capacity for readjustment. With happy-go-lucky medics like Private First Class Frenchy Poier, curly, blond-headed de Groot, and half-Indian "Smitty" from Oklahoma cheering them up, the patients gradually regained their good spirits. Many of them had recovered sufficiently to make good use of the volley court and boxing ring we had set up for their and our entertainment. The matches were short, snappy, and harmless, with the sixteen-ounce gloves we used. The bouts also served as a means of letting off steam when some of the medics got tangled up with each other doing their daily chores. Many of the ex-patients chopped wood, worked in the wards, or walked in the woods for exercise. What with poker, bridge, crap shooting, and bull sessions, days melted into weeks.

The food supply was serious. Our lack of medical supplies was even more alarming. Repeated requests for medicine at the Nip headquarters at Balanga had been met with a curt: "We have none for you. Only headquarters in Manila can issue."

We knew the Japs were lying and they knew we knew. We couldn't afford to antagonize them.

Finally Andy Rader told Colonel Duckworth he'd like to try to make it into Manila with a command car we had found and kept hidden in the jungle.

"All right," the Colonel said. "You know the risks involved. You haven't a pass and you may get shot."

We sweated Andy out for three long days. He pulled into the hospital, face beaming, car loaded with medicines, food, candy, and cigarettes. By sheer bravado coupled with luck and the foraging pass the tank general had given him, he had made the hundred-and-fifty-mile trip successfully.

I asked Andy if he had seen any white women in Manila.

"No," he said. "Not a one, Al. I imagine it's safer for them to hole up until the Yanks return."

I nodded, wondering if Hanna had "holed up" and if so, where and how she was, and whether or not… So many questions and no answers. Rader's trip reminded me of one I had taken with Hanna.

South of the Pasay suburb of Manila we streaked down a ribbon of concrete. It was the rice-planting season. The dikes were open. The flat lands were covered with water. For miles about Manila the parched rice-paddy countryside with its checkerboard of knee-high retaining walls greedily lapped up life and sustenance. Slow moving carabao plodded knee-deep in churning mud, dragging harrows behind them that looked like huge women's combs. Groups of bare-footed Filipino women clustered in the paddies, backs bent, nimble fingers busily burying tender rice seedlings deep in the muck. Clothed in brilliant red and green blouses, sheltered by wide-spreading flat rice-straw hats perched precariously on their black hair, they sang the traditional rice-planting song as they worked.

In the distance we could see the brackish waters of the Laguna de Bai covered with fish traps, flocks of tame ducks, and square-sailed bancas.

We left the flat country and penetrated low rolling hills covered with coconut plantations. On the ground, flecked by the shadows of fronds waving in the breeze, shirtless Filipinos were busily ripping of the hairy coir covering of coconuts by impaling them on an iron stake.

The terrain grew more rugged as we climbed into foothills of the Sierra Madre Range. Evergreen trees reared overhead, their trunks supported by huge buttressing skirts. In the deep shadow of the forest, the air lost its mugginess and became invigoratingly cool. Clad in a light pale-green slack suit, Hanna snuggled closer.

The road crawled along the edge of a canyon. Far below we saw the flashing silver of a mountain stream and heard the roar of waterfalls.

We rounded a curve. In the sudden blinding glare of the tropical sun pouring through a forest glade a torrent of gurgling, gushing water poured over the brink of a precipice to go tumbling wildly into space in a greenish-white cascade. Prismatically cracking the white of the sun into a myriad of transparent colors, the waters fell into the depths of the gorge below.

Cheek to cheek, Hanna and I watched the ever-changing brilliant play of colors.

With no warning the order came through that Little Baguio was to be evacuated immediately. We were to transfer as a hospital unit to Camp O'Donnell, near Tarlac. Lieutenant Fraley and his gang of wreckers went into continuous operation, salvaging everything that could be ripped loose from its moorings. With only twelve weeks of experience as prisoners of the Japs, we had already learned the difficulties involved in procuring equipment and maintenance supplies from them. Stoves, mess gear, water pipes, wire, carpenter's tools, axes, electrical bulbs and pumps, generators and scrap metal, were boxed and labeled. Secret emergency food stores buried and dispersed in foxholes were unearthed as the wrecking continued day and night. Crutches, splints, overhead surgical spotlights, operating tables, breakable laboratory equipment, microscopes, medical and surgical supplies were packed by filthy, sweat-streaked officers and men. In the wards, patients in suspension fracture frames were tenderly but expeditiously unhooked from traction and swathed in plaster of Paris so that they could be transported by truck to Manila. The American patients would be left at the Bilibid Prison and the Filipinos at the Philippine General Hospital.

It was not easy to say good-bye to some of them. "Mindoro Joe," third substitute medical orderly and first substitute chaplain on the orthopedic ward, looked at me pleadingly, his eyes a liquid brown.

"Who will say de quan (prayers) for de Filipinos when de fader (priest) is sick? Let me go with you."

"Mindoro Joe," our nineteen-year-old bantamweight, had been peacefully growing rice in his father's paddies when the war broke out. He joined the army. During the break-through at Bigaac, a mortar shell caught him in a clearing. A shearing explosion transformed his two hands into bloody pulp. After six plastic operations he was left with the palm and thumb of the right hand and three stubby fingers of the left. Waving the disfigured stumps before me, he said entreatingly: "They are no good to fight the Japs, but you know they are very good to pray."

Max Blouse also wanted to truck along with us. Sixty-two-year-old soldier of the Spanish American War days, owner of the Laguna Tayabas Bus Company, he felt that this was his fight when war was declared. Turning his fleet of busses over to the army, he volunteered and was serving as transportation coordinator near Mariveles, Bataan, when a Nip high-explosive bomb filled with picric acid put an end to his abortive army career. He was carried into the hospital in shock, his fringe of white hair stained a brilliant yellow-green, his beak nose torn and swung to the right as if on hinges, revealing the base of his skull. There was blood oozing from jagged wounds of both broken arms. We treated him for shock for hours before any attempt could be made to reconstruct his face or reduce his multiple fractures. Two days later it was evident that the blood supply to the right arm was inadequate. It was amputated at the shoulder. The bones of the left arm healed properly. The ulnar and radial nerves, which had been severed by bomb fragments, showed no sign of return to function. The arm was paralyzed.

Pointing the stump of his right arm at me, his blue eyes glinting hard, he snorted: "These slopeheads haven't got me down yet, Doc. I'll see you in Manila after the Yanks and tanks come back."

I said good-bye to Juan Romero. He was a cocky, loud-mouthed Filipino hero who had no doubt manufactured a thrilling tale of war adventure to fit his wound and limp. He had entered the hospital bleeding profusely from a deep wound in his right buttock. There was no wound of exit. It was important to determine the type of missile responsible for the wound. A high velocity bullet, for instance, might have perforated the bones to the buttock and lodged in the lower abdomen; a grenade fragment might have lodged in the deep tissues of the buttocks to give rise to local infection. I questioned him at the time:

"Were you hit by a bullet, Juan?"

"No, sir."

"Was it a bomb, Juan?"

"No, sir."

"What the hell was it?"

Reluctantly, "Jap bayonet, sir."

I suppose the Purple Heart does not differentiate between a wound of the butt and a wound of the belly. Nor should it, Juan had stood his ground long after others had fled before the flood of Nips pouring over the Bigaac-Pilar Line until his machine gun had ceased functioning.

Early in the morning, a convoy of captured American trucks arrived and ground their way surlily up the grade leading to the wards. Mattresses two deep lined their bodies to break the shock of war-torn dirt roads. Heaven-sent morphine was pumped in a steady stream into hundreds of convalescent battle casualties to soothe angry wounds and quiet rapidly racing hearts. Hands waved weakly; wan, weary faces strained into farcical grins. Others were wet with silently streaming tears. Motors started. A babble of voices broke:

"See you in San Francisco."

"Keep your pecker up, Doc."

"All aboard the Yankee Express!"

"When you get to Manila, don't do what I want to do!"

Too soon the hospital was empty. Doctors and medical orderlies stared vacantly at each other or wandered aimlessly about the compound.

The operating pavilion, sturdy throbbing heart of the hospital, had ceased beating, its shrapnel-pocked walls and loosened joists and beams bearing mute testimony to the shellacking it had received. A deepening red stain in the corner showed where Miss Nash had been "wounded" by a spilled bottle of mercurochrome. The ghosts of Colonel Schock, D.D.S., and Lieutenant Chamberlain grimly continued to reconstruct shell-torn faces. The soft patter of Filipino nurses as they circulated about the loaded operating tables could still be heard. The wisecracks of New England's gum-chewing, happy-go-lucky Miss Zwicker still echoed on the listless air.

The officers' quarters were strangely silent, the right wing as deserted as the shattered, gaping left. They were empty except for the bamboo pole that our shell-shocked X-ray man was leaving behind. No longer would our sleep be interrupted by the crashing blows he dealt our unsuspecting rats.

In a peaceful jungle clearing stood my car which I had so brutally mutilated: its tires cut, gas tank loaded with sugar, crankcase with mud, engine head smashed with a sledge. It had seen Atlanta and New Orleans, San Antonio and Mexico City. It had circled the Grand Canyon and twisted along the sheer cliffs of Yosemite Valley. It had been my second home in Bataan, my porch, my rest room, and bedroom. It was not easy to leave it behind.

Our steadily expanding cemetery had suddenly ceased its growth. There they were, about one hundred and fifty crosses in silent parade, line upon line, white arms outstretched over freshly turned earth. A huge bomb crater was beside the cemetery. The bodies in it had escaped post-mortem mutilation by a mere ten yards.

Trucks for the hospital personnel finally arrived and were loaded. Perched high on our luggage, which we were permitted to take with us, we lurched and swayed northward up the dirt road which fringed the east coast of Bataan. We traveled past towering Mount Sumat, over the shattered bridge at Limay, past deserted, burned-out villages, the bloody Pilar-Bigaac Line, bombed-out Balanga with its flattened churches and charred school buildings; past the cane fields near Abucay-Hacienda Road on to San Fernando where we rested on the outskirts of that dying city. Then we went north along the smooth concrete highway through the rice country to the tiny bamboo village of Capas, which I was to know more intimately during the next six months, and on to a winding dirt road, past a dilapidated cemetery with its gaudily painted saints, through fields overrun with six-foot-tall kogon grass to a slight rise. We came to an abrupt, grinding halt. We had arrived.

CHAPTER 6.
Camp O'donnell:
The Devil Stirs A Broth

To THE ACCOMPANIMENT OF GUTTURAL growls and threatening gesticulations, we hustled our personal luggage off the trucks and spread our belongings on the ground. Our captors flew into our possessions with unconcealed greed while we watched impassively. Choice morsels for the looting Japs were razors, razor blades, pencils, pens, soap, jewelry, watches, insignias, and underwear. This feverish scavenge ring came to a sudden halt when a bellowing noncom came clattering out of the Nip headquarters building followed by his own retinue of thieves. From his noisy expostulations and jabbering we gathered that the first shakedown was quite unofficial. We stood by while the second took place. Through an interpreter we were instructed to hand over our hand axes and G.I. knives. As our luggage was again searched, the same pilfering performance took place.

From the knoll on which the Nip headquarters building stood, we saw a panorama of the camp. In the distance were the grass-covered foothills of the Zambales Range, rolling gently down to a winding river a mile away, the chief water supply for the mess halls. To and from it crawled an endless line of tiny figures in the sweltering, fecal air, carrying water buckets suspended from bamboo poles. In a corral close by, listless humpbacked cattle grazed. There was no other sign of life in this mile-square compound, which we were told housed forty thousand prisoners. No sound could be heard from the widely spaced bamboo barracks. Only the nauseating smell of night soil and the cloying odor of death indicated that these shacks were crowded with dead and dying. Coming from the wind-swept, tree-covered slopes of Little Baguio, we studied this forlorn scene with drawn faces and sinking hearts. As we carried our duffel bags down toward the so-called hospital area, two men came out of a neighboring barracks carrying a naked corpse between them. Wordlessly and without a glance at the new arrivals, they dumped it on the ground near sixteen others stacked like cordwood, turned and re-entered.

Andy Rader and Charley Osborne, who had arrived at Camp O'Donnell a week earlier, led us to our new quarters, vacated the day before by American prisoners sent out on work details. Of wood-plank construction with nipa-palm roofs, about fourteen by fourteen feet, they housed ten men apiece. We dumped our belongings on the floor and trailed out to locate old friends.

In the rapidly fading twilight I recognized a rolling, swinging gait that could belong only to Captain Al Poweleit. As the face and figure approached, I was less certain. Only the wide-beamed, powerfully constructed bony framework remained. In the twelve weeks that had elapsed since he left Little Baguio, his body tissues had melted away to a mere caricature of themselves. Heavy frontal ridges cast his blue eyes in somber darkness; the nostrils of his button nose flared back sharply; bronze skin stretched tightly over a massive, square-cut jaw. His huge bald head was supported by a flowerlike neck. His cavernous chest was symmetrically patterned with washboard ribs. Spirit and strength were still in his bull-like voice as he bellowed, "Well, I'll be a sonovabitch!" We danced about, walloping each other on the back.

"Stay right where you are," he ordered. "Don't you remember? This is the Fourth of July. We're going to have a party!"

Off he rolled again into a neighboring bahai (shack) to return immediately with a canteen and several articles wrapped in a ragged towel. He led off and I followed up and over a little rise until we had cleared the hospital area and were in an open field. Carefully he spread open his parcel. Reverently he whispered:

"Stateside coffee. Bananas." There they were, two of them, nestling in the rags.

Squatting on my heels, Filipino fashion, I watched him as he rolled some boulders together, got a twig fire going, emptied his canteen into a tin can and suspended it over the leaping flames.

I asked him how he felt.

"Not too bad except for the trots. That's the main trouble with this God damn camp. We've all had it, from the generals down to the privates. Some of us came down with the 'squitters' in the hills of Bataan, others picked it up drinking from carabao wallows on the Death March after the surrender. The rest of us got it in this perfume palace. By the way, how do you like the smell?" he asked.

"Lousy. Smells like a lot of dead bodies soaked in night soil."

"Bright boy. Do you see those shacks?" he pointed toward the river.

I could just make their outline out in the fast-settling gloom.

"That's the Filipino camp. Beside it is the American camp. That's where they live. When they die their bodies are dumped outside the barracks to make room for those who are sleeping in the mud under the barracks. There are about three hundred stiffs waiting to be buried now. By tomorrow morning they'll total four hundred. And most of them are covered with their own excrement. I haven't seen so much of it in all my life. If it rains tomorrow we can't bury the dead because the graves get filled with water. If it doesn't rain we can't bury them all because there aren't enough well men to dig that many holes."

In the flickering firelight his eyes glittered wildly and his voice cracked. "Nice place we have here," he muttered.

As we drank our coffee and finished off with the bananas, I got the story out of him piecemeal.

He had left Little Baguio on April 9, 1942, with a G.H.Q. group including Tank General Weaver to whom he was attached as medical officer. North of Balanga he was separated from his group. He trekked along the now infamous one-hundred-and-twenty-kilometer Death March from Bataan with thousands of other captives to San Fernando. Sick and well, they streamed along on little food and less water, with constant pressure on them by the Nip guards to keep moving. Feet blistered, the prisoners straggled on in thin, poorly guarded groups. Jovial and placid by nature, Al suddenly went berserk when he saw a limping G.I. being clubbed to death by a slopehead. Al had worked his way through medical school as a semi-professional boxer and had not forgotten all he had learned.

"I uncorked a right and caught the bastard flush on the jaw. It lifted him off his feet. He dropped to the ground without a sound. I dove for him and twisted his God damn head until I could feel his cervical vertebrae grate and slide over each other. Then I tossed the body and rifle into a bamboo thicket, picked up the punchy G.I. and moved down the road."

Nightmarish days followed one after the other until he reached San Fernando. Together with one hundred and twenty others, he was stuffed into a tiny metal box car for a day's ride to Capas. One hundred and seventeen crawled out alive. Then came a five-kilometer hike to the camp itself where, footsore, hungry, and crazy with thirst, he stood with a silent, broken host under the tropical sun for hours, waiting for the Nip prison commander to make his appearance. He finally came, a short, squat, evil-eyed Nip, his ugly face screened by long mustaches, and made his speech of welcome. Al said that, though it was delivered in Japanese, it dripped hatred and venom.

Carrying their dead and dying, herded like cattle, this shambling mass drifted away, the Americans in one direction, the Filipinos in another. Into dirt-covered, deserted barracks they crawled, packed by the hundreds, until all available floor space was filled with begrimed, sweating bodies. Still they came, dragging themselves under the barracks to get away from the burning sun. Those who could get no shelter staggered out into the fields to drop exhausted into a profound, dreamless sleep. Day after day they poured into this crowded compound until an estimated forty-five thousand Filipinos and eight thousand Americans were within the wire perimeter of its fence.

There was no fuel to boil the heavily contaminated river water used for cooking, nor any water with which to cleanse cooking utensils and mess gear. There were no tools to dig latrines, nor oil to burn them out and keep them properly sterilized; no lumber to construct overhead shelters to prevent the straddle trenches from flooding, no wire screens to protect the food from flies, no medicine to treat those with diarrhea, no bed pans to receive the droppings of those too ill to move, no soap to wash clothes, bodies, and floors covered with dripping night soil. There was nothing at all to sustain life except a blinding hatred for the Nips. This criminal negligence had more to it than mere Japanese inefficiency. Time and again requests for food, medicine, and tools by ranking American officers were turned away with a curt, bland: "So sorry. We can do nothing now."

The camp became one vast sewer, foul and stinking. Clouds of flies buzzed everywhere: in the latrines, where they dropped their eggs in teeming filth; on the faces of those in coma, rimming their lips and drinking from their half-open eyes; over open, dripping ulcers of arm and leg; in filth-soaked clothing. They settled in an almost solid, quivering mass on the rice buckets as they were loaded by shovel from the steaming kwalis (open kettles), refusing to rise as they were waved away by K.P.'s.

Eating became a tricky maneuver; one hand rapidly shoveled rice from mess kit into mouth while the other moved back and forth over a rag with which the rice in the mess kit was kept covered.

During the first few days there was little or no food available because of the lack of cooking facilities. The camp was still in the process of construction and by no means completed when hostilities began. Abandoned by the Philippine Seventy-first Division when the Japs drove south from Lingayen, it had lain deserted until it became a concentration camp for prisoners.

Using shovels made from mudguards of abandoned cars, the inmates dug dhobie clay from near-by rice paddies and constructed stoves large enough to hold large shallow iron containers about four feet in diameter. On these primitive ovens rice and water steamed, stirred by bamboo poles, to make the staple dish lugoua (rice gruel). Long straggling lines of prisoners waited for hours in the broiling sun or torrential rains to receive their watery portion twice a day. Anything that could hold water served as mess gear—helmets and Klim cans as well as the standard U.S. mess kit which the men pounded thin and rounded out so that it could hold more.

To this diet was occasionally added brown sugar, Camotes (sweet potatoes), and a marsh weed, konkon, more commonly called whistle weed, because uncooked, it was almost tough enough to whittle into long narrow whistles. Made of indigestible fiber, it acted like sandpaper on bacteria-torn, ulcerated intestines. On three occasions in twelve weeks carabao were slaughtered and issued, a quarter of a carcass to about five hundred men, enough to make a thin meat gravy. As the weeks went by, the alarming death rate stirred the Nips sufficiently to increase the rice ration so that steamed rice was served twice a day and lugoa for breakfast only. After a homemade baking oven was constructed, rice flour was issued for a period of a month and baked into small buns.

This diet was totally inadequate to meet the bodily requirements for protein and vitamins. This deficiency increased the cases of diarrhea. Pellagra, a disease caused by the lack of nicotinic acid obtained from meat, fish, and vegetable protein, was present in Camp O'Donnell in all its manifestations: dermatitis, diarrhea, dementia, and death. Nicotinic acid increases the resistance of the mucosa, the lining of the intestines, not only to infection, but also to the normal digestive action of the intestinal juices and their abrasive action. Lacking it, the mucosa of the intestinal tract ulcerates. The intestines become so irritated that food passes through them almost in an undigested state. This was evident from the human droppings that were everywhere.

Lack of protein was again responsible for the appearance of beriberi, with its concomitant waterlogging of all tissues of the body and destruction of nerves. The explosive character of its appearance and spread was almost epidemic in nature. Small wonder that the earlier students of this disease considered that it was caused by some unknown bacteria. Only in the last generation has it been proved to be due to the lack of vitamin B1.

Lungs loaded with tissue fluid fell easy prey to pneumonia. Hearts weakened by prolonged starvation suddenly dilated and stopped beating. Men standing quietly in the chow or water line toppled over dead. Others straddling slit trenches slithered into their fecal graves. Still others struggling back from a work detail would silently lie down on their filth-covered pallets and die. Sometimes they were hauled in coma to the hospital and deposited in whatever space was available, often in the mud under the elevated hospital floor. There they made their fight for survival during the starlit night. In the morning medics and doctors as emaciated and disease-ridden as the survivors, patiently and wearily disentangled the dead from the living. The pulses of the living were so feeble and respirations so shallow that it was not always easy to make the differentiation. On scraps of paper the medics copied the serial numbers of the dead which had been painted on gaunt chests with the pitifully tiny supply of iodine and gentian violet husbanded on the long, long road from Bataan. The least that could be done was to notify wives and mothers in far-away America that their husbands and sons were dead, that they were not missing, that they had fought their fight and were at last in no pain.

These men had lived and fought in the mountains of malaria-infested Bataan. They moved to live in O'Donnell near the malaria-infested foothills of the Zambales Range. Without mosquito bars and prophylactic quinine, those that had escaped the disease in Bataan soon came down with it. Racking chills, chattering teeth, sudden peaks of raging fever took place every second or third day with concomitant exhaustion due to the toxemia of the disease and the rapid combustion of body tissue.

If the Angel of Death ever had a caldron of victims ready for him, it was in Camp O'Donnell during these first twelve weeks after the surrender. Amoebic and bacillary dysentery, beriberi and malaria ravaged the starved, exhausted, beaten men who lacked food, shelter, clothing, medicine, and not infrequently the will to live. Heartbroken by their defeat, bodies broken by the Nips on the March, hungry, overwhelmed by their isolation, with no hope of immediate recapture, with nothing to look forward to but more thirst and starvation, it was easy for men to turn their faces to the wall, refuse rice and water for forty-eight hours, and pass away. Why all of them didn't die remains a mystery to those of us who watched and tried to help make their last death agonies less painful. The death toll rose—fifty, two hundred, four hundred lifeless skeletons to be buried a day—until it reached a peak of five hundred and fifty. Death, not life, had become the norm for the camp. In a brief twelve weeks, twenty-seven thousand Filipinos and seventeen hundred Americans had been crucified by the Japs, deliberately, maliciously.

A fine mist began to fall as Al finished his tale. The moon hid its face behind scurrying clouds. The crickets and bullfrogs in the low ground filled the air with night sounds.

After a short silence he said: "If the slopeheads don't release your hospital and medical supplies and increase the chow, we're done for."

"Do you think they will?"

"I don't know. They've been emptying the camp steadily during the last month. They're sending all American prisoners out on work details or to Cabanatuan Prison. There are about nine hundred left who are able to walk, and they're scheduled to leave tomorrow at four A.M."

"Are you going?"

"No. Major Ruth, Captain Berkelheimer, Major Smith, Captain Reid and a couple of other docs and medics, together with the hospital kitchen crew, the burial, pump, and truck details are being left behind."

"How do you feel about staying?"

"It looks like I'm getting screwed. Everybody wants to get out of this death trap. It may turn out O.K. The old Jap C.O. is leaving too, and the new bastard couldn't be any worse. It looks to me as if something is in the wind. The Nips in Manila keep howling in their newspapers about how they love their Filipino brown brothers and how they want to cooperate with them, to make them happy. But out here in O'Donnell the Filipinos are dying like flies. The double talk may have become sufficiently obvious to impress even the Nips themselves. It may be that they have sent you people down here to clear up a stinking mess and to prove to the Filipinos that they are receiving preferential treatment while the Americans are being herded into Cabanatuan Prison to die."

"Sounds possible," I said, stretching myself wearily. "How's about leading me back to my mansion, Al?"

Back we went to my bahai, where I crowded in among nine others. Wrapping my blanket about my shoulders I lay down to tumble and toss through a restless night, made hideous by nightmares.

I was walking down Peachtree Street at noon. The sidewalks were filled with well-dressed men and women leisurely going about their business. I turned near the Henry Grady Hotel and entered Doc Taylor's drugstore to have a coke with him. Coming from the glare of the street into the shade of the interior, I blinked my eyes. As they accommodated to the gloom, the faces of the soda jerks, saleswomen, and customers gradually transformed themselves into grinning Oriental caricatures. These people glanced at me and then looked meaningfully at each other. I turned quickly and fled from the building into the security of the street. But that was also filled with slant-eyed bow-legged men and women all staring significantly at me. As I crossed the street from Davison-Paxon's Department Store, the earth yawned open. Down I slithered and tumbled into a gaping cesspool, landing with a thump on a projecting ledge. I sat there bruised and gasping for breath. I let out a piercing scream for help. Immediately the edge of the deep crater was surrounded by hissing, high-cheeked Orientals waving their fists threateningly. Then the faces vanished and the walls of the cesspool reverberated with the sound of their pounding feet. They marched round and round this crater's edge. The walls swayed crazily. Rocks and dirt showered down upon me. The ledge on which I rested cracked neatly and I plunged headlong into the foul pool below, clutching wildly at thin air.

I awakened with the sound of marching feet still pounding in my ears to find myself lying in a pool of water that had collected from the dripping roof. A steady drizzle was falling, only partially obscuring stars and moonlight. On the road past the hut came a long column of men, the last of the ambulatory Americans leaving camp. Shoulders hunched forward against the falling rain, shirts and shorts in tatters, the more fortunate with a canvas shelter half wrapped about them, they lurched by without a word. Nearly a thousand of them stumbled and splashed through the muddy puddles in a steady stream. Like automatons they moved forward to meet their individual fates.

CHAPTER 7.
From St. Peter's Ward to the Underground

THE NEXT MORNING WE ASSEMBLED under Andy Radar. Spruced up in our best clothes, we fell into columns of four and marched to the Nip headquarters to be addressed by the new commanding officer. We halted on a driveway facing the single-story wooden structure and snapped to attention when he made his appearance. Tall for a Nip, about fifty-five years old, somber, frozen-faced, Colonel Ito spoke in short staccato sentences translated by an interpreter.

"You have been sent here by the Imperial Japanese Forces as a hospital unit. There are many sick and dying in this camp. You must do your best to cure them. You will not be interfered with in your work. All hospital and medical supplies will be released to you immediately. Do your best. Take care of your health. Finished."

He turned stiffly on his heels and departed. As we marched back, an excited babble of voices broke out:

"What about that?"

"Do you think he means it?"

"It's a trick!"

"What a break!"

"Don't believe it. We won't see any of our stuff."

And so it went, hope against cynicism, wishful thinking against the black picture of death that spread itself about us.

In the steady drizzle we sloshed back through the slippery gumbo and ever-deepening pools of water. We climbed the rickety stairs and entered the U-shaped hospital shed. The rain poured through the fragmented palm roof upon forms lying huddled on the floor. There were hundreds packed together on either side of the central aisle, each wrapped in a filthy army blanket, head resting on some rags, eyes open and staring, a rusty tin can with water at his side. The oppressive silence was broken only by the raging of a haggard, wild-eyed Thirty-first Infantryman held down by a couple of medics.

"Look out, Jim! Duck! There's a God damn Jap in that mango tree! I'll get the bastard!" And he lifted his arms as if he were sighting along a rifle.

The other patients lay motionless on their pallets, paying no attention to him and less to us as we moved down the ward. We stopped by a door at the far end of the north wing of the hospital.

"This," said Sergeant Pendley, "is St. Peter's ward."

In the dimness of the interior, I counted twenty-two naked forms in a room about thirty feet square into which wind and rain came in gusts. Some lay comatose, flat on their backs, breathing imperceptibly, mouths open, the whites of their eyes rimmed with fat green blowflies. Others were lying on their sides breathing with irregular, rasping, mucous-filled gurgles. They were all gaunt and emaciated, their shaggy hair plastered with feces. Huge, eroded pressure ulcers had formed over their tail bones. One curly-haired youngster, his belly bloated with fluid, his legs and feet so swollen that the skin was cracked and oozing serum, was on his knees, pipe-stem arms extended, staring vacantly into space. Another was squatting, lips and forehead distorted with pain, clenched fists plunged into his emaciated abdomen, a trickle of bloody mucous inching down his legs. A tiny runt of a fellow was resting on his knees and elbows, each vertebra outlined in the curve of his back, head drooping limply, eyes closed. In the corner were two skinny wrecks in ragged pants attempting to force a little rice and water into the mouth of a patient lying on his side. He savagely fended them off, his jaws tightly clenched.

"O.K., Bill," one of them said soothingly, "O.K. Now take a little of this and you'll feel better."

"The hell I will," he rasped through clenched teeth. "The hell I will."

"Come on, Bill, just a spoonful. The Nips are going to hand out a lot of medicine that's just come in. You're going to be all right."

"That's a lie and you know it, Lang," he boiled. "I don't believe you or those God damn yellow bastards. I'm fed up. I'm through. For Christ's sake, take the God damn stuff away and let me die!" Flailing about wildly, he sent the mess kit of rice clattering on the floor.

I stood there, letting this scene photograph itself on my brain. I knew I would never forget it. I wanted to remember.

"Those are the Lang brothers," the sergeant said. "They're two of a damn small group who have come into this ward as patients and lived to tell the story. We've had more than eight hundred come through this room on a one-way ticket from different parts of the camp in two months. They last a couple of days and then are buried in Blue Hill behind the hospital. These Lang boys aren't medics. They volunteered to work in St. Peter's ward after they got better. The fact is they practically live in it day and night. They feel that they might save a few who come in, like they were saved."

"What other help do you have?"

"Medics come and go. They work awhile, get sick, cash in. We get replacements. It's practically impossible to keep clean and protect your own health," he said apologetically. "We don't get enough to drink. We don't have enough water to wash ourselves or our patients unless we can catch some rain water. We try to keep the floors clean by sanding and scraping them."

"How about blankets for the poor devils?"

"We've only got a few. We hand them out to the men we think have the best chance of making the grade. Even if these boys got blankets, they'd be filthy in a day. We haven't any soap."

"How've you been able to stay alive, Pendley?"

"I almost conked out with the 'runs.' I went from one hundred and sixty pounds to ninety pounds in a month. Major Smith, who's in charge of the ward, was able to smuggle in some emetine for me. I'm O.K. now. Smitty's quite a guy. He's worked on this ward since it opened and hasn't stopped yet."

"Has he gotten any medicine from the Nips?"

"Hell, no. The docs were finally able to get the Nip's permission to send work details out to collect guava leaves that the Filipinos say are good for the trots. We make tea from it. It's no damn good, though."

"Then what's the use of walking miles to collect the junk?"

"Listen. The Filipinos in the villages around here hate the Nips as much as we do. A lot of them have sons and husbands dying in Filipino prison camps. When the work details scatter in the woods to pick leaves, they are met by civilians who load them up with medicine, canned goods, and fruits which our men carry back in their sacks covered with guava leaves. We split the proceeds; that's how we get some of the little medicine we have."

"Do you get anything in through the American truck drivers who carry rations in from Tarlac?"

"Some of them are damn swell. But some of them are bastards. If you've got the dough, you can buy a can of corned beef for fifteen bucks, canned sardines for ten bucks, a sulfa or quinine pill for a buck apiece. It's dog eat dog for some of them. On the other hand, many of them charge just what they pay for the stuff on the outside. Major Smith and some of the other docs buy up what they can. They get some medicine for nothing from some of the truck drivers."

"Well," I said as we walked out of the hospital, "let's hope to God the slopeheads keep their promise and release our supplies."

"If they don't we might as well call it a day," he replied.

With a shrewd insight into Nip psychology, Andy Rader was able to size up the Nip executive, commissary, and medical officers with whom he would have to deal. Soon he had them eating out of his hand in spite of the handicap of language. Working day and night, he had drawn plans for a central hospital area to house the acutely ill. It also would include buildings to house surgery, pharmacy, X-ray and other special departments. He drew plans for subsidiary hospitals to accommodate thousands of patients. With tall, deliberate Major John Ralston and impulsive Major Ruth, who supervised sanitation, he surveyed garbage and sewage-disposal areas. With Claude Fraley and the pump-house gang, he figured on laying new water pipe lines to supplement the completely inadequate water supply we had. He beat and banged away at the Nips for a more adequately balanced diet. In between times he slept. When Colonel Duckworth arrived with fifty-five more medics several days later, after a stopover in Manila, a widespread program was available for his criticism and approval. It was then up to the Duck to get the Nips to sanction the plans. They did.

The setup called for four sub hospitals, each to house a thousand patients, and the main hospital, which would take care of five hundred of the worst cases. We had forty doctors, three dentists, and one M.A.C. officer to staff the hospitals and act as administrators, sanitary, and laboratory technicians, maintenance, supply, and mess officers.

We had about one hundred and sixty medical corpsmen to serve as wards men, surgical assistants, laboratory helpers, wood-choppers, latrine diggers, and cooks; they worked on burial details, ration runs, building construction, and maintenance. They laid water and sewer pipe, built homemade showers, strung electric wire and generated power. They worked day and night, rain or shine, sick or well, on short rations. They bitched and griped, but they put out. If they hadn't, we would have all perished in spite of Colonel Duckworth's leadership and the good luck we had.

There wasn't any time to waste. The rainy season was about to begin. Sewage disposal and a more adequate water supply were priority items if we and our patients were to survive. In the dhobie clay we dug deep latrines, ditched about to prevent flooding and roofed for protection against rain. Latrine box seats, constructed out of scrap wood, were placed over the trenches and banked with earth to make them fly proof. Germ-laden flies breeding in night soil, carrying dysentery germs into the mess halls, were our greatest enemies next to the Nips.

With the three-inch pipe we had transported all the way from Little Baguio, Fraley ran a new pipe line from the pump house a quarter-mile away to the various hospitals. As life-giving water flowed from taps throughout the area and in the buildings themselves, patients took a new lease on life: no more standing in line for hours in the tropical sun or drenching torrential downpours. We crowded patients into one ward while the other wards were hosed down and scrubbed with Lysol. We set up showers between buildings, dug drainage ditches, constructed board walks, made wooden windows, repaired leaking roofs. Everything we used we had brought with us—tools, hose, and pipe. Our medics scrubbed the starved, begrimed skeletons with hot soap and water until they writhed with pleasure. For the first time since the war started they found themselves between clean sheets on a soft mattress in a hospital bed.

"If I ever get home, I'll never get out of bed again" sighed an emaciated corporal. He died a week later.

In addition to forty-five hundred Filipino patients we had one hundred and fifty Americans who had been too sick to move when the Nips sent all other Americans to Cabanatuan Prison. In spite of the food and medicine we poured into them, eighty of them died in the first month after arrival. Tuberculosis, uncontrollable dysentery, and advanced beriberi got them. The others managed to cling to life.

We tore the guts out of a long rambling building facing the main hospital wards to set up a laboratory, pharmacy, X-ray room, dental office, and operating pavilion. We whitewashed the walls, scrubbed the floors, but never got rid of the rats and bedbugs. Again five operating tables stood spick-and-span with their gleaming spotlights beside them, flanked by dozens of white-enameled cabinets filled with surgical supplies. We set up our electric sterilizer, later to serve as my private pressure cooker. Silent Sergeant Brenner, Private Ruby, curly-haired St. Burns, Pharmacist Mate Blondy de Groot, and sad-faced Jones worked and sweated like stevedores getting the operating rooms ready.

We unloaded our thirty-two truckloads of medical equipment and supplies and divided them between the five hospital units. Included were four truckloads of our precious emergency rations which we had unearthed before leaving Little Baguio. These included some flour and oleomargarine, canned fruit, vegetables, corned beef, pressed ham, and coffee. We stretched this chow out for our acutely ill patients over six months until British bulk Red Cross and individual American Red Cross parcels came in shortly before the Christmas of 1942.

A Diesel-engine generator which we had brought from Little Baguio was set up. Soon the steady whirr of its motor filled the hospital area. The buildings were flooded with light, X-ray machines sparked, refrigerators chilled carabao meat, the whistle on our electric steam sterilizer blew its piercing note, and a trickle of water flowed out of our distillation apparatus. Private Mathe set up the two-ton lathe we had brought. Before long he was repairing and making surgical and dental instruments and pipe fittings. Our X-ray doctor was still with us, nutty as ever about flies and rats but taking good X-ray plates.

Working constantly, exposed to thousands of disease-ridden patients, eating a meager diet of rice and scraps of carabao meat coming from kitchens infested with swarms of blowflies hatched in the feces-covered area, we fell sick by the dozens. Many of us who had contracted malaria in Bataan once again came down with recurrent racking chills and fever. Colonel Schock huddled in bed grunting with belly cramps. Long-nosed Captain Pizer, our scholarly pathologist from Los Angeles, lay in a semi-comatose delirium for weeks. Captain Browe, close-lipped New Englander from Burlington, Vermont, started out with a faint tinge of jaundice which deepened steadily into a startling, brilliant orange. We thought he had yellow atrophy of the liver, usually fatal. He turned death's corner by a hair's breadth. Not so with Private First Class van Deck, who died of the same disease, and Corporal Jollif, who keeled over with sudden heart failure.

During the first two months at least a third of the medical personnel were out of commission with acute bacillary or amoebic dysentery of an unusually severe type. It is a well-known fact in bacteriological circles that germs increase their virulence when passed from one body to another. These germs afflicting us had plenty of opportunity to become tough and nasty. They had passed through the bodies of approximately twenty-seven thousand Filipinos and seventeen hundred Americans who were buried in mass graves behind the camp.

I had at first felt contempt for patients who in their flight toward the latrine had suddenly stopped, squatted, and excreted on the spot. I raged: "How the hell can these weak-willed bastards expect us to get this camp cleaned up if they continue to crap all over themselves?"

I learned better when I was guilty of the same misdemeanor several days later myself. Apparently the bugs irritated and stimulated the smooth muscle of the lower bowel to such an extent that it was humanly impossible to prevent the explosive expulsion of its contents, just as it is impossible for a woman to prevent the expulsion of a baby when the smooth muscle of the pregnant uterus begins to contract. I finally made the latrine. A full moon shone down on the desolate fields of pampas grass that filled the prison camp. It rode high across the horizon in a steady arc and disappeared. As the dawn broke, etching Mount Pinatuba, I still sat on the latrine, bowels cramping, afraid to move.

The Duckworth-Rader combination continued to play the Nips as anglers play a fish. Colonel Duckworth continued to live in his bahai in austere isolation. All subordinate Nips attempting to give him orders were frosted out. They learned to go to Andy Rader's quarters. Our C.O. held intermittent solemn conclave only with Colonel Ito. From time to time new batches of Filipino prisoners numbering in the thousands arrived in camp after an exhausting trip from Mindanao and the Central Philippine Islands where they had been captured. Some of us were delegated by the Duck to meet and examine them. We sent the worst cases directly to the hospital.

One day the Duck received a directive to send one major, three captains, and two lieutenant physicians to Nip headquarters to check a small batch of new prisoners. He did so, but immediately sent a letter to Colonel Ito protesting the tone of the directive and its contents. He said briefly:

It will be impossible for me to carry out the work of treating forty-five hundred prisoners sick in this hospital if you order my officers away from their duty in large numbers and by rank. As Commanding Officer of this hospital, this decision must be left to me.

Colonel Ito visited him personally and apologized. We were never troubled again. On Sundays thereafter, in fact, Ito regularly paid Colonel Duckworth a brief, formal social call. Knowing the Oriental's custom of returning present for present, he sent Ito a huge birthday cake weighing seventeen pounds. The next day we got in return an extra cow, eight sacks of flour, and three of sugar—not a bad investment.

We ran into one problem that gradually became very troublesome. Under constant hammering by Andy Rader, the Nips issued us medicine in weekly installments, including quinine of which we were desperately short, but no sulfa drugs. After the hospitals were set up the Nip guards came sneaking in at night to get treatment for gonorrhea and syphilis, which were rampant among them. Soldiers with venereal disease are severely punished in the Jap Army. They are broken one grade, often beaten, restricted to the prison area for a month, given no treatment, and are prevented from returning to Japan if they still have the disease! We had so little sulfa that it was urgent to get these Nips off our necks. But it's not easy to argue with an armed Jap. The Duck complained to Colonel Ito, who ruled that any Nip guard found in the hospital area would be thrown in the brig unless he had a letter from headquarters authorizing him to go to the hospital for medical or dental treatment. That helped, but it didn't solve the problem.

I was studying in the operating room one evening, as was my custom. We had a few novels and textbooks. To keep from going nuts, most of us began a course of study ranging from astronomy to architecture. I spent a couple of hours every night studying Japanese and Spanish. We had plenty of Spanish lads among our medics and even more Nips in the area to practice on. I heard the stomping of feet on the board walk outside of surgery. The door was flung open. In walked a Nip, a two-star private, obviously drunk, grinning and smirking, carrying a bottle of beer under his arm.

"Kon ban wa," I said. (Good evening.)

"Kon ban wa."

"Dozo suwaru kudasai." (Please sit down.)

"Beeru suki masu ka?" he said, plopping the bottle on the table. (Do you like beer?)

"Hai, arigato gozaimazu." (You bet. Thanks a lot.) Then came a lot of palaver from him: How many children do you have? Have you any pictures? How do you like life without women? How often do you masturbate? Do you like the Japanese? When will you go home?—the usual line of baloney and preliminary stuff that preceded a demand for medicine.

Finally I asked, *"Nanda?"* (What can I do for you?) *"Chimpu byocki,"* he said grinning. (I've got gonorrhea.)

"Ah so ka. Okino doku de gozai masu." (Oh, is that so? I'm very sorry indeed.)

"Kusuri to tchiusha agette kudasai." (Give me some sulfa pills and injections.)

"Dekimasen. Nipponzin taiso no tegami arimasu ka." (I'm sorry, I can't do it. Do you have a letter from your C.O.?)

Eyes squinting evilly, slobbering lips pulled back in rage, drawing bayonet from scabbard, he bellowed: *"Bakero, Ima shin-*

de imasu!" (You God damn fool. Give me that medicine now or I'll kill you!)

It was about eleven P.M. Not a soul was around. I drew 5 c.c. of distilled water into a syringe and pumped it into his vein. Then reaching into the table drawer, I gave him two dozen bicarbonate of soda pills which we had grooved so that they resembled sulfa pills.

"Kono kusuri taihen yoroshi, itsu taksukan jidosha sigoto wo shimasyo," I said. (This medicine is good only if you take plenty of exercise, especially on a bicycle.) It was undoubtedly the worst advice any patient with gonorrhea ever got.

All smiles again, he bade me *"Sayonara."* (Good-bye.) This system of disposing of Nips who wanted sulfa pills I found used in every prison camp I visited. At Cabanatuan Prison several of the G.I.'s went into the drug business. They carved a mold out of hard wood and sold thousands of imitation sulfa pills made of starch to the slopeheads for a dollar apiece or the equivalent in food.

It was a bitter psychological struggle for survival that we waged. Eventually it bore fruit. For weeks our diet included rice three times a day, konkon, watery soup, and an occasional scrap of carabao meat. Gradually it increased in quality and quantity as the reluctant Nips put out small weekly installments of oleomargarine, coconut oil, sugar, lard, and flour. We kept howling about the impossibility of curing beriberi without more protein and were rewarded by the arrival of a herd of emaciated Brahma cows and carabao. From then on we got a meat issue regularly—a cow every other day divided among six hundred men. Since these animals dressed down to about two hundred pounds of meat, the handout amounted to about five ounces per person every two days. Small as this was, it made an appreciable difference in the health of the camp. Our deadly monotonous fare during this period was as follows:

For breakfast, a mess kit full of lugoa, one teaspoonful of sugar, one sweet roll, and coffee made from the Filipino coffee bean, later from burned rice.

For lunch, half a canteen cupful of vegetable soup made from konkon weed or camote tops, upo (gourds) or mongo (green cow beans), and occasionally onions; a mess kit full of steamed rice, and one small slice of bread.

For supper, a mess kit full of steamed rice, a slice of roast or small hamburger meat or stew, two small slices of bread. On alternate days, instead of meat, we had a bone and chittling soup.

In addition to this issue our two supply officers, Max Andler and Captain Fred Nazyr, a dentist from Omaha, Nebraska, did a good job between them in stealing the Nips blind. Both had learned enough pidgin Japanese to get along well with the Nip noncoms in charge of the commissary. Max was a big-boned, happy-go-lucky chap with a line of chatter that the Nips fell for. Fred had something even more valuable—a wavy, luxurious blue-black beard that covered his face and fell to his chest. The Nips, most of whom were hairless, couldn't keep their eyes from it or their fingers out of it. Max would first give the Nip noncom a line of soft soap to get him in a good humor; then together they would figure out the weekly allowance of rice, vegetables, flour, oil, and sugar. After the calculations on the abacus (counting beads) were completed, our ration detail trooped in to carry out the issue while the Nips checked them off. Fred and his wonderful beard then came into view. It was more than the Nips could resist. As they clustered about to play with it, Max and his gang carried away everything they could lay their hands on. The booty was considerable. They pulled the same gag while getting our meat issue—one large emaciated cow or two small ones every two days. Frequently they and our cowboys—tobacco-chewing Private First Class Ivy, ex-fiddler from Arkansas; cagey Mullinder from Alliance, Nebraska; and slick Corporal Aquila from San Jose, California—returned from the corral splattered with mud, triumphantly leading two large cows by their homemade lassos.

The diet edged its way upward. We received some eggs and canned milk issued by the Nips for the sick. As the sanitation improved the swarms of disease-carrying flies disappeared. The death rate plummeted from its level of five hundred and fifty a day to five hundred a month, and finally to five a month. During the last two months at O'Donnell we had no deaths whatsoever. In part, the drop in the death rate took place because the weakest had died off; in part it was due to the more adequate supplies Colonel Duckworth squeezed out of the Nips; in part it was due to the improved sanitation and water supply. The camp was still a museum of deficiency diseases, but under sufficient control to permit life.

The doctors chosen as chiefs of the subhospitals were efficient and industrious men: Berry, Schmayla, Smith, and Keltz. Major Wilbur Berry had come up the hard way, working for a livelihood while going to a Middle Western medical school. Highstrung, but holding himself under excellent control, he kept a shrewd eye on his doctors and corpsmen. Captain Schmayla, with his mashed-up nose wrinkled in perpetual good humor, was especially loved by his Filipino patients whose psychology he understood so well. Major Smith of Miami, Florida, baldheaded, his face made chubby with the swelling that goes with beriberi, was also a past master of chiseling extra chow from the Nips. Captain Charlie Keltz was blindly loyal to Colonel Duckworth. Under these men and their assistants, thousands of sickly Filipino patients shuttled into the hospital were treated and discharged alive.

During the first few months the death rate was so high that the Japs never had an accurate count of the number of patients in the hospital. They were too afraid of contracting disease, to make the count themselves. They relied on our figures. We purposely gave them inaccurate tallies showing fewer patients on our totals than we really had. We did this because of the escape situation. The Japs divided the American doctors and medics into groups of ten: "Blood brothers" we called each other. If one of us escaped, the other nine were to be shot. We were also held responsible for patients escaping from the hospital, which they did in droves. At twilight, dozens of Filipino civilians from neighboring villages drifted toward the Nip guardhouse outposts bearing vegetables for sale. They also carried Filipino civilian clothes hidden away.

While the Nips were occupied buying food, Filipino prisoners and patients rapidly shed their army clothes, slipped through the barbed-wire fence, put on civvies, and then drifted out of camp with the food peddlers. By reporting more deaths in the daily tallies than actually occurred, we were able to cover up the escape of hundreds of Filipinos from the hospital. As the number of deaths in camp dwindled we had increasing difficulty in reporting these escaped prisoners as deceased.

We were finally caught with our pants down. One day, three Filipinos escaped from the hospital when no deaths had occurred. The Nip executive ranted and raved. Colonel Duckworth and Andy Rader desperately tried to pacify him.

"You have been negligent in guarding your patients," the Nip screamed. "Three Filipinos have escaped from this camp for the first time since it was opened. I must inform the Japanese headquarters in Manila. I have lost face. You must be punished. I must kill some of you American doctors and medical corpsmen so that the others will be more efficient."

To help him in his face-saving efforts Andy explained: "Of course, you know these three prisoners were insane. Nobody but a madman would ever dream of escaping from this most carefully guarded Jap prison camp."

Quick to catch the drift the Nip muttered: "Yes, they were insane. Yes. Yes, of course, they were insane."

Carrying on smoothly the Duck interjected: "If we can receive your permission to build a strongly constructed jail in the hospital, even the insane will not escape."

"You must do so immediately." Turning black with anger again he roared: "You and some of your doctors will be shot if any other escapes take place. In the future your men must set up a patrol in and outside the hospital buildings to prevent escapes. I hold you personally responsible."

The Japs had a complicated guard setup. A Nip patrol made its rounds outside the rickety barbed-wire fence surrounding the hospital. They also kept watch from five-story guardhouse towers. Scattered about in the deep pampas grass outside the compound were machine gun replacements which had us under point-blank fire should we riot and rush the fence. Now we were compelled to supplement their efforts. In addition to our professional work we became jailors. Our patrol setup was almost as complicated as theirs. One medic and two patients stood guard all night in each ward. There was a roving patrol of medics within the barbed-wire fence. An officer of the day was appointed for each sub-hospital. There was also a super O.D. who wandered back and forth between the sub-hospitals.

This business cost me a broken arm. In spite of the increase in our diet, many of us, including myself, had developed night blindness because of the lack of vitamin A found in butter, milk, eggs, and animal fats. Connecting the wards there were ramps ten feet high which had no protective banisters. On the nights I was duty officer I usually corralled a medic to lead me in safety from one ward to another. One moonless, drizzly night I tapped my way with a piece of bamboo through the silent ward, unable to find a guide. I cautiously edged on to the board walk leading to the psychopathic ward, one arm outstretched. I stepped headlong into space. A stabbing pain radiated from my hand into my chest as I landed on my outstretched right arm. My head crashed against the sun-hardened clay. When I again struggled back to consciousness, Frenchy Poier was standing over me muttering, "I'll be a sonovabitch if Doc hasn't broken his arm." Two months later, the arm having been very well set by Joe Bulfamonte, I was able to take over my surgical work again.

Surgery at O'Donnell was entirely different from the work we had previously encountered. It also differed from the normal run of surgical work performed in civilian practice. Joe Bulfamonte, "Kewpie" Poweleit and I tried to figure out bizarre diagnostic surgical problems as they were presented to us. During the first few months we all had the usual manifestations of scurvy due to lack of vitamin C: bleeding gums and black-and-blue spots on the arms and legs. We had never seen the surgical aspects of this deficiency disease which attacks the smaller blood vessels and capillaries so that they become fragile and rupture easily. We couldn't explain the clinical picture some patients presented on any other basis. They came in with spontaneous Charley horse, extensive swelling and excruciating tenderness of the calves of the legs. At operation we found huge clots of blood clinging to the muscle fibers. Frequently the clots would be floating in ounces of pus. Several patients exhibited a diffuse peritonitis similar to that seen in a ruptured appendix. At operation the abdomen, was filled with bright red blood oozing from many tiny capillaries of the peritoneum lining of the abdominal cavity. Others had palpable masses (similar to an appendical abscess) which were caused by blood clots deep in the muscle (iliopsoas) in the vicinity of the appendix. These patients did well on the native calamense (lime juice) we smuggled in. Patients who simulated acute meningitis didn't do so well. At autopsy they showed extensive oozing of blood from small capillaries into brain tissue, causing its softening and destruction. Filipinos by the hundreds had painful swollen testicles which we thought was caused by hemorrhage, the result of vitamin-C deficiency.

They had their own explanation: "The God damn Japs are putting poison in the rice so we lose our manhood."

Frequently these testicles were so destroyed by abscess formation and secondary infection that it was necessary to castrate.

After doing so for a Filipino who took his loss with the greatest of equanimity I asked him, "Joe, would you like to look at your egg?"

"But yes, sir," he replied passively.

I signaled to one of the medics to get me a hen's egg that had just arrived from a grateful patient.

"Here it is, Joe," I said, handing it to him and turning toward another patient. Ten minutes later as the litter-bearers were about to return him to his ward I remembered the egg, my first in five months.

"Hey, Joe!" I hollered. "How about returning that egg?"

"But, sir," he said, turning his egg-smeared face toward me, "You said it was mine!"

All our surgical problems were not caused by deficiency diseases. Captain Rolando Dudutag of the Philippine Army came in. I had known him before the war.

"Captain," he said, "the Japs are organizing groups of Filipino prisoners into propaganda corps. They are to travel about the country and speak in small and large towns. They are to extol the virtues of the Japanese and urge Filipinos to give up guerrilla warfare. The Japs promise to release these prisoners after the speaking tours are finished."

"Well?" I asked, studying his face.

"They have asked me repeatedly to lead one of these groups. I have refused many times. Now they are angry. They say they will kill me if I refuse again."

"What do you want me to do?"

"Hide me in the hospital."

"You don't look sick. They'll find you here. They'll beat you and raise hell with me."

"Then operate on me. Do anything," he pleaded, "but help me to remain an American."

I operated on him. I took out a normal appendix.

It was increasingly difficult, I found, to reconcile civilian medical ethics with prison ethics. I had deliberately given a Nip soldier advice which I hoped would have disastrous consequences; now I had performed an unnecessary operation.

One night after supper, "Kewpie" and I took our usual stroll over to the Filipino prison camp to pick up local gossip and war news. In this camp there was a Filipino captain in G-2 work whom we made it our special business to visit. He had operatives covering all Jap activities of Manila into the upper provinces as far as Lingayen, Aparri, and the Cagayan Valley. By banca (native sailboat) and carabao cart these operatives traveled back to Camp O'Donnell with their reports. At night they snaked their way through the Jap prison guards into camp where they lost themselves among the thousands of Filipino prisoners. They spent a few days in camp giving their boss detailed accounts of troop and ship movements, then slipped out of camp again. The captain compiled their reports. By similar messengers he transmitted them to Filipinos who were U.S. Secret Service men in Manila. They relayed the reports to the States via submarine or secret radio. The Nips never caught on.

We moved briskly down the road in the fast-falling twilight. Then we stopped short. A Nip guard had lined up ten slender emaciated Filipinos. He knocked them down like tenpins with his scabbard.

"What's the matter, Joe?" we asked one of them when the guard had left.

"He said we did not salute good, sir. We are a patient people with long memories," he added grimly. "We will not forget. We shall teach him the American salute."

We bumped into Dr. Medina, the Filipino X-ray man whom I had met on the road in Bataan and had talked into joining General Hospital No. 1. He was haggard, his glossy black hair turning gray. I looked at him shamefacedly.

"You are very angry with me?" I asked.

"Oh, no, sir," he reassured. "I shall be very proud to tell my children I worked in the American Hospital in Bataan."

Try as they might the Nips could not shake this stolid loyalty to America. They attempted to demonstrate the might of Japan to the Filipino prisoners. Nightly they showed movies of the fall of Hong Kong, Singapore, and the Dutch East Indies. Eventually they permitted the Philippine Red Cross to bring truckloads of clothing into the camp; they increased the Filipino prisoners' diet; they let them play volley ball and baseball; they organized track meets; they brought in professional entertainers; they finally released them by the thousands. It was all wasted motion. The Filipino hatred of the Japs burned more steadily and brightly.

As night fell, the pitch darkness was broken by the flickering light of hundreds of campfires. About them wandered brown-faced Filipino prisoners, fly swatters in hand.

"What are you cooking, Joe?" we asked a ragamuffin with an unruly shock of black hair.

"Sir, we are roasting grasshoppers and frogs, sir. We are very fortunate today, sir, because we have captured a dog in our dog trap." He pointed to the strips of meat broiling in the hot wood ashes. "We Cagayanos are having a festival tonight. We would be honored to have the American doctors eat with us."

We followed him to a small bahai filled with twenty of his countrymen. White teeth flashed a welcome in the flickering light of a wick burning in a tiny can of coconut oil. As the night deepened we sat about softly singing the songs we liked but never knew we loved until the loneliness of prison life overpowered us: "Suwannee River," "Carry Me Back to Old Virginny," "Home Sweet Home." The little wick spluttered out and its light was replaced by the white beams of the tropical moon pouring through the holes in the Nipa roof. Tears rolled slowly down the haggard faces of soldiers whose veneer of hardness had been melted by isolation and despair. With guitar softly strumming and voices blended in rich harmony, we sang of home far away.

About November, 1942, everything broke wide open for us in a big way. After incessant needling, the Nips finally consented to open up a commissary store for prisoners. By properly greasing the palm of the Nip commissary officer and noncoms, we were able to buy large quantities of fruits, vegetables, eggs, chickens, carabao meat, canned milk, fish, and corned beef. Colonel Duckworth had funds available for the purchase of this produce. He had been able to smuggle money into camp concealed on his body when he first arrived. This fund was supplemented by money smuggled into camp later on through the underground. From the same source most of the prisoners received limited funds by which they were able to make small purchases. The morale of the camp picked up dramatically. Patients who had not cut their hair for months complained bitterly about their physical appearance. It was necessary to appoint barbers in the various wards to keep patients from griping. Needles and thread appeared out of thin air. Raggedy-assed soldiers busily patched their shredded trousers and multicolored clothes. I went into the surgical ward. There were two patients who had been on the verge of death a week ago. Now they were leaning on their elbows on adjacent beds making feeble passes at each other.

"What the hell's going on here," I bellowed. "What are you two nuts fighting about?"

"That bum," pointing an accusing finger at his ward mate, "said anybody who comes from Arkansas is ignorant. That's my home. I won't let any God damn mule from Missouri—" He fell back on his pillow exhausted.

We had to get the boxing gloves out again to let medics and patients let off steam. We leveled volley ball courts and made a baseball diamond. Life was beginning to look up.

The Philippine Red Cross had tried unsuccessfully for months to get into camp, and finally succeeded. Soon white-haired Tony Escoda and his beautiful wife, Josefa, were frequent visitors, unloading food and medical supplies at the Nip headquarters building from their tiny broken-down truck. Before the war, fifty-year-old Tony had worked on the Manila Daily Tribune while his wife was active in the Catholic Women's League. Following the surrender, they devoted all their money and energy to keeping prisoners alive both through the Red Cross and the underground. Soon stems of bananas by the hundreds and scurvy-curing crocks of native lime juice were being delivered. Bottles of quinine and life-saving sulfa drugs came in. Tubes of morphine and codeine arrived cunningly secreted in bananas.

The Filipino Women's Federation finally got permission to set up a canteen in the little railroad junction of Capas seven miles away from camp. They occupied a two-story frame building, the lower floor of which was a canteen where they were compelled to serve Nip soldiers with refreshments, this being the only basis upon which the Nip C.O. would let them function. Ostensibly they served as an information bureau for Filipino families inquiring for relatives in the prison camp. They also fed new batches of Filipino prisoners when they unloaded from box cars. Actually, they were a blind for the underground, which originated in Manila, for the transfer of food and medicine into O'Donnell. Charming, vivacious, twenty-five-year-old Spanish mestiza Pilar

Campos, was one of the ringleaders. Daughter of the president of the Bank of the Philippines and former society reporter on the Herald, she pawned her jewelry to buy medicine for us. She organized a group of Filipino girls who wrote notes and sent food to American prisoners, strangers to them. They fed their bodies and re-built their morale. To avoid identification, these girls signed their notes "Screwball No. 1, No. 2, No. 3," and so on.

Chaplain Frank Tiffany had several underground contacts that sent in hundreds of pounds of food and thousands of pesos weekly. One of his contacts was a woman of Italian descent who masqueraded as a Filipino. In addition to smuggling in food to O'Donnell she ran a cabaret for Nips, whom she pumped for information when they were drunk. This intelligence was relayed by our G-2 in Manila to Australia. We referred to her as "High-pockets" because the notes and money she carried to us were hidden in her brassiere. Another was a red-haired woman of Polish descent, Mrs. Utensky, married to an American sergeant captured on Corregidor. She remained foot-loose on a phony Lithuanian passport. Finally, there were three Spaniards—Mr. and Mrs. Joaquin Mencarini and Ramon Amusatagui, a handsome Basque.

Our end of the underground was handled by our own truck drivers who picked up parcels from the Filipina canteen in Capas while carrying loads of rice and wood back to camp. It was a thrill to have Private First Class Russell poke his head into my bahai and whisper, "I've got a parcel for you, Doc." I hurriedly unwrapped it. There were three cans of corned beef, a can of tiny sausages, one of Klimm milk, and the most beautiful chocolate cake I have ever seen or will ever see. A tiny note fluttered from the wrapping. It read:

MY DARLING AL:

I finally located you after a dreadful five-month search. They told me you were killed in Bataan. I did not believe them. My brother and I have joined the underground. We have Austrian citizenship papers, so we are free to move about. Tell me what you need and I will send it. I love you.

HANNA

P.S. Do not write my address on any notes.

My eyes misted at the sight of her scrawl. Her eyes and lips were painfully vivid to me again.

I sent back a note through the underground. I thanked her fervently for the chow and cake. I asked her to wait for me. I warned her to stay away from underground work; she had experienced her share of excitement and danger. From Vienna she had escaped the Hitler terror by way of Brussels, France, Italy, and finally Shanghai. A long trip for a girl to take by herself. That ought to be plenty for her, I thought, for the rest of her life.

I broke the glad news of the food parcel to the nine men living with me in our tiny bahai. I told them we'd have a real party that night. Later in the afternoon Father Blank took me aside confidentially.

"Al," he said, his forehead wrinkling as he chose his words carefully, "I'd like to speak to you a minute, if you don't mind."

"Of course, Padre, what's the trouble?"

"About this party tonight, I sure appreciate the invitation. But I don't think I can take any of the food. You doctors who are doing physical labor as well as professional work need it more than I do. Holding Mass several times a day doesn't wear me down. I just couldn't face those sick, hungry boys in the wards if I ate any of that extra chow. I want to live as they live, hunger as they hunger, and suffer as they suffer. Please don't be offended, Al."

"Padre," I said, and my voice was husky, "I've met some wonderful people during my lifetime, but I never expected to meet a saint."

That night we clustered about our little table in the flickering light of a single candle. Padre ate. The spirit was willing... .

We got the word from the canteen in Capas that individual parcels sent from Manila were piling up by the hundreds. The last link in the underground had temporarily broken down. Our truck drivers who had picked up the parcels on their trips back to camp were being shaken down.

"Is there anything you could do to get the stuff in?" they asked.

I racked my brain trying to figure out an answer. Finally I decided to ask Lieutenant Fugi, Nip supply officer, if he would drive me to town. I knew him well after having treated his face, which had been lacerated in an auto accident.

"No," he said promptly, "I cannot do it. It is against military orders for prisoners to be taken out of camp."

Toward the end of our stay in O'Donnell he saw fit to reverse his decision when he fell sick with jaundice. I was a frequent visitor at his house in Capas when I was ordered to treat him.

I was not able to ask Dr. Yashimura, physician for the Nip guards, for help. He had been transferred with Andy Rader, Charley Osborne, and twenty-five medics to the Davao Prison Camp in Mindanao. He was one of the few Japanese gentlemen I met in three and a half years of prison life. Tall, handsome for a Nip, courtly, he had been a gynecologist before the war. He was not bitten by the Bushido bug. "Captain," he would say when I attempted to pump him for information about the war, "let us talk about medicine, music, and anthropology. In fact, let us talk about anything but the war. Then we will remain friends." During our first four months at O'Donnell he was of the greatest help in procuring medical supplies.

Dr. Takenoshita had replaced him. As Nips went, he wasn't bad. At least he did not interfere with Colonel Duckworth in the running of the hospital. Not particularly interested in medicine, he devoted his week-ends in Manila to strictly amatory pursuits. He occasionally dropped into the operating room to watch an operation. After it was finished he regaled me with stories of his latest conquest. To believe him, one would be convinced he was the modern Oriental Casanova. He spoke some English and German. With the help of the pidgin Japanese that I had picked up, which always put him in good humor, we could understand each other.

"Dr. Takenoshita," I asked one day, "did you have a good week end in Manila?"

He made a wry face, "No, I didn't, Captain. The charming mestiza I met two weeks ago has not yet succumbed."

"Have you tried buying her some clothes?" I asked.

"Ah, yes," he sighed, "I have brought her some dresses but it has made no difference. She said she had plenty of dresses. She said she might look with favor on me if I brought some silk stockings." He added sadly: "It is impossible to buy silk stockings in Manila."

The germ of an idea began to propagate in my mind. "Dr. Takenoshita," I began cautiously, "I know where there are some silk stockings."

He looked at me incredulously. "What, here in prison camp?"

"No. But if you get me into Capas I can get some for you, providing I can bring back some food parcels."

He meditated awhile, sucking through his teeth, head cocked. "Tomorrow at two o'clock I shall take you."

When our nurses had left Little Baguio for Corregidor the night before the fall of Bataan, they had taken only a few of their personal belongings. They left behind a great many locker trunks filled with their clothes. When we subsequently left Little Baguio for O'Donnell, we took everything that was loose or that could be ripped from its moorings, including these trunks. After our arrival at O'Donnell we stored them in our supply shed. They were still intact. I had received one note from Miss Frankie Lewey, interned with the other nurses at Santo Tomas, Manila, bewailing the fact that they were running about in tatters. After our contacts had been established I had made up bundles of shoes and clothes and sent them from O'Donnell to Capas by Private First Class Russell, one of our truck drivers. A Filipino civilian, Al Obin, routed them into Manila where I hope they eventually landed in Santo Tomas. It had been pleasant to have some contact with women, even if it only meant rummaging through their clothes. Some of the girls had beautiful undergarments, and there were still dozens of pairs of silk stockings in the trunks.

The next day Dr. Takenoshita and I were driven in his command car into Capas. I had the silk stockings tucked under my shirt. I was jumpy and I think he was. It was the first time I had been outside barbed-wire fences in five months. It was more than pleasant to pass by little clusters of bamboo shacks and see gayly clad Filipinos with huge, flat, rice-straw sunbonnets perched precariously on their glistening black heads. Bare-bottomed children played in the streets. I envied the withered old Filipino squatting on his heels as we rode by. He could roam from one end of the island to the other, even though it was occupied by the Japs.

I directed the Jap driver to pull up in front of a small bamboo shack, the ground floor of which was open to the streets. This was the headquarters of the Filipina Women's Federation, the end of the underground which originated in Manila.

"This is where my friends work. They operate the canteen for the Nipponese soldiers. They live in the rooms above the canteen," I explained to Dr. Takenoshita.

"Ush," he hissed. (O.K.) "Go. We will pick you up late this afternoon. Don't leave the rooms. You must remain upstairs. If you are discovered I cannot protect you."

Trembling inwardly, I walked past the Nip guards seated at their bamboo tables. They looked curiously at me and the Jap command car and turned their heads away again.

I tiptoed upstairs and entered a spacious living room.

There were three Filipino girls talking quietly to each other, young Lulu Reyes and Pilar Campos, whom I had met in Manila before Pearl Harbor, and lovely Benilda Castañeda, one of my surgical nurses at Little Baguio. When they saw me standing silently at the landing of the staircase, they let out a yelp and hustled me into a tiny storeroom.

"Jesus, Maria, José!" they exclaimed. "Have you escaped? Shall we get some Filipino clothes for you? What do you want us to do?" They hugged and kissed me.

"No," I said, "I'm not escaping. The Jap prison doctor brought me here."

"Why? How? What for?"

"He has a sweetheart in Manila and wants some silk stockings for her, so I made a deal with him. If I get him the stockings, he will let me bring back some of the packages you haven't been able to smuggle into camp for us lately."

"But we don't have any stockings," Benilda said, her face falling.

I took two pairs out from under my shirt. Their eyes widened in astonishment. I told them how I happened to be in possession of the priceless commodity.

"How long can you stay?"

"A few hours. We'll have to watch through the window for the return of the Jap command car. It'll stop in front of the canteen."

"How thin you are! We must hurry!" They dashed out of the storeroom and returned with platters of food. I gorged myself on chicken and pork adobo (sweet and sour pork), stuffed fish, lumpia (a cake like a Mexican tortilla), and fruits during the next two hours. As I ate I related the experiences of the Hospital No. 1 unit since its departure from Bataan. They told of their experiences in Corregidor and life in Manila since the surrender.

Then Benilda spotted the command car pulling to a stop below us.

I walked downstairs, a mobile grocery store, bank, and post office. In my shoes were dozens of tiny notes folded to the size of postage stamps: these were for Filipino and American prisoners. My hatband was lined with Japanese-Filipino currency, fifty- and hundred-peso bills, to be distributed to individuals, a list of which I was also given. In both hands I carried woven fiber carryalls loaded down with dozens of parcels containing food and medicine. Under my right arm I carried a small stem of bananas.

I loaded the parcels into the car and got in. After we took off I slipped a small package to Dr. Takenoshita sitting beside me.

He opened it and grinned broadly when he saw the silk stockings, nodding and chuckling to himself.

We reached camp safely. I returned the salutes of the Nip garrison very primly as we passed through the gates. I paid off the Nip driver of the command car later with a bottle of gin I bummed from one of our truck drivers.

I was able to make the same trip four times before we left O'Donnell.

We went through an earthquake that was scary but did no harm, and a typhoon which blew down several wards, killing two Filipino patients, yet the last two months in this camp were the most comfortable in our entire imprisonment. The basic food issue was adequate to support life. We even managed, with the additional food smuggled in or purchased openly in the commissary, to regain a little weight. When Red Cross medicine and food in bulk and in individual packages arrived in December, 1942, we felt we were in the clear. Our status also changed. Instead of being captives with no rights we were treated as prisoners with certain privileges. Theoretically, the Japs paid us the same rate they paid Nip officers of equivalent rank. Actually they paid us 40 pesos ($20) a month. They said they had opened savings accounts in Tokyo for the remainder of our salaries.

The news had also definitely taken a turn for the better. We got verbal reports on Nip military activity in Luzon from our Filipino G-2. We were able to get the Nip version of global warfare from Manila papers sneaked into camp daily. We got the American version of the same events from the short-wave radio set we had smuggled into camp with our medical equipment. Claude Fraley and Jack Lemire did the listening. They spread the news quietly. We silently rejoiced when we heard of the Battle of Midway. We held our breaths while the marines got a precarious foothold on Guadalcanal. We knew of the gallant defense of Port Moresby and the retreat of the Nips in New Guinea. We were convinced we would be free within a year.

The morale of the camp was sky high. The shows, reviews and burlesques we put on in the mess hall were enthusiastically received. The more risqué the better. We had plenty of women's clothes and several very good female impersonators.

On Christmas Eve we had a splendid service, sang Christmas carols, gave and received gifts. We ate the best meal I ever had in prison camp, including some of the swell meals I had prepared myself, using the steam sterilizer in surgery as a pressure cooker. For supper the patients and staff had tomato soup, roast carabao, brown gravy and mashed potatoes, creamed asparagus, white bread, and raisin pie. At eleven o'clock we had coffee and chocolate cake.

After Christmas the Nips released thousands of Filipinos weekly to their homes. They sent many other thousands out to work in mines and lumber camps as labor battalions. It was evident to us that our days in O'Donnell were numbered.

In the second week of January, 1943, Colonel Duckworth spoke to us: "This camp is to be abandoned in three days. The General Hospital No. 1 Unit will be broken up. I am being sent to Bilibid Prison with a small group. A larger group will set up a small hospital in a compulsory military training camp for Filipinos near Cabanatuan. The rest of you will go to the Cabanatuan Prison Camp. I don't know whether we will ever meet again. You have worked well together during the dangers of war and the evils of prison life. I am proud of you. Good-bye and good luck."

CHAPTER 8.
Cabanatuan Prison: The Devil's Brother Does The Cooking

THE TURMOIL OF BREAKING UP our hospital unit at Camp O'Donnell began again for others, but not for me. It was almost worth having my arm in a plaster cast. Fortunately the doctors and medics were in fine physical shape after two months of fairly adequate Jap rations, supplemented by the life-saving Red Cross chow. There were hundreds of grateful convalescent Filipinos who were anxious to help—and did. Under our supervision they toiled and sweated far into the night, anxious to show their appreciation for their recovery. One of them was retired, fifty-five-year-old ex-Sergeant Moreno of the Twenty-seventh Cavalry. He had been one of our mess attendants in Little Baguio. He went about his work stolidly packing surgical equipment.

"Sergeant Moreno," I said, "this is a happy day for you. Tomorrow you will again see your wife and six children."

He looked up and said quietly, "But, sir, I shall not see them tomorrow."

"You told me they lived in a village near Fort McKinley. It shouldn't take more than a day to get there by train. They are well and alive?" I asked, puzzled.

"Ah, yes, sir, they are well, thank you sir. But I shall not see them. The God damn Japs will not let me go."

Before being released, all Filipinos had to sign a statement renouncing their loyalty to the United States and pledging allegiance to Japan.

"Moreno," I said, "if you remain here or are sent to a labor camp after we are gone, you will die. The Japs will not give you medicine when you become sick."

"Yes, Captain, I know that, but my heart does not let me sign this paper," he said slowly.

"But, Moreno," I pleaded, "thousands of other Filipinos are signing it with their tongues in their cheeks. They leave to join the Philippine constabulary so that they can have a gun when the Yanks come back. Many will go back to their provinces to get strong again. They will join guerrilla bands in the mountains. Sign this scrap of paper. Uncle Sam will understand it was signed unwillingly and in bad faith. You are worth more to us alive than dead."

"Captain, I was in the Philippine Scouts for thirty years before I retired. I cannot sign."

And he didn't sign. Nor did hundreds of other Filipinos, whose consciences were stronger than their fear of imprisonment and death.

The trucks shuttled back and forth to Capas all day loaded with bed patients. Thousands of ragged, convalescent Filipinos shuffled out of camp in a brown stream flowing to the railroad junction seven kilometers away where they were met by friends and relatives. One wisp of a lad, about eighteen, took a different kind of trip. The joy of reunion was too much for his weak heart; he died at the prison gates in his mother's arms.

Tony Escota, his slender wife and their Red Cross workers bustled about with bamboo platters loaded with bananas, fried chicken, and rice cookies. Kind-faced women of the Philippine Women's Federation dispensed hot tea and water as the dusty, wind-swept plaza filled with thousands of prisoners, weary and bedraggled after their hike from O'Donnell under the hot sun. There was loyal, devoted Benilda Castañeda and quick-witted Gregoria Espanozo, two of our Filipino nurses in Bataan. We could only smile, nod at each other and cautiously whisper words of encouragement, since we were under the very eyes of the sour-faced Nip guards parading about with fixed bayonets.

The whistle of the wood-burning, narrow-gauge railroad engine could be heard in the distance; soon a long train of freight cars drew into the station. We hastily gave our last morphine injections and applied the last bandages to our ex-patients. We loaded them carefully into the tiny, windowless steel freight cars. The empty plaza glared at us as we departed for camp again.

At four o'clock the next morning the medical personnel of the hospital assembled to load our equipment for transport to Capas. A booted Nip officer carrying a two-handled samurai sword appeared, accompanied by his interpreter.

"Your equipment and supplies will not be moved today. We shall ship it to your new camps later. You will carry only your personal belongings. Fall into columns of four and march to Capas," he finished brusquely.

We arrived at Capas under the flickering light of the stars, alarmed, disgusted, and dismayed at the loss of our irreplaceable medical and surgical supplies.

"Just about the time I think these bastards are human I catch sight of their tails," grumbled Gus disconsolately.

"Don't worry about it, Gus," soothed Tarzan. "They may send it later."

"Sure. And they may kiss you on both cheeks just before they cut your neck off."

The train was waiting for us. About a hundred and thirty strong, we climbed into two freight cars. Colonels Duckworth and Schock, accompanied by several medics, had left the day before for Bilibid. Two armed guards crawled in moodily after us and blocked the open door with their bodies.

The piercing blast of a steam whistle cut through the silent air in answer to the distant crowing of a cock. The engine puffed and snorted. The car couplings strained and rattled as we slowly picked up steam and drew away from O'Donnell forever. Stretched out on our luggage we grumbled about the close quarters and the heat. We napped intermittently. Clanging and rumbling over the uneven roadbed, the train traveled slowly south through the sun-parched rice country of Bulacan and crawled over temporary wooden bridges that spanned the muddy tributaries of the Pampanga River. We caught only glimpses of tiny clusters of bamboo shacks until we reached the main railroad junction at Bigoa, where the train stopped with a lurch.

"Everybody out for the seventh-inning stretch," was the order passed from mouth to mouth.

We clambered out, eager to escape the humid, foul-smelling odors of the box car. The glaring blast of the midday sun blinded our eyes. We scuttled for the shade of the railroad platform that was already crowded with hundreds of Filipinos waiting patiently for their trains. Fruit and food vendors dressed in colorful, netlike blouses and wrap-around skirts busily plied their trade. A tiny Filipino boy about ten years old approached our group carrying a basket filled with hard-boiled eggs, baked sweet-water fish, and bananas. We looked questioningly at the guard. He nodded his head.

"What's your name?" I asked.

"Pedro," he said, and added softly: "Mother told me to tell you to be brave, sir. You will soon be free, sir. She said the Yanks have killed many Germans in Africa and soon they will come back to the Philippines, sir."

Over our secret radio we had already heard of the invasion of Oran, and of Casablanca and the Allied drive into Algiers and Tunisia.

"Do you like the Japs, Pedro?" I asked.

His little face tightened. "No, sir, they beat me and my companions if we do not bow to them. When the Yanks come I will join the Scouts and kill many, sir."

I tried to pay him. He shook his head doggedly and slipped something into my hand. "My mother said you must take this, sir." It was a ten-peso bank note.

Bellies filled with good things to eat, arms loaded down with mangoes and bananas, we piled back into the freight car. For hours we traveled toward Mount Aryat, a huge, wooded, volcanic cone. We crawled through fifty miles of sun-baked flatland covered with the brown parched stubble of cut rice stalks. We gradually swung east of this peak which in solemn majesty guards the central plain of Luzon. As the sun dropped into the China Sea we pulled into the destroyed metropolis of Cabanatuan, whose burned-out warehouses and bomb-shattered churches lay scattered about the city in disorder. In the dimly lit station we sorted ourselves out quickly. Ten doctors including myself and twenty medics were to go to Prison Camp 3. The rest of the detachment was earmarked for the main American internment set-up at Camp 1. There was time only for a hasty handshake before we filled our trucks and were off again. We were carried east into the gently rising foothills of the Sierra Madre Range. A two-hour ride past multiple roadblocks brought us close to the farming community of Bagabad nestling at the base of giant mountains which reared their heads in unbroken alignment, the eastern escarpment of Luzon. The poorly focused headlights of the truck picked up a line of barbed wire behind which the barracks of the prison camp lay huddled. We dumped our belongings on the ground and strolled into the gloomy compound—Camp 3, a division of Cabanatuan Prison.

A Filipino in his early twenties greeted us. "The Japanese officers have already departed. You came very late. We can speak freely. I am Lieutenant Estrada, formerly of the Philippine Army. I am here already six months with five hundred Filipinos. The Japs are 'reconstructing' us."

We asked him what "reconstruction" meant.

"They give us many lectures about Japan and Japan's Coprosperity Sphere. They show us many movies of Japanese victories. They give us Japanese military training. They tell us we are their brothers. Then they beat us."

"Do you think many of your boys are falling for this line?"

"Oh, no, sir," he replied quickly. "These Filipinos have been sent here from O'Donnell and they already know the God damn Japs very well. The chow is better here. But they are beaten more often because all military commands are given in Japanese, which they do not learn very well, sir. They all want to go home."

As a matter of fact, most of them took French leave. During the Christmas holidays of 1943 two hundred and twenty-five prisoners, presumably indoctrinated with Japanese Bushido, were given a furlough—only twenty-five returned. The others fled to the hills with their families.

"I have a note from Chaplain Cummings in Bilibid Prison," Lieutenant Estrada told me, producing a folded scrap of paper from his shoe.

Glancing about to assure ourselves of privacy we read:

DEAR AL:

I am feeling well. My arm has healed and I can use it without pain. After I left Little Baguio I went to Bilibid. I got along fine. I was able to visit Filipino priests in Manila a few times until I got caught smuggling food and medicine in under my cassock. That was tough luck because I can't get out any more. The news is good.

The Nip fleet got smashed at Midway and was turned back in the Coral Sea. They lost thirty ships in the second battle off the Solomon Islands, many of which are in our hands. They are taking a whipping in New Guinea. Everything is looking up. There are rumors of a landing on the Celebes and Borneo.

Good Luck.

FATHER CUMMINGS

"Who gave you this note?"

"The Philippine Women's Federation have set up a canteen a mile down the road. One of the ladies gave it to me. Her name was Benilda Castaneda."

"What about that!" Gus Laudicina crowed gleefully. "What a system! What a setup! Good chow, good news, and contact through to Manila even before we've unloaded. That sure is hard to beat."

It was hard to beat. In every prison camp from Davao in southern Mindanao to the civilian internment camps in Baguio in northern Luzon, Filipinos rallied to our cry for help. The men went into the mountains to join some of our American officers who had never surrendered. They harassed Nip lines of communication, ambushed their trucks, and made it necessary for the Nips to garrison the islands permanently throughout their length and breadth. In addition to this they supplied our intelligence officers with detailed information concerning the disposition of Japanese forces.

The Philippine women took over the job of keeping us alive. Sex-conscious as the Nips are, they were won over by the smiles, the flattery, and if need arose, the bodies of these brave women. It was ludicrous to see hard-boiled Nip noncoms smirking like schoolboys while they were being twisted about their dainty fingers. Many women had already been killed during the Nip occupation of the Islands. Lovely Miss Conchita Pan, a member of the Philippine Women's Federation, was dragged through the streets of Manila and publicly executed on Dewey Boulevard when she was caught smuggling food for American prisoners. These women knew they were flirting with death. They were prepared to continue to do so indefinitely.

We created a hospital to accommodate a hundred patients mildly ill with malaria and dysentery. The water supply was good. Flies were nonexistent. We had enough medicine given to us by the Nips for our immediate needs. Before our departure from O'Donnell, Colonel Duckworth had divided our remaining stores of medicine between all members of the hospital unit to be carried on our persons and in our luggage. Because of his farsightedness we were able to keep these supplies in reserve. The chow was adequate but dull: rice and carabao stew twice a day. Since we still had the same Nip noncom officer we had had in O'Donnell, Lieutenant Max Andler was able to use the same food-stealing technique on him with the same success. With the food we could purchase at the Filipina canteen and smuggle in, we were indeed sitting pretty. We met Hutchinson and Snyder, American prisoners. They served as utility men for the Nips, generating the power and running the water pumps for the camp. Because of their relative freedom of movement they were able to put together a short-wave receiving set. They listened in to Stateside broadcasts every night, although their quarters were surrounded by Nip-occupied buildings. Again our news sources could not be improved on. With little work, plenty of free time for crap shooting and bridge playing, with opportunities for swimming in a lake nearby, we were living, relatively speaking, like kings. A Nip armed guard accompanied us to a neighboring swimming hole. Arriving there, he delegated one of us to protect his rifle while he paddled in the water like a puppy.

It was too good to last. Two weeks later we were ordered to leave. Disgruntled by the news that we were to be sent to Camp 1 and replaced by another group of medics, we regretfully packed our belongings and waited for the trucks to arrive. They were neither long in coming nor in departing. Again we swung through the foothills of the Sierra Madre Range, this time heading toward the city of Cabanatuan. In and out between the rounded hills sparsely covered with hardwood evergreens, we rode on the open truck through clouds of dust until we caught a glimpse of the flat rice country in the distance.

We climbed up the last low-lying knoll from which Camp 1 spread itself at our feet. An eight-foot-high barbed-wire fence enclosed a half-mile square area. About it, at hundred-yard intervals, reared a four-story wooden guard tower with its Nip guards bearing rifles and submachine guns that glinted wickedly in the brilliant sunlight. Two hard-packed dirt roads divided this enclosure into three equal segments. We learned later that in the segment closest to us lived five thousand American prisoners. This area was covered with neatly aligned, widely separated barracks of frame construction. About sixty feet long, each barrack accommodated a hundred prisoners on its double-decker bamboo floor separated by a central aisle—just about enough room to turn in while lying down on the un-mattressed deck. The central segment included the Nip barracks, guardhouse, mess halls, and drill field. Beyond this, on the far side, was the hospital area with its twenty-five hundred patients. In all, the view was almost as unappetizing as our first view of O'Donnell.

I was riding in the cab of the truck beside the driver, Private First Class Saver of New Hampshire, a short, wiry-looking fellow with crooked nose, crooked teeth, and smiling lips. "Doc," he said, "I suppose you know you're in for a shakedown?"

"By whom and for what?" I snapped.

"Well," he coughed, embarrassed, "the Nips will shake you down for weapons, but an American interpreter, an officer in the marines, may shake you down for medicine or anything else he wants."

"Who the hell does he think he is?" I snorted.

"I don't know, but he's got a tough reputation around here. Most of us can't figure out if he's a Jap or an American from the way he slings his weight around. He spent years in Japan as a language student—sent there by the navy, you know. When we surrendered in Corregidor he let the Nips know quick how good he was with their lingo, and they put him in charge of a lot of us. In fact he had a hell of a lot of authority. He threatened to turn us in to the Nips if we didn't obey him. They say he beat up a few of the boys. I don't know for sure. I do know he ate a hell of a lot better than we did after the surrender, and he isn't doing bad here. He's skinny, though. They say he has a nervous stomach. He'd be a God damn sight more nervous if he knew what we planned to do with him when the Yanks get here!"

I handed him my haversack stuffed with several bottles of quinine, sulfa drugs, and surgical tools. "How's about ducking this stuff until after the inspection?" I asked.

"O.K., Doc," he answered cheerily, stowing it under his seat.

We lined up and were counted off by the Nips. The marine officer, a small, wizened pip-squeak of a man in khaki shorts and shirt, his head covered by a marine officer's hat, barked at us. "Open your duffel bags and spread out your gear."

We still had plenty of gear to spread. We had lost practically nothing since the war had ended for us. In all our transfers as a hospital unit we had been able to truck our personal belongings. We had husbanded and patched our clothes carefully because it was evident that we would receive none from the Nips. Besides the army clothes I had a complete civilian outfit that Hanna had smuggled into Camp O'Donnell. I also had a phony Swiss passport from her. This was my ace in the hole. I had sworn that I would never permit myself to die in prison like a starving rat. If the prospects of life in prison became black enough, I had plans to hide out in Manila for the duration of the war as a Swiss citizen. My physical build was not against it. I knew enough German and French to make the plan workable.

The Nip guards began the old pillaging and looting routine while searching for arms. As usual, mirrors, razor blades, cigarettes, and playing cards dissolved under their hands. To avoid a more complete search we put photographs on top of our gear. Like children, the Nips are fascinated by pictures of people and places. Snapshots of pretty women almost always put them in a good humor. They were diverted by this effective smoke screen. My shakedown was superficial. The guard passed along. I followed him with my eyes breathing easier. I had a hammer, a hatchet, and a straight-edged razor in my belongings. I turned to see the marine officer pawing through my clothes.

"I've already been inspected, sir," I said politely.

"I'll tell you when you're through," he said.

Reaching into the tangled mass of clothing he slipped a bottle of surgical sulfanilamide powder out of a sock in which it was hidden. He found two tubes of yellow oxide mercury eye ointment in the toe of a shoe. Finally he located a bottle of iodine wrapped in a towel.

Boiling-mad, I said, "What the hell's the idea?"

He looked at me coldly. "It's none of your God damn business. If you want to argue I might get him to take you on," pointing to the Nip guard with a fixed bayonet.

He barked: "Inspection finished. Pick up your gear and move on to the hospital area."

Fussing and fuming, I loaded up and moved across the Nip parade ground. A dry voice hailed me: "Hello, Al. How are you?"

It was Colonel Craig, whom I had last seen operating in the Sternberg Hospital in Manila when the war started. His pipe-stem arms and legs looked pinned together under the sun-bleached army shirt and shorts. His hair had grayed. His face was deeply furrowed.

"Fine, Colonel. How've you been?" I looked at his right arm that dangled beside him, limp and distorted.

"Can't complain; I'm still alive," he said. "Had some trouble with the arm. Beriberi I guess. It's coming back fast since we got some Red Cross medicine. How'd you make out with the inspection?"

"Not too bad. I left my haversack loaded with medicine with one of the truck drivers. The inspection officer picked up a few items. Does he turn those supplies over to the hospital?" I asked.

"Hell, no. They're for his own use. Why, his bahai looks like a regular pharmacy. We've tried to buck him but he's thick as thieves with the Nips. He'll have to wait until after the war before he gets his—if he's still alive," he added grimly.

He told me what happened to him after the fall of Bataan.

"After Hospital No. 2 broke up we were trucked to San Fernando and rode in freight cars to this camp. We weren't allowed to take any equipment with us. There were about five thousand Americans here captured on Corregidor. They looked hungry but not in any great danger of dying. I guess they must have eaten better than we did in Bataan," he grinned. "There was a hell of a lot of canned food left in the tunnels of Corregidor when they surrendered. Well, thousands marched into Cabanatuan Prison later from O'Donnell. I guess I don't have to tell you what shape they were in. They were in even worse shape when they arrived here, if that's possible. Most of them had dysentery, many had malaria. With few exceptions, they all had scurvy and beriberi to boot. Yet some were actually smiling when they arrived."

I looked at him incredulously.

"Sure, smiling and laughing. They never expected to get out of O'Donnell alive. They thought that once they got to Cabanatuan their troubles would be over. You know the dream: plenty of chow and water, a real hospital, soft beds, clean linen, and all the medicine they needed. A prisoner's paradise. They got plenty of water here but very little else. The chow was standard: lugoa in the morning, steamed rice for lunch and supper, konkon, camote tops or mongo-bean soup daily; a spoonful of sugar every third day, hardly any proteins at all."

I asked about the hospital setup.

"You'll see it in a few minutes. It hasn't changed much since it was established in July. The little medicine we carried in on our bodies was soon used up. It was practically impossible to squeeze any more out of the Nips except a little quinine. The hospital served as a stopping-off place for dying and bedridden men who were not strong enough to stand in the chow and water line.

"The wards are numbered from one to forty. We have a ward similar to your St. Peter's. We call ours the Zero Ward. It was a busy place. A thousand prisoners died in June, a thousand in July, and just about another thousand have died in the last six months. It was a tough job finding men strong enough to carry the corpses out of camp on our homemade litters and dig the graves. So bodies were always lying around the camp. Most of them passed out with dysentery, malaria, and starvation. In August the death rate began to drop. The weakest had faded out of the picture.

"Sanitation and fly control improved. We thought the worst was over. The Nips finally consented to set up a canteen and we were able to buy small amounts of fruits, vegetables, and canned goods. That is, those of us who still had money or could borrow some. If you or your friends didn't have any, it was just T.S. Then the Manila underground began to function. We were able to smuggle in some good medicine. Do you remember Dr. Watrous who practiced in Manila before the war?"

I nodded.

"Colonel 'Shep' Fields, your boss at Santa Escolástica called him in to see a patient whose upper tooth he had just extracted. Watrous looked at the gray-green scum about the socket, smelled it, and said it was diphtheria. We thought he was crazy. But that's what it was. It spread through camp like wildfire. Not the mild type we see in the States either. I don't quite understand why it was so bizarre and deadly. Men who came down with it had the most curious lesions—may be that their resistance was so low that the germ which hits the tonsils in the usual case could grow anywhere—lips, cheek, tongue, sinuses. Why, we even had patients with the germ growing and developing dirty-gray ulcers in the conjunctiva of the eye and on the penis under the foreskin. These men were extremely toxic. Hundreds died in a few weeks of kidney trouble and heart failure."

"What about antitoxin?" I asked.

"For weeks we got nothing. Colonel Jack Schwartz, who is in charge of the hospital, and Major Watrous haunted Nip headquarters begging for it. The Japs finally broke down and sent some in from Manila. We got a microscope, slides and dyes to make throat smears throughout the camp. We isolated a number of early cases who pulled through. We also found plenty of carriers of the disease who had no symptoms. The epidemic gradually petered out."

I interrupted, pointing to a long string of men trudging toward us, their heads and shoulders hunched forward, carrying huge loads of cut dried grass on their backs.

"That's the hay detail," he explained. "They are the light-duty men. They walk out into the fields, cut kogon grass with their bolos, and haul it back to camp to feed the carabao herd." He pointed toward a man-made pool in which dozens of these wide-shouldered beasts were wallowing.

I noticed that all the men were barefooted.

"The shoe situation is bad enough. The Nips make it worse. They won't let our men wear shoes while they are working. They say the shoes must not wear out. The same thing is true for our heavy-duty men who are working out in Farmer Jones's garden."

"Farmer Jones?"

"He's a retired American soldier who's farmed in the Philippines for many years, a dhobie citizen. He joined the army when the war started. About October of 1942 the Nips couldn't tolerate the idea of thousands of sick prisoners doing nothing but dying so they started a farm in these rice paddies. The hell of it is, there's an undercrust of lava ash deposited in these parts when Mount Aryat exploded thousands of years ago. They made Jones responsible for growing vegetables in this impossible soil. They sent thousands of these sick men to slave under the broiling sun every day. It might have worked out well, except for lack of tools and water. Although they have about three hundred acres under cultivation, they haven't any plows or tractors. The men scrub around in the dirt with sharp sticks and hoes they fashion themselves out of scraps of metal. Because there was no irrigation system, when the dry season started all watering had to be done by hand. It's a long carry from the river. Strange as it may sound, they did grow some crops of sweet potatoes, corn, and garden vegetables. We don't get much of our crops. The Nips load most of it on trucks and haul it to their own garrisons in Cabanatuan. Personally, I think the food the men actually grow and eat doesn't replace the muscle and the body tissue they burn while working. You may have a chance to see how heavy the work is yourself," he added, grinning.

"Hell, no," I said hastily, "I don't know anything about gardening."

"Maybe you'll learn. There are plenty of officers, chaplains, doctors, and medical corpsmen working out there. As a matter of fact, the Nips insisted on the hospital supplying five hundred convalescent patients a day for the farm. Jack Schwartz howled so long and loud at the Nip administration headquarters that they revoked this order after two days. He's got plenty of guts; so has Colonel Beecher, the marine officer in charge of the camp. Both of them have often been slapped around by the Nips for 'complaining and using arrogant language.'"

I asked if any American prisoners had been executed. "Plenty," he said. "Five G.I.'s were caught at night trading jewelry for food with Filipinos through the barbed-wire fence. They were tied to stakes outside the camp near that building," pointing to a barracks, "and for forty-eight hours they went without food and water. Then they were shot. We buried them where they fell. In August the Nips claimed that two patients had escaped from the hospital. The 'blood brothers' of these men were corralled for execution. The execution date was actually set when the bodies of the two men were found. One had dropped dead in the high kogon grass near his barracks; the other had fallen into a latrine."

"Later that month three officers tried to escape at night. They crawled into a ditch leading to the fence and lay low, waiting for a chance to make their getaway. The Nips had forced us to establish a patrol inside the fence to prevent escapes. Actually, we were being forced to guard our own men. One of our M.P.'s making his rounds found it necessary to urinate. Unfortunately the stream landed on these officers who lost their heads and raised hell with him. The M.P. urged them to return to their barracks, pointing out that if they escaped the twenty-seven men in their three shooting squads—you know we were divided into 'shooting squads' of ten—would be executed. They scuffled with him until the Nip guards came tearing down the field. The officers were thrown into the brig." He added slowly: "In full view of the camp they were beaten with clubs for forty-eight hours and then shot. I still don't know how they lasted so long. They were battered beyond recognition."

"Well, Colonel," I said, nauseated by the recital, "I guess that's all I can take for one day. See you later."

I began thinking of ways and means to escape. From Colonel Craig's recital, there were more doctors and medics in camp than were needed to treat the sick. I wouldn't feel as if I were deserting patients who needed me. If death from starvation in camp were inevitable, I should prefer to sweat it out with the guerrillas in the mountains or take my chances as a phony Swiss citizen in Manila.

My medics hauled my luggage to the hospital head-quarters and then took off to scout the camp.

Colonel Jack Schwartz, who had been one of my chiefs at Jai Alai, greeted me. I don't think he weighed more than ninety pounds.

"You're looking fine, Al," he said wistfully. I had gone up from a hundred and twenty to a hundred and forty pounds during the last two months at O'Donnell.

I nodded, somewhat apologetically.

"I've had amoebic dysentery off and on," he said. "I'm better since the Red Cross chow and medicine came at Christmastime. We got quite a bit of stuff—vitamins, sulfa drugs, quinine, morphine, and some surgical stuff. You know Colonel North, don't you, Al? He comes from your neck of the woods?"

He was from Georgia. I had met him in General Hospital No. 2 in Bataan.

"He's all right now, but he was plenty sick with dysentery for a while. He's had to operate without gloves, gowns or sterilizers. He's got what he needs for the first time in more than six months. His hands have been full: amputations for uncontrollable, spreading ulcers of the feet, perforated peptic ulcers of the stomach, amoebic perforation of the bowel with abscess formation or peritonitis. Handicapped as he was, it's amazing any of his starved patients pulled through. Many of them did die."

I asked if he was still losing weight.

"No, Al. I've been gaining since Christmas, 1942. We got three Red Cross individual parcels each—they total about thirty-six pounds—and a lot of bulk food. It was a lifesaver for many of us. We've had only thirty deaths in February, and will have even fewer next month. We've been able to issue extra food in the galley almost every day for the last two months, mostly in the form of stews. It's a great help. Many of the men still can't eat steamed rice straight in sufficient quantities to keep alive. With the stew to flavor it, they can swallow it. Many are gaining a little weight. We're stretching out our Red Cross chow to make it last as long as possible. Nobody knows when the Nips will let more come in."

"How many patients do you have?"

"It varies. Colonel Craig is in charge of all medical work. Through the dispensaries on the work side of the camp, he can keep about three or four hundred in quarters every day. We have about twenty-five hundred in the hospital now. The Nips are raising all kinds of hell about the total here. They hound me every day to discharge men to duty from the hospital. You see, they regularly send work details from this camp to labor in different parts of the island—Nichols Airfield, Clark Field, the Pasay Naval Airport, auto and truck reclamation in Bataan, road building in Tayabas. They sent one group of six hundred to Mukden, Manchuria, and fourteen hundred to Japan, mostly technicians. A thousand are being shipped to Japan next month. Would you like to visit the Land of the Rising Sun?"

"Hell, no, Jack. I'm a lousy sailor," I replied hastily. "I made one mistake when I volunteered for service in the Philippines. There's not much danger of my volunteering to go to Japan."

"There's not much danger of our sending you yet," he said slowly. "They permit us to send only two doctors with every thousand prisoners, and no chaplains. Many of them have begged to go but the Nips won't listen. Except for a few who hold services, many doctors and chaplains work on the farm. There isn't much surgery being done except for outright emergencies that Colonel North and Lieutenant Sauerwald handle. I'll have to put you on a medical ward."

That was O.K. with me. Anything was better than working on the farm detail under a blazing sun.

"The acute medical cases are sent to wards run by Major Kagy and Lieutenant Schultz. These wards get all the medicine they need and all the extra chow their patients can eat. The rest of the medicine is parceled out in small amounts to the other wards every week," he said apologetically. "Since Christmas we have been paid about forty pesos a month. The rest goes into Nip bank deposits. We finally got the Japs to permit us to draw on these personal bank accounts to purchase eggs for the patients. This is a voluntary contribution made by practically all officers in camp. We buy thousands of eggs from Filipinos every week for the hospital. They are allotted to the wards, depending on the number of needy patients. You will be issued a share for your ward weekly.

"Your patients will be chronic ones with dysentery, malaria, scurvy, and beriberi. Your job will be to see that the medicine is dispensed honestly by the medics, a few of whom are shifty customers. See that the patients swallow their pills rather than hoard or trade them off for cigarettes. They're still pretty well whipped down physically, and even more depressed mentally. Not as bad as before Christmas, but low enough."

His gentle face crinkled: "A kindly word and easy handling will do as much good as medicine. They're lonesome for their folks. They've received no mail. The food situation is better, but they're still hungry. They have no music to hear and no books to read. Dull weeks stretch into deadly dull months. They sit around with nothing to do, waiting for the next meal. The boredom is overwhelming. They're irritable, moody, and suspicious. They've seen some of their own G.I.'s and officers act like animals, conniving for a little extra chow and stealing medicine from those who needed it more. They don't trust anybody. They've lost faith in their friends and themselves. Don't expect them to behave like soldiers. They're broken-down, disillusioned, unhappy, sick children and must be treated as such. Be kind to them; be gentle. They need all the help you can give them. We're glad to have you and your men in camp. You're all in good health and spirits and should do some good. I hope to God you can."

We shook hands.

CHAPTER 9.
Carabao Wallow

I STROLLED THROUGH THE HOSPITAL area past long lines of men standing passively in front of the galley, mess kit and canteen cup in hand. Tanned nut brown, hatless and shoeless they stood, chests exposed to the hot rays of the sun, loins covered with a pair of sun-bleached, ragged shorts cut down from army trousers. Skin and bone, pipe-stem arms and legs, without muscle on their shoulders or flesh on their buttocks, they stood shifting their weight from one foot to another. Their prematurely aged and drawn faces showed neither anger at the long wait nor pleasure for the anticipated meal. There was no banter, no small talk, no loud voice, no laughter, no cussing. They stood silently, the picture of complete indifference, utter boredom. The line shuffled along to the serving door where the rice was being dished out with a homemade wooden paddle. Extending their mess kits, they said briefly, "Hit it light" or "Hit it heavy." They passed along a line of servers to receive two spoons of corned-beef stew, a spoonful of marmalade, and a half-cup of mongo beans. They straggled away to wolf their chow near their barracks, squatting on their haunches or sitting on tiny stools they had knocked together.

I passed row upon row of barracks of standard construction separated by strips of hard-baked clay ground over which gusts of hot wind blew clouds of dust in twisters which danced bizarrely through the area. At Ward 17 I inquired for Lieutenant Dale Henry, the barrack leader. Each barrack had an officer-patient who was responsible for roll call and maintenance of order. He was about six feet tall, wiry, with well developed torso. Arms and legs were covered with steel-like bands of muscle: not an ounce of fat.

A smile lit his face as he shook my hand and said: "Glad to see you, Doc. Hope you like it here. How've you been?"

"O.K., Henry. How are the folks back home in West Virginia?"

"All right, I guess. Haven't heard yet. I sure miss them."

"How long have you been on this ward?"

"About three months. I think I'm just about ready to leave the hospital and go on a work detail."

"I wish you'd hang around until I get broken in. I've been working with Filipinos so long that I feel like a real sunshiner. I like them a lot but it's swell to be with Americans again. What do you think our men need most, Henry?" I asked.

"They need a lot of things—good news, clothes, food, and tobacco, to name a few. What I think they need most is sympathy, encouragement, and entertainment. They've been pushed around so much that they don't trust anybody. They're confused and sullen. They've got beriberi of the brain. They either mope around by themselves or spit like cats at each other. Not all of them: there are some with plenty of pepper and fight, but they're mostly on the work side of the camp. Most of these boys in the hospital are whipped down so badly that they can't snap out of their gloom by themselves. A lot of them are young kids who've always had an easy time of it in the States. Since the war they've had to eat too much misery at one sitting. Now they sit around on their backsides, if they have any muscle to sit on, all day long, thinking about home. There's plenty of water, but they've lost the habit of washing. There's plenty of wood laying around to make a pair of clogs, but they haven't enough push left in them to make a pair. It's easier to go around barefooted. They're not really shiftless. They've just lost the old punch. It's got me beat," he said, scratching his head.

"What about the officers?" I asked.

"Some of them aren't much better," he said cautiously, watching my face. "Especially when they get sick. We had an officers' ward for a while. They raised so much hell demanding special privileges, more chow and medicine because of their rank, that Colonel Schwartz finally had to break it up. Now they're distributed through the hospital. It's worked out better that way. They were getting in their own hair, pulling their rank on each other."

"How's the tobacco situation, Henry?"

"Pretty lousy. The men have finished off their Red Cross cigarettes. There's not very much coming through the commissary, so even the boys with money are hard up. We used to get in some long brown dhobie cigarettes, but no more. Some Rositas come in. They're good. Mostly, we get in 'Green Deaths,' a God-awful tobacco wrapped in cardboard tubes that're tipped with green. Most of the men go snipe-hunting for butts. By common agreement the area is divided into strips for foraging. God help anybody that encroaches on some other guy's strip."

"What goes on by way of entertainment?"

"They've organized a swell jazz band and a glee club that puts on shows on the work side of the camp. They come over to the hospital every two or three weeks. The men are crazy about them. Too bad we can't have more of the same thing. The chaplains put on services in the hospital area on Sunday. They're well attended and appreciated. In fact, there are a hell of a lot of guys going to church that never went before. I guess it must help pull through the tough grind."

We went into the ward and found Corporal Berry dispensing medicine. He was a tall, silent, poker-faced Texan who could be relied upon to carry out orders. I checked through the records of his hundred patients and had them pass before me so that I could associate their records with their names and faces. There were a smattering of old-timers who had lived in the Philippines for many years. The rest of them were young. Many were from the West and Southwest, representing National Guard units that had been sent to the Philippines before the outbreak of the war. Hair long and uncombed, clothes ragged and dirty, they filed by, not particularly interested in me. They crawled back to their bamboo slats and listlessly stretched out again. Here and there a few were carving wood pipes or playing cards. For the most part, they lay immobile.

I asked Henry to round up a few men who appeared more alert. I had some dhobie coffee brewed and passed some cigarettes around. There were several older men. Captain Ingerset was a two-fisted, barrel-chested Norwegian-American with a hard-boiled face and horny hands. He had piloted a small navy tug across the lonely wastes of the Pacific from San Francisco to Manila just before Pearl Harbor. He walked with a roll and talked the crusty, salty language of the waterfront. He had gone to sea forty years ago in a four-master. He had come up the hard way. He wouldn't take back talk from the devil himself. Although he was in his fifties he was a fool for work. His very activity shamed the younger men into action when we began repairing the ward. Mr. Trapp was a civilian who had been installing special radio equipment in submarines at Cavite Navy Yard before the war. He was a thin, wizened little man with a bald head, huge red-gray beard and a twinkle in his eyes. A sailor, retired because of disability, he had lived in the Philippines for years. During his youth he had played bits in stock companies in the States. First Machinist Mate Sergeant Harrison, assistant barrack leader, was about thirty, a wisecracking, tobacco-chewing sailor of the new school. He had diabetes. We had a nightmare keeping him in insulin without which he would have promptly died.

Another patient, Lieutenant Abe Schwartz, ex-supply sergeant of the Thirty-first Infantry, referred to himself as a second-class second lieutenant. A friend of Father Cummings, who had baptized the three children born to his Chinese-Filipino wife, he had visited me at Little Baguio. Black-haired, sharp-eyed, with aquiline nose, his real character was portrayed in his generous, laughter-loving mouth. Full of fun and mimicry, he helped us forget the present.

Sergeant Abie Abraham, a short, swarthy and stocky Syrian-American Catholic, had also been with the Thirty-first Infantry. Professional boxer in the States, he remained in the boxing game as a trainer and instructor in his outfit in the Philippines before the war started.

We shot the breeze for a while, talking about the latest "scuttle" and getting acquainted. For a starter, I said: "I've called you men together to get some advice on how to run this ward. You've all been here a long time. You know the ropes better than I do. I've checked over the men in this ward superficially. It's quite evident to me that very few of them are seriously ill. They're all undernourished. Most of them have the runs, beriberi, pellagra, and malaria. Yet with medicine and chow coming in, I don't think many of them are going to die. But a lot of them act as if they don't give a damn if the sun rises or not. Do you have any ideas as to how to make them snap out of it?"

"Kick 'em in the butt," growled Captain Ingerset. "Shake 'em up and keep 'em busy. They're too God damn sorry for themselves."

"You can't do that," protested Schwartz. "They're just a bunch of young kids who've had a rough deal. They haven't got over it yet."

"Nuts," responded Ingerset. "I'd like to have 'em on a four-master, beating around the Horn, and show 'em what a real rough deal is."

"What do you think, Mr. Trapp?"

"Well," Trapp said slowly, stroking his beard, "I think they're both right. These men will have to be pushed and led at the same time, rewarded for good and punished for bad behavior. You'll have to go very slowly. They'd be suspicious of Jesus himself if He were to lead them by the hand."

"I'd like to see this ward become something like a community club or company playroom," interrupted Sergeant Abraham. "Let 'em forget that this is a hospital. Let 'em think of it as a place where they can play games, entertain their friends, work out in the little gym. Let them forget they're in prison. If I go slow, I can steal enough wood in camp and logs from the wood choppers to build a café alongside our barracks where they can eat in the shade. I'm planning to open a roadside café in Manila after the war. I might as well get a little practice now."

I nodded my approval and looked questioningly at the others.

"O.K. by me," was the answering chorus.

"What are you going to call the joint?" asked Corporal Holliman of Richmond, Virginia. He was an old patient of mine from Little Baguio. When our nurses left for Corregidor before Bataan fell, we were short of help. Soft-spoken and gentle-handed, he was a godsend to our helpless patients on the gas-gangrene ward. He worked constantly, washing, feeding, and encouraging.

"I don't know," I replied. "What do you think of having a name competition thrown open to everybody in the ward? We might give the winner a can of corned beef. I've got some chow I smuggled in and I'll probably get more."

"That's swell," said Trapp. "I'd like to chip in, too." He tossed twenty pesos on the ground where we were squatting in a circle. It had no sooner landed than the ground was littered with bills. I counted ninety-four pesos. This was just the beginning of our war chest.

Lieutenant Henry announced the competition. We received only twenty-four entries in a ward of a hundred patients: a lousy showing, indicating the lethargy into which these men had sunk. We studied the entries carefully. Some I still remember were "Beriberi Inn," "Bum's Haven," "The Bitching Bahai," "Filipino Flop House," "Bedbug's Paradise," and "Carabao Wallow." We chose the last because a carabao is happiest when wallowing in his mudhole. We hoped the men would be as strong as that beast when they left their wallow in the hospital. The name stuck.

Trapp came to me one day and said: "Doc, I think we can get these men behind us most quickly if we supply them with free tobacco."

I agreed. From my own experience and observation I knew smoking was an effective way of curbing the pangs of hunger.

"Well," Trapp said, pulling at his beard, "I'll buy several packs of shredded Alhambra tobacco out of the war chest—let's say two pounds—and put them in a box in a corner of the barracks. Anybody in the ward that wants to roll a smoke or fill up their tobacco pouch will be welcome to it. No questions asked."

He did so. The patients began to perk up and take notice.

It soon became evident, however, that our expenditures for tobacco would make an excessively big dent in our funds. I went to visit Ted Lowen on the work side of the camp. He was a muscularly built civilian with a twisted, punched-in nose and a pleasant smile under a crop of shaggy, gray-streaked hair. Before the war he ran a night club and gambling joint in Manila called the Alcazar. He had owned several clubs in California. He left the States for Manila before the war. He knew all the angles. If anyone had received training in the States to live the life of a prisoner of war, it was he. As supervisor of a construction gang in camp he got to know the Nip noncoms. They soon ate out of his hand. He never met a Nip who couldn't be bribed, if the bribe was large enough. Before long he had contact with Filipino friends in Manila. The rest was easy. He passed out bribes lavishly: a gift of a watch to the Nip noncoms, rings for the Nip guards. Food and money began to flow into camp by way of the American truck drivers who drove in daily from Cabanatuan to our prison camp. During the year I was in camp he was able to smuggle in literally tons of food and hundreds of thousands of pesos. I am certain many prisoners would have died without his help.

The day after I first approached him with our tobacco problem he sent over a huge rice sack filled with cured leaf tobacco, about thirty pounds. This was the first of many shipments. I never learned what strings he pulled to get them, but the Carabao Wallow never lacked tobacco during the year of Our Lord, 1943.

With the patients acting a little less surly, we thought it was time to put pressure on those who had lost all interest in their personal appearance. With clothes that Private First Class Liebert collected from our old medics who had come with us from O'Donnell, plus the clothing I had brought in my trunk, Henry announced another competition—a clothes-patching one this time. A time limit of one week was set, with thirty-two articles of clothing as prizes. Owners of the most neatly patched clothes received a prize of one article of clothing. To avoid recrimination in this competition, the judges included one officer, one noncom, two G.I.'s, and myself. We had plenty of needles but very little thread. We manufactured more by unraveling torn shirts. The appearance of the men perked up: so far so good.

There were many men who didn't know how to sew and, furthermore, didn't give a damn about repairing the rags they were wearing. To handle this group I approached Private "Queenie" Blank, a marine from Shanghai. He was a tall, emaciated youngster with long, disheveled hair, soft, expressive brown eyes, and full lips with a sullen twist. His face, arms, and legs were a mass of impetigo sores.

He had exhibited homosexual tendencies since adolescence. When he was about sixteen he had worked as a female impersonator in a notorious restaurant in San Francisco. Before the war he ran away from home and joined the marines. He spent several years in Shanghai where it apparently was easier for him to express his abnormal sex drive without excessive comment. As a prisoner, in addition to hunger and starvation, he had to endure the taunts of his fellow prisoners because of his peculiarities.

"Queenie," I said, "what are you thinking about?"

He raised his sullen head: "What difference does it make to you?"

"Not much. I thought I'd shoot the bull with you for a while, if you don't mind."

He softened up a little. "I was thinking of what some of my boy friends in the States would think of me if they saw me now. I look so ugly." His large brown eyes filled with tears. "I was thinking of what nice clothes we all had. Wherever I look now, all I see is dirty, ragged men. It's horrible."

"Queenie," I asked, "do you know how to sew?"

"Why, yes," he answered, brightening up. "I love it."

"How would you like to be the barrack's tailor? You can charge the officers a reasonable fee for your work, but you'll have to do the work for the rest of the men for nothing. In fact, you'll have to pester them to get their clothes patched. If they want to tip you, that's O.K. by me."

"What kind of tip?" he asked coyly. "Sure, I'd love the job."

He did a swell job, nagging and pestering the men in the barrack to get their clothes patched. Business got so good that I gave him an assistant, a silent, stolid American Indian, named Luan, who actually used to be a tailor.

The next job we tackled was that of making wooden shoes or "go aheads," as we called them. Most of the men had no shoes and walked about on the dust-covered ground on bruised, infected feet. There were plenty of odd pieces of wood to be scavenged about the camp. We sawed them into appropriate lengths for men who wanted to make clogs. Henry announced a shoe-making competition with three prizes for the best pairs made: first prize—a can of corned beef; second prize—a can of fish; third prize—a dozen bananas. The clogs were shaped by hand with the hatchet I had smuggled into camp. We stole a second from the Japs.

Again we ran into the same residuum of men who were clumsy with their hands or were out-and-out shiftless. Our best shoemaker was a retired soldier, Sergeant Nester. About sixty-two when the war started, he had enlisted and fought through the Bataan campaign. More than six feet tall, body and extremities deeply tanned, he had a flowing mustache and long white beard parted in the middle *a la* Chief Justice Hughes. He consented to be our cobbler. Squatting on his heels, his corded hands grasping wood block and hatchet, he patiently chipped away, fashioning the wood to fit the normal curves of the foot. His output was two pairs a day when he worked steadily. To complete the wooden shoe he needed tire casings which he cut into strips and tacked in a loop into which the toes could snuggle across the front of the clog. We got casings from the truck drivers. In a month everybody on the ward was shod.

Sandy-haired Corporal Marlin E. Sargent of Hagerman, New Mexico, was lying on the bamboo slats in the ward, staring at the deck above him, a smile flitting across his thin, freckled face.

"What's the big joke, Marlin?" I asked.

"I was just thinkin' of a little ol' barber shop I used to work in back home," he drawled. "It sure was swell to stand there stroppin' the ol' razor and shootin' the bull with the customers. Yes, sir, I'm agoin' to get me my own shop when I get back."

We made Marlin the barrack's barber. He used the straight-edge razor I had smuggled in and a mess-kit G.I. knife honed down to a fine edge. We needed a pair of scissors. We tried to make them out of scrap metal but without success.

I wrote to Hanna for the first time since my arrival at Cabanatuan. I told her about my transfer from Camp O'Donnell and the lousy setup in Camp Cabanatuan, where many doctors were doing slave labor. I told her about receiving the pair of red socks she had sent me and kidded her about the color. I reminded her of a trip to Baguio when we had shopped in the gay native market; a dance at the Polo Club when she was dressed in sheer white; a symphony concert in Manila when she wore a crescent of red Camellias in her hair. I guess I got sentimental about seeing her again. I asked her to send me some carpenter's nails and a pair of scissors, also some lipstick and rouge for our female impersonators in the shows we put on at the Carabao Wallow.

Several weeks later I received a package and a note:

AL, DEAR:

I read and reread your note a dozen times, until I memorized it. Then I had to destroy it. The Japs search our house so often trying to get something on my brother Fred and me. Fred was finally sent to Fort Santiago dungeon where he was tortured for weeks. They didn't squeeze any information out of him about you know what. [His activity with the Filipino guerrilla band called the Blue Eagles.] He is home now, very weak and sick. My folks are well and send their love.

I think of you every day. I sit on my doorstep when the sun goes down into Manila Bay and dream about you.

Life in Manila under the Japs is filled with uncertainty and sudden death. I need you to keep my sanity.

P.S. I sent what you asked for.

We gave the pair of scissors to Staff Sergeant Stevens of Estancia, New Mexico, who did the haircutting. He and Marlin were specialists, referring trade to each other. Captain Ingerset built them a couple of rickety barber chairs which could be raised and lowered by a screwball "Rube Goldberg" contraption. The same system of remuneration was followed: officers paid, enlisted men tipped if they had anything. Thereafter, anybody with disheveled hair or unshaven face got hell from barrack leader Henry or myself if they didn't get cleaned up.

The work of building the Carabao Café continued under Captain Ingerset, Sergeant Abraham, and two middle-aged, retired ex-sergeants whom we called "Mike and Ike," or the "Two Dwarfs." I don't remember their names.

They had settled and lived in the Philippines for years before the war. Both were short, heavy-boned, and had tiny, pointed beards. One had a red beard on a lantern jaw and the other had a blond wisp on a square jaw. They had both been carpenters. They loved the sound of a hammer rapping on a nail.

The café ran the whole length of the barrack, about sixty feet. Against the wall of the building they first built the Greasy Spoon Annex, a series of sixteen tiny side-arm tables for two, similar to the Thompson Spa variety. Men of the lone-wolf type were assigned to these tables. They were quiet, retiring soldiers who preferred to eat by themselves or with one friend. They didn't like a lot of noise and small talk. Running parallel to the Greasy Spoon was the main café with a center table for four, flanked on either side by two tables for eight men each. The wide aisle between the café and the Greasy Spoon was filled with six tables for two. The legs on all these tables were made of logs that Sergeant Abraham had "borrowed" from the wood choppers; the table tops were made of many small pieces of packing cases carefully joined together by the Two Dwarfs.

We needed wide planks for seats both in the café and the annex. We hunted high and low without any luck. The only boards available were twenty-foot-long, two-by-six planks which lined the filled-up, deep, abandoned latrines near the barbed-wire fences. Their ends protruded some two feet above the ground, much too short for use if sawed off.

I was eyeing the planks longingly one day when Captain Ingerset came rolling toward me.

"What's on your mind, Doc?" he asked in his brusque manner. "You look as if you're between a sweat and a fit."

"Captain," I said, "we need those planks to finish our café, and I'm damned if I know how to get them out."

"Jesus Christ," he bellowed, "you can't use *them*. They're covered with night soil."

"They are now. After we get them out, scrape them with sand, and sun-dry them for a few days they'll smell as sweet as a baby's breath. Can you get them up?"

"If you want them," he sighed resignedly.

And he did. We got a long chain from the truck drivers and a fifteen-foot two-by-four plank to be used as a lever. Resting one end of it on a log, Ingerset wrapped the chain about it and one of the planks sunk in the ground. With eight of the strongest men in the barrack heaving upward on the long end of the lever, we gradually eased the plank out, inch by inch, under the broiling sun. It worked. Our seating problem was solved. In all, we were able to seat ninety men. The overflow, usually newcomers, ate their meals sitting on the park-type benches the carpenters had constructed—two at either end of the barrack.

Sergeant Abraham and Private First Class Muldovan, a handsome young air corpsman, both had ideas about beautifying the café. They stole enough two-by-fours from a pile of scrap lumber near the Nip guardhouse to extend the roof of the barrack over the café itself. By splitting long bamboo poles lengthwise they obtained flexible strips which could be bent. They tied these with bits of wire (stolen from the barbed-wire fences) to the uprights sunk in the ground about the café, transforming them into a series of arcades. Then they latticed the bare areas between and above them. As a finishing touch they covered the roof with similar strips of whitewashed bamboo.

Captain Jim Brennan, M.C., my roommate, who was decorated for heroic action in Bataan, supplied the almost nonexistent whitewash. Signs were hung from both ends of the ward announcing that the Carabao Café was open for business.

The Dwarfs were in their glory when wood was available. It wasn't long before they had it all sawed into proper lengths and nailed into place. They appeared every morning to stand silently before Ingerset, hammer in hand. They didn't say a word, but waited patiently for a work assignment while he paced up and down irritably, trying to find something for them to do.

"Why don't you say something?" he bellowed exasperated. "I'm no brain trust! Find something yourself!"

But they waited for his ideas. He had plenty of them. He hauled up enough planking from the abandoned latrines to floor completely the dirt-covered central aisle of the ward. The Dwarfs constructed a wash rack behind the barrack for the few men who had helmets which they used as washbasins. For the others they built a series of teeter-boards to which a canteen could be attached. When the teeterboards were tilted by hand, water flowed out of the canteen. Weighted by a rock, the board flipped upright when hand pressure was released. They improved our rack for drying clothes. They built a homemade shower by punching holes in the bottom of a fifty-five gallon drum and suspending it by a rope passed through a pulley carved out of wood. They cut the bamboo sleeping platforms in the ward into segments. These could then be carried out and doused with boiling water to kill bedbugs which swarmed all over the place. The Dwarfs were unhappy when work ran out.

We felt that the time was now ripe for full-time participation in this reconstructive psycho and physio therapy. The men had reached the stage where they passively trusted us and were vaguely grateful for the comforts they received. Many of them, however, still lay about on their backsides with nothing to occupy their minds or strengthen their bodies. They were still bored to death, lonesome for home.

To rouse them I asked Captain Lawler to take over the job of indoor entertainment officer. He was a thin, active-brained recent West Point graduate who had been with an artillery unit in Bataan. Under him and Sergeant Abraham, a series of weekly competitions in indoor games was organized with three food prizes for each competition. Everybody in the barracks who could crawl out of bed had to enter at least one competition: bridge, cribbage, pinochle, chess, checkers, monopoly, and that famous navy game, acey-deucy (something like backgammon). Men in the barrack made all these games, including several handsome pairs of dice carved out of carabao horn. The dentists at the clinic drilled the dots on them and plugged them with white cement. Egged on by Lawler and his gang of assistants, attracted by the food prizes, the men soon filled the café, where they sat for hours, studying their chessboards intently or talking enthusiastically to the rolling "bones."

The evenings were especially dull after the fast-falling tropical twilight had plunged the camp into darkness. We had few books. We had no electric lights. These prisoners had fought and re-fought the Bataan and Corregidor campaigns since the surrender. They had heard each other's stories a dozen times over. There was nothing to do but dream of home as the stars twinkled above. To dissipate this nightly pall of gloom, I asked Master Sergeant Jackson to take over the job of evening entertainment officer. He was a strongly built, professional Marine, about forty years of age. Prison fare had blinded his eyes so that he no longer could read. It had not broken his spirit. Carrying his well-molded head on erect neck and squared shoulders, he was a stalwart figure of manliness. He had one of the finest minds and memories I have ever seen. Editor of the Shanghai Marines' Walla Walla, brilliant student of military history, he gave fascinating lectures, without notes, on the campaigns of Caesar, Alexander, Pompey, Genghis Khan, and Napoleon. Together we arranged a program of evening entertainment, some elements of which would be attractive to all men in the barracks:

> Monday—lecture; Tuesday—carabao sing and Major Bowes program; Wednesday—lecture; Thursday—quiz program with prizes; Friday—carabao crap game with prizes; Saturday—formal entertainment by camp jazz band, theater group or glee club; Sunday—no entertainment, the men usually going to religious services.

Sergeant Jackson hustled about the camp lining up speakers for the talks. They were poorly attended at first, but soon they became a source of endless conversation among the men in the barrack. Instead of lying on their butts wrapped in lonesomeness or beefing about the chow, they turned out to listen, learn, and discuss what they heard. The talks covered a wide range of subjects: astronomy, radio, coal mining in the States, gold mining in the Philippines, life among the pagans in Luzon, trapping in the Rockies, fur trading in Mongolia, horse raising in Kentucky, cattle breeding in Louisiana—all by men who were experts in their field. When a speaker cancelled out, Jackson filled in with a military talk or I with a medical talk.

Sergeant Danforth, with his sweet Irish tenor, led the sings and conducted our Major Bowes programs. Captain Lawler handled the quiz programs. One of our Southern boys supervised the crap games. As the months rolled by, many of the leaders in this organizational work returned to duty. We always found replacements. The entertainment work went on.

To balance the indoor program, Corporal Holliman and black-haired, toothless Private First Class Greenley of West Virginia organized an outdoor program. They cleared a wide strip of land of kogon grass on the far side of the barracks along its entire length. Using dhobie clay, strips of bamboo, and bits of pipe, they constructed a nine-hole miniature golf course with hazards sufficiently treacherous to make Bobby Jones's hair turn gray. Fashioning a knife from a piece of scrap steel sharpened on a rock, they whittled out wooden golf balls and clubs, including a set for left-handed customers. We used these until we were able to smuggle in some putters and golf balls from Manila six months later. After par was established, anybody who shot under it was entitled to a prize of one duck egg. It wasn't long before we had to handicap some of our young golfers to avoid going bankrupt.

Holliman and Greenley wove some rope into quoits and set up two sets of these. They bent segments of one-inch pipe into horseshoes for those who liked "barnyard golf." Soon competitions in outdoor sports were in full swing, with money and food prizes as usual. This setup was properly labeled the Carabao Country Club.

I was more than satisfied. Straggling, forlorn, lonesome men had a home where they could live in modest comfort within the confines of a Japanese prison camp. They became a cleaner, healthier, more lively, more self-respecting group. They had a club to which they could invite their friends for a cup of dhobie coffee and an old-fashioned bull session. During the evening they entertained themselves or were stimulated by talks on subjects far removed from prison life and war. With minds occupied, they lost their lethargy and much of their loneliness.

All this work and organization had been done by a small group of men on a volunteer basis. The time had come to test the others in the ward; to see if they would participate positively under orders in the attempt to rehabilitate themselves. Could soldiers who had been degraded to a level lower than animals again raise themselves to the status of disciplined men? Would they obey orders given to them by us who had little or no authority to enforce them? True, we had our own M.P.'s in camp. We had our own brig which housed offenders against the peace and crooks caught stealing chow from our galleys and from their brother prisoners. Provost marshal court-martial proceedings for serious offenders were held. Yet, officers generally throughout the camp were extremely hesitant to put fellow Americans in jail within a prison camp.

Not at all sure of what the outcome would be, I checked over my hundred patients. I classified them into three groups according to the state of their physical health: no duty, light duty, moderately heavy duty. The moderately heavy duty men, of course, were those who were awaiting discharge. Discharge days from the hospital came at regular intervals set by the Japs. Roughly, the hundred fell into three equal groups.

The next morning I spoke to the men at roll call.

"I have divided you men up according to the state of your physical condition. The groupings are posted on the café bulletin board. I suggest you check there after I'm finished talking. It's my belief that your convalescence will be speeded up if you do some work to limber up your muscles while you are resting in the hospital. Many of you have been in the hospital for months. You'll find it pretty rough going when you hit the farm again. Muscles go soft quickly. The work I have planned to toughen you will involve gardening about the wallow for the heavy duty men and maintenance of the café and country club for the lightweights. This work is compulsory. Every man fit to do a little work will be assigned to these details—officers included—except for the men who have special duty jobs like the barbers, tailors, and carpenters. If any of you are assigned to heavy duty and don't think you can handle it, see me. I'll have you shifted to light duty. If any of you prefer to be transferred to another ward in the hospital, let me know about it."

There was a buzz of conversation as the formation broke up. Three men asked for a transfer. I was able to arrange the transfers through Colonel Jack Schwartz, who knew about the program and approved it.

There were two men on the ward who were expert gardeners and landscape artists. One was Colonel Ball, a short, wiry, red-faced man with a bulbous nose and shortsighted, peering blue eyes. He had been an artillery officer in World War I and had been decorated for bravery by the king of Belgium. In the Bataan campaign, his artillery outfit with their old-type 75's and 105's were in large part responsible for keeping the Japs at bay for months. Querulous but kindly, sporting a huge, rolled straw sombrero which shaded his lobster-colored torso, chewing a wad of tobacco constantly, he was the spark plug of the gardening work. A confirmed bachelor who had lived for years in Hawaii, flower-growing was his hobby. He was really a professional; he had developed new strains of gardenias and chrysanthemums.

The second gardener, Sergeant Melody (I have forgotten his real name), was about thirty, a shy, blue-eyed, skinny fellow with thinning sandy hair and a golden smile. He had supported his widowed mother for years. From her he inherited a love of flowers.

Sergeant Walter Bird, ex-service man, World War I, of Decatur, Georgia, took over the job of developing a lawn in front of the ward. He had with him a group of old-timers, including Sergeant "Buster" Keaton, a middle-aged plethoric Georgian with old-fashioned white goatee and mustache. This lawn was not easy to develop or maintain. During the dry season it needed tons of water to keep it green. During the wet season the grass roots drowned if the plot wasn't properly ditched and drained.

They dug up the area with pick and shovel, removing a surface layer of tough lava ash. Scurrying about the hospital with homemade litters, they collected heaping loads of fine grass turf. They carefully matched them together and tamped them with a homemade log tamper. From Farmer Jones I got some canna-lily bulbs which we planted as a border to the grassy plot. Properly watered, they grew like weeds to the height of five feet with their colorful flags of orchid-shaped, red and yellow flowers clustering in their broad green leaves. The border was then edged with whitewashed stones. In the center of this grassy plot, sixty by forty feet, was a solid centerpiece of brilliant blue strawflowers. Near it dangled a split log on which was burned with a hot wire the words "Carabao Range."

Lieutenant Schwartz developed the garden at the rear end of the wallow. He called it the Carabao Corral. It was so designated by a sign hanging from the top of a rustic entrance made of bark-covered branches. There was a little swinging gate of the same material with carabao-leather hinges. This plot, about the same size as the range, was surrounded by a miniature corral about which entwined a native climbing ivy with its tiny red and yellow trumpet-shaped flowers. A graveled path led into it to a centerpiece which our cobbler, Sergeant Nester, constructed. This was a waist-high tower of mortised rock, its crevices covered with bits of moss. Surmounting it he modeled a medieval fortress out of dhobie clay with narrow, slit-like, barred windows, gun emplacements, and wooden doors which could swing open.

Nester also constructed an accurate sundial and placed it on the roof of his castle. The path in the corral led to a bower with its love seat. Soon this was shaded by the broad leaves of a rapidly growing native vine. From it grew a gourd with a sponge-like matrix. Opened and exposed to the sun, its meat rotted away so that we could use its fibrous framework as a sponge. The borders of the grassy corral and its graveled path were lined with yellow and lemon-colored marigolds. Colonel Ball, who worked the flower seed beds, had selected seeds which grew the double rather than the single type of marigold.

Sergeant Abraham was not to be outdone. His group developed a grassy strip running parallel to and outside the café. It had a border of gaily-colored zinnias with a centerpiece of golden-flowered lilies. They constructed arcades of bamboo leading to the entrance and exit of the wallow. These, and the roof of the café itself, were soon covered with rapidly growing Upo and Umpalaya vines with their huge, luxuriously green leaves and gourds shaped like a breadfruit dangling from the trellises. Colonel Ball, who knew orchids, pestered the life out of the woodsmen who went out into the forests every day. They eventually collected orchid plants for him. Soon they were hanging in the café, carefully wrapped to charred branches with the fibrous coir of the coconut.

Corporal Holliman wanted something different. After his country club was lined with strips of grass and edged with whitewashed rock, he planted the corners, exits, and entrances with tropical tree-seedlings, orange, lime, and papaya. Some of the papaya trees were shoulder high before we had to move the café to a new location.

When all this landscaping was finished, many of the men wanted to develop vegetable gardens. We divided an area extending from the country club to the barbed-wire fence into twenty-four plots, each about twelve feet square. With seeds smuggled in from Manila, each patient owning a plot planted what he wanted: corn, peanuts, camotes, Chinese lettuce, radishes, onions, and native spinach. When a patient owning a plot left the hospital for duty, he sold it to one of his friends. Tobacco was usually the medium of exchange. Some very cagey maneuvering took place during these real-estate transactions.

One of the more serious problems in the development of this landscaping project was the procurement of gardening implements. We were able to borrow some from my roommate, Jim Brennan, who was in charge of the hospital sanitation, but they were not enough. We developed our own tool factory under Corporal John Padgett of Pahokee, Florida. He was recovering from an infection of the brain involving the cerebellum, which houses the centers of muscular coordination. He was a dark-haired, sad-faced fellow who spoke in a jerky, spasmodic manner. He had worked on a railroad and loved tools for what they would do. In spite of the coarse tremor of his hands, he turned out rakes, trench shovels, hoes, grubbers, and scythes. He made them out of scrap metal and fitted them cleverly with tree branches for handles. With constant use these broke down. He was kept busy repairing them. He was stuck for a long time when he tried to make a pick. Our foragers finally unearthed some rusty, two-inch pipe which he bent at right angles and flattened at one end. It was a clumsy tool, but it worked.

We established a special foraging department. Two professional ex-hoboes took over the job. One was "Pappy Hokum" Kiser who claimed Melba, Idaho, as his birthplace. He had taken to the open road when he was fifteen and was called "Little Sister" by his brother hoboes in the States. He was really tiny, less than five feet. He looked like a pixie, with sandy hair growing from both sides of his head to meet at a crest in the center. His eyes were bright blue and sharp, his nose a little nubbin, his lips pursed quizzically. A wispy, blond, pointed beard waggled back and forth when he talked. We gave him a brilliant-green sport shirt which he wore constantly, the tails dangling to his knees. His assistant was Private Howard, a tall gangling lad of twenty-four with disheveled hair, crooked teeth, and gentle manner. These two, who had lived by their wits for years, could see prospects for profit and trade in junk we all passed daily in the hospital rubbish dump. Neither was unhappy nor depressed by prison life. They had both seen hard times and were accustomed to them. They lived for the moment and never despaired of the future.

They left after breakfast to forage. They returned at lunch with scraps of metal for the toolmaker, nails for the carpenter, and buttons for the tailor in addition to odds and ends they had picked up for themselves. I made a big stink about needing sheet metal to cut into shovel patterns. After dark they returned, rolling a fifty-five-gallon gasoline drum which they had scrounged from the Nip garage.

For some reason unknown to me, they collected little boxes of tooth powder the Nips gave to us. It was so abrasive none of us wanted it. One day, Pappy returned, his pants bulging.

"What have you got there, Pappy?"

He plunged his tiny, grimy hands into the pockets and withdrew them filled with prune pits.

"What the hell do you want them for?" I questioned. "Can't tell now," he said secretively, pulling at his little beard.

The next day he came toward me carrying something wrapped in wide banana leaves.

"What've you got today, Pappy?"

"Baked a pie for your birthday, Doc," he said, his sharp eyes twinkling.

It was a banana-custard pie with a shell of rice-flour dough. The frosting was made of Red Cross butter whipped up with penoche (native cane syrup). It had a delicious peppermint flavor. On it were sprinkled some roasted grated nuts.

"Prune pits?" I asked, pointing to them.

He nodded. "It's damn good, Pappy. Where did you get the peppermint flavor?"

"Japanese tooth powder."

Breaking the men into this form of community living and cooperative work was not easy. They had lived like lone wolves too long to become Rotarians overnight. As the weeks rolled by, the halter we placed on their shoulders gradually ceased rankling. They saw grass, flowers, and climbing vines take the place of the dusty, sunbaked ground around the barracks. They began to take pride in their work and the work of the specific detail they were on. I could overhear them boasting to their friends who visited them how much nicer the corral looked than the range or vice versa. To stimulate the competition between the groups, Colonel Ball made a formal inspection of the garden plots every month. The men working on the plot that showed the greatest progress were given a hot-cake breakfast on Sunday. With money from our war chest we bought cane syrup, eggs, and rice. The men dampened the rice with water and ground it into flour, by rolling it with empty quart bottles. The hot cakes weren't hard to take.

New men coming into the ward were broken in slowly. They lay about for a week, unassigned, to absorb the atmosphere of the wallow. Then, if they were well enough, we assigned them to a project. Occasionally, they asked for a transfer to another ward rather than do their share. Similarly, I transferred them if they did too much growling and bitching. During the thirteen months I ran the ward, we asked for no help from our provost marshal in disciplining the men. If a soldier was recalcitrant or if we caught him stealing from his bedmates, we set up our own kangaroo court made up solely of G.I.'s and noncoms. The accused chose his own defense lawyer. They preferred the kangaroo court to being reported to the M.P.'s. The punishment was either extra night-guard duty or latrine duty. Sometimes the culprits were roughed up.

On one occasion, one of our patients fell afoul of the law. The Nips had finally issued Red Cross shoes to the men on the work side of the camp and a smaller number to the hospital. I gave one pair to Sergeant Bogart, a short, sullen, irritable ex-machine gunner who had been repeatedly decorated for bravery while fighting for the Thirty-first Infantry on Bataan. Like so many others, Bogart was a tobacco fiend. He sold his shoes to a friend for a carton of dhobie cigarettes.

Captain Francis, the provost marshal, learned about this and was instructed to put him in the brig. The Nip headquarters were especially nasty about the sale of these shoes because they eventually landed in the hands of Filipinos via the Nip guards. Similarly, our American headquarters took a poor view of the transactions because there were not enough shoes in camp for all the workers. The sentence in these cases was three weeks on rice and water in the brig. Bogart had just recovered from a serious bout of beriberi involving the heart. I was afraid he might suffer a relapse on this limited diet and kick off. I thought I was justified in trying to get him off. I saw Colonel Schwartz and explained Bogart's condition to him.

"Al," he said, a tired smile playing over his face, "everybody in camp has beriberi. We can't let him off on that score. This stealing of shoes and selling them to Filipinos and Nips must stop. We haven't any replacements."

"You're right, Jack," I answered, trying another angle, "but I think Bogart has had such serious beriberi that it's affected his brain. I don't think he's responsible for his behavior. What about letting the psychiatrist see him?"

"O.K.," he answered begrudgingly.

"Bogart," I said the next time I saw him, "in view of your war record, I'm going to help you beat this rap."

"What can you do about it?" he said, sullenly.

"If you cooperate we can put on an act. From now on you're nuts. You're crazy. Do you understand?"

"You mean all I have to do is act natural," he said morosely.

"Hell, no! Act violent, fly off the handle. Don't pay attention to what anybody says to you. Just sit like a bump on a log. Captain Blank, the psychiatrist, is coming to examine you. If you convince him you're nuts you may beat the rap."

"O.K., Doc. That won't be hard."

Captain Blank, a scholarly but offensive doctor with few friends in camp, came to see Bogart. Sitting behind Blank so that he could not see me, I coached Bogart through the interview by hand signals and grimaces. He put on a vivid, dramatic performance of a man completely indifferent to his surroundings. Bogart had never heard of the term "schizophrenia," but his characterization was a textbook picture of this mental derangement. If he's still alive he ought to go to Hollywood. I read Captain Blank's consultation note.

> **Sergeant Bogart is suffering from a mild form of manic-depressive psychosis or schizophrenia precipitated by malnutrition and prison life. He is not responsible for his behavior. At present he is not a source of physical danger to himself or others. He does not need housing in the psychopathic ward.**

The case was squashed. I never had any more trouble with Sergeant Bogart.

Contributions to our war chest came in at irregular intervals from officers who were getting paid by the Japs, from G.I.'s who were experts at crap shooting and poker playing, and from the old-timers on the ward who had underground connections in Manila. We used half of the money to buy extra food from the commissary for our weakest patients. The other half we distributed as food and money prizes in various competitions. During the existence of the Carabao Wallow, we spent more than five thousand pesos at a time when money was not easy to get and had great value in terms of food. This may be one reason, in addition to a better issue of chow and more adequate medicine, that we didn't lose a patient on this ward.

The beautification and café idea originated almost simultaneously throughout the hospital area. The demand for tools, seeds, and flowers was so great that Colonel Schwartz appointed a beautification officer to synchronize plans for landscaping. The hospital area, half a square mile of old rice-paddy land, was converted from a dusty, sun-baked plain into a wide-spreading garden. Wards competed with each other for more startling or intricate landscape designs. Captain Clayman, recreation officer for the hospital, started inter-barrack competition in indoor games. Father Talbot, our genial hospital padre, held a series of competitions with money and food prizes open to the whole hospital; these competitions included poetry, music, short stories, and handicrafts. The last was especially successful with intricate items submitted: carved chess sets, rings, trinkets, cribbage boards of carabao horn, jewelry, religious ornaments, wristbands hammered out of scrap metal, honest-to-God guitars made of sheet metal, violins carved out of hardwood. He carefully labeled and stored them. I hope he was able to get them back home.

The hospital census gradually dwindled from twenty-five hundred to six hundred. The Nips insisted on cutting down the size of the prison compound. The hospital moved to the work side of the camp. We transported the café to the new hospital area. It had previously been blown down twice by typhoons and rebuilt. We recreated garden plots about our new café. When the hospital census shrank to three hundred we moved again, carrying with us every precious scrap of wood. We transferred our flower seedlings into new gardens.

During this year we gave a barrack party about once a month, with an especially big blowout on Thanksgiving and Christmas. I remember the first party mainly because it was the first. Mr. Trapp, through the good services of Ted Lowen and by some very fancy sleight of hand of his own, smuggled a hindquarter of carabao into camp. We cut the best pieces into small steaks and broiled them. The rest of it went to make a rich, thick carabao-meat stew with plenty of garlic and onions.

We bought a quarter of a sack of rice. For two days the café was filled with patients busily dampening rice on the café tables and rolling it by hand with a bottle into a coarse flour. They mixed the dough with soda-bicarbonate pills chiseled from the hospital, sweetened it with cane sugar, and let it ferment overnight. The next morning we baked it into thick, heavy, but substantial rice cakes.

We had the woodsmen bring in some evergreens which we draped throughout the cafe. Sergeant Abraham and his gang covered the large tables with white bed sheets I borrowed from the operating room. Using cut pieces of bamboo as flower vases, Sergeant Marsden filled them with gaily-colored zinnias and marigolds for table centerpieces. From my trunk I dug up several long white candles which I had saved for surgical emergencies. We made some bamboo candlesticks. At "chow down" the men collected their rice servings from the galley and saved them for the party. Seated at their accustomed tables they awaited the arrival of the guests—Colonel Schwartz, Colonel North, Father Talbot, Chaplain Tiffany and myself. I arrived decked out in a complete civilian outfit: tie, shirt, suit and shoes. When I removed the raincoat which covered the costume, the men whooped and hollered as if a movie actress had appeared in their midst. It was the first civilian suit they had seen during a year of imprisonment. (The next day rumors spread throughout the camp that a Red Cross representative had inspected the hospital.)

As dusk fell and the moon sailed overhead we ate by candlelight, faces shaved and shining, hair brushed, clothes patched. Everybody was polished up. The waiters served each patient a small broiled steak, a half canteen cup of carabao-meat stew poured on the rice, a canteen cup of mongo-bean, carabao-bone soup, a huge chunk of rice cake, and hot tea sweetened with penoche. We handed out cigarettes and cigars. The waiters were dressed in the style of the Gay Nineties, with forelocks slicked down over foreheads, huge, black charcoal mustaches, and hospital bed sheets for aprons. Towels were draped over their arms. Sergeant Abraham bustled about happily, greeting and seating his customers. Bellies loaded, we sat back and watched the entertainment by the flickering light of the candles in the flower-bedecked café.

Mr. Trapp, dressed as an old bum, was the master of ceremonies. A hillbilly trio led by Private Tolliver of Texas, sang dreamy cowboy melodies which Staff Sergeant Marsden of Norfolk, Virginia, accompanied on our homemade guitar. Tall, serious Major Hubbard, M.C., recited "The Face on the Barroom Floor" and "Alaska" in his deep resonant voice.

Luan and Saraceno, dressed in full regalia and war bonnets, stomped an Indian war dance about a campfire burning just outside the café. Captain Ingerset, Sergeant Keaton, and Sergeant Bird, as a trio of drunken sailors, tried to tear down the joint. Sergeant Abraham took them all on in an uproariously comical boxing bout. Queenie brought the house down when "she" entered, head covered with a turban, face made up, dressed in a colorful evening gown "she" had created. One skit followed another.

We sang the ballads and songs we all loved, as the candles spluttered in their drippings. Led by slender Captain Ranson, M.A.C., with his vibrant baritone, we finished off by singing "God Bless America." For one night, a hundred men forgot they were in a miserable Japanese prison seven thousand miles from home.

CHAPTER 10
Cabanatuan Prison: Work Side

THE DIESEL ENGINE GENERATING ELECTRIC power throbbed a steady beat in spite of the coconut oil that was being burned for fuel. The wooden walls of the flimsy shack vibrated with its thunder. Two men with smears of oil on their faces busily regulated fuel valves, cursing steadily under their breaths.

"God damn it to hell, how do these slope-headed monkeys expect us to keep electricity going throughout the camp if they don't give us proper fuel? This engine is just about ready to burn out."

A duckling waddled clumsily through the open door. It watched the mechanics until a young puppy, wagging its tail briskly, dashed at it, barking wildly. The duckling backed hastily into a corner, neck extended, bill snapping viciously, while the puppy attacked and retreated.

A Nip guard slipped in stealthily, head twisted over his shoulder. He dropped his gun and hastened to a small alcove containing a homemade electric hot plate.

"Yoroshi Ka?" he asked. (Can I use it?) Lieutenant Dick Hedrick, who was seated opposite me playing acey-deucy, nodded. The Nip extracted three eggs from his pocket, scrambled them, wolfed them down, and departed smilingly.

"Those bastards are almost as hungry as we are," Dick remarked. "They're in and out of here all day with food to cook." He got up to speak to a Nip noncom who poked his ugly head through the door.

The shack had been thrown together and covered with a roof of scrap tin when American prisoners first arrived in Cabanatuan. In the corner was a double-decker, homemade wooden bed in which the two night-shift men were still sleeping: Jerry, a sailor, with his tousled red head nestling on his arm; and thin-nosed Captain Bob Miller, formerly vice-president of the Philippine Education Company, the largest jobber of schoolbooks in Manila. Two other canvas-covered frames with mussed-up blankets lined the wall. Under the beds on the dirt floor were worn-out leather shoes, skivvies, tin cans, a stem of bananas, a pile of empty beer and geneva bottles, and a half-filled sack of rice.

It was twilight. I had visited all afternoon on a pass issued by Colonel Jack Schwartz and countersigned by the Japs. This authorized me to leave the gates of the prison work camp to visit the powerhouse, presumably to administer medical service. Since this hut was in the Nip inhabited area outside the prison camp proper, I always felt a little uneasy, even though protected by the pass.

The acey-deucy game continued while Dick Hedrick spoke steadily in a low monotone. He was a handsome six-footer with black wavy hair, flashing eyes, and a bubbling personality. The only offspring of a Danish father and an American-Jewess mother, he had directed a flourishing auto agency in Manila before the war. When the Japs occupied the country, his mother was interned in Santo Tomas. His lovely Spanish wife was free to roam in Manila.

"Al," he said rapidly, "you know the Gekko (lizard) that lives in this bahai?"

I nodded.

"He sounds off every night. When he sounds off seven times, that means good news. He did last night. I listened in to KGEI, San Francisco, again. The news is great. The big show has started in Italy. You remember I told you we went to Sicily in July, 1943, and landed in the heel of Italy on September 3? Well, we landed in Naples yesterday. Italy has surrendered. It's the beginning of the end, Al. In the East the Russians have retaken most of the

Ukraine. They are approaching the neck of the Crimean Peninsula. In the Solomon area we've cleaned up Munda and Vella Lavella. We're getting set to hop into Bougainville."

"Jesus Christ," I exclaimed, "maybe the camp won't go wild when this news breaks!"

It did. When the men returned late at night—exhausted, depressed, and broiled by the sun on the farm details—they had a shot in the arm waiting for them. They sat about in small groups speculating anxiously about the news.

"One down, two to go."

"Look out, Hitler, we're on your tail."

"Do you think they'll put the heat on in the Pacific now?"

"Jesus Christ, it will be swell to be back home again!" "Honey, you'll see me in 1943."

News was more than food and drink to us. It sustained us. It kept us hanging on grimly when the Nips went on the warpath in camp. It was our very life. We had to have news to keep going. We got it by all kinds of trickery. I believe there were three secret radios in camp. I had contact with only one. When the American Navy prisoners came to Cabanatuan from Corregidor, they brought a set, its parts spread among many men: one carried a radio tube strapped to his crotch; another an amplifier under his armpit; a rheostat was slipped into a false sleeve; wire was strapped around a waist; condensers were carried in shoes. In the dead of night they sweated under blankets by candlelight to put it together. And it worked!

"Dick," I once asked, "how the hell did you get the parts to your radio?"

"I forced the Nips to give them to me," he smiled broadly.

"Quit your kidding and give," I protested.

"You see, we generate two kinds of power here," he said, pointing to the Diesel engines. "One is direct current for the lights on the barbed-wire fences and the perimeter watchtowers. The other is alternating current for the Nip barracks and administration buildings. When the Nips listened to Tokyo on their short-wave sets, which use alternating current, we poured a little direct current through the wires. Radio condensers and tubes burned out. The Nips hotfooted it down here the same night, cussing the lousy radios; they wanted us to fix the sets. They knew less about radio repair than a batch of idiots. We said we'd fix 'em if they'd get the parts from Manila. When they brought parts we kept them but told the Nips they were the wrong kind, and sent them back for more. For several weeks we listened on the repaired radios which we finally returned to them. We worked the same stunt several times until we had enough parts to build our own set. Red Keyes and I have had some narrow escapes listening. We've never been caught yet," he finished, knocking on wood.

Chaplain Tiffany also got radio news smuggled in from Manila. These were in the form of weekly digests sent in by Tony Escoda or the Mencarini group of underground workers. They were studied carefully by our news analysts. We plotted the progress of the global warfare on maps smuggled into camp. We tried to read between the lines of speeches by Roosevelt and Churchill. We argued about the terms of the Casablanca Conference in January, 1943, and the implications of the Teheran Conference in November, 1943. We moaned about the strikes in the Detroit area and shredded John L. Lewis verbally. We tried to figure out what a "zoot suit" was, but couldn't.

In addition to the radio news and Chaplain Tiffany's news digests, the truck drivers and the "Carabao Clipper" (carabao supply carts) smuggled in the Nip-controlled Manila Tribune newspaper, printed in English. The Jap communiqués about the Russian front were fairly accurate, but the retreat of the Germans was described as "elastic withdrawal for strategic purposes." Russian victories were heralded as victories of people with "Oriental blood and courage." They religiously avoided anti-Russian propaganda. Obviously, they didn't want a war on their Manchurian border. Their news from China was grossly exaggerated with overwhelming victories reported, but few territorial advances.

The Jap press and newspapers first castigated American soldiers as "degenerate cowards." Later, as the war progressed in New Guinea and in the Solomons, they printed horror stories depicting Americans as "inhuman gangsters and brutal animals" who tortured and killed all prisoners. All naval battles ended in complete victory for the Japs, including the second Battle of the Solomons in which we sank twenty-eight Jap transports and warships off New Britain. Throughout our imprisonment we were never more than a week behind the news.

Back in 1942, for a few months after the establishment of the Cabanatuan Prison, a Jap noncom was in charge of ten thousand American prisoners from colonels down to buck privates. He had little control over the Nip garrison which was officered by a Jap lieutenant. It was during this period that the death rate was thirty a day, and beatings were at their worst. At that time it was apparently the will of General Homma, the Japanese High Commander in Manila, that all prisoners in Cabanatuan were to die of disease or starvation.

We got the word that a high-ranking Nip officer was going to take over the camp. He turned out to be Lieutenant Colonel Mori, a stubby slopehead with a bristling black mustache, who ran a bicycle shop in Manila before the war! He had a large garden planted near his quarters and a miniature Mount Fuji built in its grounds around which he stumbled, clothed in a black kimono, drunk as a hoot owl. Conditions in camp remained desperate.

We didn't get much help from higher ranking Nip officers. In September, 1943, a Japanese general inspected the camp. Colonel Beecher, a two-fisted, square-faced Marine officer, accompanied him on an inspection tour of the work camp which was divided into three group areas. The American commanders of these groups were warned sternly by the Japs not to talk to the great mogul unless spoken to. Nevertheless, pointing to many prisoners who were too ill to stand in ranks during inspection, one of our officers said to the Jap general, "We have many sick in this camp."

"Why?"

"This is why," the American officer answered bluntly, pointing to the noonday meal of rice and camote-top soup.

"The prisoners are sick because they need more exercise," snapped the general.

The prison farm came into existence to supply this exercise. The Nips arbitrarily assigned a slave-labor quota. This quota had to be filled, regardless of the physical health of the prisoners. They lined up, the sick and the well, the blind and the weak. They were counted off and marched out in the heat of the rainy season to slosh in the mud, digging drainage ditches and dams in the designated farm area; digging furrows in the tenacious rice-paddy clay, using pickaxes on the lava-ash undercrust. It was back-breaking, heart-rending work at a pace set by sullen-faced, sadistic Nip guards, many of whom were Formosans, as wicked as the Nips. With the American capacity for choosing pictur-esque names, it wasn't long before the farm guards were properly labeled: "Air Raid," "Charlie Chaplin," "Big and Little Speedo," "Web Foot," "Beetle Brain," "Many Many" (many heads down, many butts up), and "Donald Duck."

Donald Duck, who spoke a few words of English, once asked suspiciously: "Why am I called 'Donald Duck'? Who is Donald Duck in America?"

The prisoner reassured him. "Don't you know? He's a famous Hollywood actor."

Softening, the Nip asked, "Does he make much money?"

"Of course. Millions every year."

The Nip grinned proudly. Thereafter he insisted upon being addressed by this monicker—for a while.

To impress us with the might of Japan, the Nips showed us moving pictures twice a month depicting their victories: the fall of Singapore, Hong Kong, and the Dutch Indies. Attendance at these shows was voluntary. To draw a crowd they also showed cartoons including "Pinocchio," "Pluto," and "Mickey Mouse." Several Nip guards were regularly detailed to be present at these performances, apparently to prevent riots. To our dismay, the Nip "Donald Duck" was present one evening when the "famous Hollywood actor" Donald Duck appeared on the screen. The prisoners under the jurisdiction of his Jap namesake had a rough time the next day.

To fill the increased quota of workers during the dry season, when all watering was done by hand, ranking officers, chaplains, doctors, and medics were ordered out to sweat and strain under the broiling sun. As the hospital census shrank, more and more doctors and dentists gave up the stethoscope and forceps for a pick or shovel. They learned to adapt themselves as well as the other prisoners who had already hardened their bodies to heavy labor. The doctors changed professions, when G.I.'s working beside them dropped of sunstroke.

Physical treatment of prisoners depended in large part on what detail they worked. Most of the beatings took place on the farm where the Nip guards vied with each other in demonstrating their ability to wield a pickaxe handle on the backs of the prisoners. We never had any trouble in the hospital proper. There were too many sick in our compound. The Nips were scared stiff of contracting diseases. The prisoners on the smaller details also had relatively little trouble. The men learned how to soft-soap the Nip guards and noncoms. The woodcutters left in their trucks every morning with a few guards who welcomed the opportunity of stretching out in the shade of the forest and falling asleep while the trucks were loaded with logs. Similarly, the hay detail had relatively little trouble. Men working the tailor and cobbler shops, which were established after Red Cross equipment came into camp in December, 1943, developed protection by doing odd jobs for the Nips. Americans who worked as servants for Nip officers received plenty of abuse but few beatings. Men who worked in our galleys and on ration runs had little or no contact with the Japs.

When thousands began work on the airport near the camp, Colonel Beecher convinced the Jap headquarters that the work would be facilitated if we used American prisoner supervisors. They consented to a trial of this system, provided a daily work quota was met. The Nip guards were instructed to maintain a perimeter guard about the prisoners who were leveling the field with pick and shovel. They were ordered to refrain from min-gling with them. This system cut down considerably opportuni-ties for beatings.

The garage mechanics and the truck drivers were the fair-haired boys of the Nips. They got away with murder —ate well, lived like kings, and lorded it over the rest of us. We needed their help to smuggle contraband from Manila. We paid through the nose for it. Some of them became big-shot black marketeers, sell-ing food and medicine at fabulous prices, while men hungered and died of disease in camp. Other truck drivers were square shooters.

The work of the underground outlined previously contin-ued on a magnified scale. The Philippine Women's Federation again established a canteen for the Nips at Cabanatuan and again used it as a blind to which food and medicine were shipped from Manila. "Highpockets," Dr. Tony Escoda, Mr. Amasatagui, Mr. Mencarini, Hanna Kaunitz, and their groups functioned quiet-ly and well. Various underground Filipino Masonic orders or-ganized in Manila for relief work. They sent thousands of pesos into camp monthly which Captain Bob Miller distributed to needy Masons and non-Masons. The same type of Masonic relief work went on in Santo Tomas, the American civilian internment camp. Mr. Kennedy, who handled the receiving end of the work there, was finally picked up by the Nips and thrown into the Fort Santiago dungeon for six months. I don't know if he is still alive.

From Cabanatuan the contraband flowed into camp through different channels. If one was blocked by the raiding Nip secret police, another was used. It was risky, scary, dangerous work. Many heads rolled in the dust before it was finished. Much of the contraband was picked up by truck drivers on their daily runs from Cabanatuan City. Nip noncoms who worked in the garage knew about the deal. They were paid off.

Filipinos hid packages of contraband in the forest where the prisoner woodcutters worked. They were then concealed under logs which were loaded on the trucks. The prisoners stuffed small items, like notes and money, into the hollow center of bamboo trees when they brought a load in.

Most of the contraband came in through what we called the "Carabao Clipper." As gasoline ran low in the Philippines, the camp supplies were hauled from Cabanatuan City by carabao carts. Early in the morning a long line of solid-wood-wheeled, low-slung carts hauled by huge-shouldered carabao with wide-spreading horns went down the dusty road, driven by prisoners and Nip guards. In the evening they returned with contraband hidden under loads of rice sacks. Back to their corral outside the camp they were driven. The unharnessed beasts made a beeline for a little man-made pond where they wallowed happily. The drivers hid the contraband until they could conveniently slip it into camp. They carried in money and notes concealed in their clothing. Most of these drivers were civilians and solid citizens who asked for no cut in the proceeds. One of the ringleaders of the Carabao Clipper was a handsome young German refugee, Ben Hessenberger, who had come to Manila just before the Nips made their first landing. He volunteered for service immediately and served in the Bataan campaign. He was gracious and generous; a brave man.

Once in camp, notes and parcels went to several distributing agents of whom Chaplain Frank Tiffany and Colonel Mack were the most active. Chaplain Tiffany was a tall, kindly, brown-eyed, lantern-jawed man in his early forties. He had worked for years as a farm hand in Canada and the Northwestern states until he felt the call of God. At great hardship to his wife, tiny daughter, and himself, he trained in a school of divinity. He entered the Presbyterian Church. He talked rather than preached in the little churches he built with his own hands as he moved from one prison camp to another. He spoke simple, kindly words of love and encouragement. Colonel Mack, another distributor, was a hard-boiled, brusque soldier who had been in the army for many years. Both moved about the camp like postmen, delivering mail. Notes, money, and packages were in cloth sacks they carried openly. Understanding Jap psychology, they found it safer to use this method than to attempt to conceal them. We waited impatiently for the mailmen to make their rounds.

"Anything today, Frank?"

He nodded. It was another note from Hanna containing a fifty-peso bill.

MY DEAR AL:

I hope you get this money for your 1943 birthday present. It gets more and more difficult to send packages. I hope you can buy some food. I am well. The family sends their best wishes. Maybe we shall spend your next birthday celebrating at the Manila Hotel. How much longer is this going to last, Al dear? At sunrise I look out into Manila Bay for Uncle Sam's ships and planes. At night I still look for them. I know they will come. But they must come soon. Ugly rumor has it that all able-bodied prisoners are to be sent to Japan. How can I help you if you are sent away? The nights are long without you, darling. I send you a thousand kisses.

The Jap guards were tightening up all along the line. It was getting more and more difficult to smuggle in large packages. The price of contraband food skyrocketed. I was able to buy four eggs, a papaya, and a dozen bananas for the fifty pesos ($25).

I wrote Hanna that through friends at the prison headquarters I knew I was not on any of the alerted lists waiting to be sent to Japan. I told her to keep waiting and praying.

I was sure the Yanks would crash into Manila Bay before the Christmas of 1944.

A Georgia-born Negro, Sergeant Bell, had a more direct contact with the underground. After World War I he retired from the army and settled in the Philippines. He raised one family. After the death of his wife he remarried and raised another. In spite of his advanced age—he was about sixty-five—he insisted upon joining the army. He retreated with the troops to Bataan. His young Filipino wife learned he was a prisoner in Cabanatuan. She found a little deserted bahai near the camp. She set up housekeeping for her two boys, aged eight and six. Every night at twilight Sergeant Bell began his vigil sitting on a box latrine twenty paces from the barbed-wire fence facing an open field. As the light began to fade his wife came tripping down the gravel road nearby, a load of garden produce balanced on her head as if she were on her way to market. He could see her and she could see him. That was the only minute in the day for which they both lived. As the dusk deepened, he saw a carabao, goaded by his older son and mounted by his younger, enter the field, stop to graze awhile, and move toward the fence. With the Nip guards grinning and watching the fun, the kids grimaced and hurled bits of rock and sticks into the compound at Sergeant Bell sitting on the latrine, yelling at the top of their lungs in Tagalog, telling their daddy how much they loved him. Night fell. Sergeant Bell sat on the latrine, black chin cupped in black hand until the Nip guards moved on. Then he picked up the bits of rock wrapped in pesos and notes of love.

Father Budenbrook used the underground and the direct approach to bring aid to the prisoners. He was a tall, white-haired, rosy-cheeked padre, wearing the sweeping, brimmed black hat with round crown and black cassock of his order. For twenty-three years he worked and lived in Christ the King Cloister in Manila, in an order of German priests. He hounded the Nip headquarters for permission to bring truckloads of food and clothing into the American prison camps openly. They turned him down repeatedly. He always came back with another request. Before the Christmas of 1943 he appeared again, hat in hand.

"May I have permission to bring Christmas gifts to the American prisoners in Cabanatuan?" he pleaded.

"You are a German. You were born in Germany. You have a German passport. Germany is at war with the United States. Why should you help your enemies?" the Nip commandant stormed.

"Because I am a priest. I have no enemies," the Father said quietly.

They granted him permission to bring one truckload into the camp on Christmas Day. When he arrived, the parcels were destroyed by the Nip guards in full view of the prisoners in Cabanatuan.

In camp the heavy hand of death dropped intermittently. Months passed in 1943 without executions. Every two or three days the Nip guards on the farm detail beat up a prisoner without killing him. Colonel Beecher protested these beatings. He got his face slapped for his pains. The beaten men recovered from their injuries and went back to work. All of us who had contact with the unpredictable, vacillating psychology of the Nips, who were given to sudden outbursts of rage followed by presentations of cigarettes, expected to get licked some time in their prison career. We tried to adjust ourselves to the inevitability of a whipping. But it was hard to stomach the executions of the weak, the innocent, and the insane.

During 1943, to the best of my knowledge, three killings took place. The farm details fell into columns of four. They marched barefooted to the farm gate where the Nip guards counted them off in batches of a hundred. On their return at the end of the work day the same procedure took place. If the count was wrong, these men waited in line until the error was corrected; usually, a prisoner had returned in the wrong batch. On one occasion the count was not correctable. A detail of Nip guards, accompanied by several ranking American officers, returned to the farm area to search for the missing prisoner. Overcome by the sun, he had fallen into a furrow between the rows of tall corn. On his hands and knees he was crawling to camp. After the Jap guards finished with him, they carried him back; his thigh bone smashed, belly full of bayonet wounds, skull crushed. I saw him in the morgue.

The poverty-stricken Nip guards were avaricious traders for watches and rings. The hungry prisoners were eager traders for food or money with which they could purchase sustenance. Trading went on day and night in spite of the orders of the Nip administration forbidding the practice. It was dangerous, but hungry men will perform dangerous deeds.

One of our medics, Private First Class Blank, an American of Mexican descent, was a trader, but a careful one. He made friends with a Nip guard who patrolled the beat outside the barbed-wire fence near the hospital. For more than a year he traded with him and nobody else. They were buddies until one night in June, 1943, when a Nip guard officer surprised them on his patrol. Before the surprised Blank knew what was happening, his Jap buddy dragged him through the barbed-wire fence, threw him on the ground, and began struggling with him. They brought Blank—now an escaped prisoner—to the guardhouse, beat him well, and shot him.

It may not be just to denounce a nation because of the short-comings of an individual. Nevertheless, our contacts with the Nips over a period of three and a half years forced us to accept their promises with the greatest of circumspection. Promises made by many were made in good faith—at the time they were made. However, altered circumstances, as in this instance, regularly resulted in an about-face which their flexible consciences tolerated. Their promises were not binding.

The third execution concerned an insane prisoner. Captain Blank had a lockup for psychopathic patients, a wooden shack with heavily barred windows and doors. It housed about fifteen psychopaths. Under the stress of the Bataan-Corregidor campaign and the strain of prison life, I am sure many more prisoners had cracked up. During the first six months of prison life, with disease, starvation, and death rampant, most of these unfortunates died. There were no facilities for their care. If they preferred to get soaked by walking for hours in tropical cloudbursts and dying of exposure, there were others who welcomed the extra space in crowded barracks made available during their departure. If they refused to eat, there were thousands of starving prisoners who welcomed an extra portion of rice. It was the survival of the mentally fittest. The more seriously cracked personalities perished.

The medics took the psychopaths out of the brig twice a day for roll call during which time they could stretch their legs. None of them was violent. Several had attempted to commit suicide. One tall, emaciated lad had unsuccessfully attempted to gouge his eyes out with a fork. In a second attempt he had cut his throat with a sharpened mess-kit knife. When the roll call terminated, instead of returning to the ward he straggled toward the barbed-wire fence. In full view of the Nip guard on a watch-tower, he climbed the fence and disappeared in the high kogon grass nearby. Apparently he had deliberately exposed himself to rifle fire to end his life. The Jap guard must have been dreaming of cherry blossoms back home. He didn't see him. Our hospital C.O. immediately reported the escape to the Nip headquarters. They ranted and raved. The escape had taken place in broad daylight. Manila headquarters would certainly rub their noses in the dirt. For two days they scoured the camp and its surroundings unsuccessfully. On the third day our own men found him while they were working on the farm. He was in wretched shape. He had kept himself alive by grubbing for camotes. They carried him into the Nip headquarters alive—and out, dead.

We all showed signs of personality change due to beriberi, pellagra, privation, and isolation. We became suspicious and hypercritical of each other. Packed in crowded barracks, we lacked privacy more than anything else. After years of this life it was difficult to tolerate the presence or conversation of even our best friends, except in small doses. Bitter arguments over stupid trifles raged constantly. As the diet picked up and the health of the camp improved, fist fights broke out like a rash all over camp.

They were not limited to G.I.'s. I'm not a pugilist, but I had a scrap with an officer in a latrine when I saw him using pages of a *Reader's Digest* for toilet paper at a time when reading material was worth its weight in gold. The scrap didn't last very long. I got licked.

It was fascinating to watch the impact of prison life and starvation on men who during prewar days had become addicted to alcohol, narcotics, and sexual promiscuity. Men who had been steadily drinking themselves to death before the war found themselves unable to obtain the flowing cheer for the first time in their lives. Chronic alcoholics, who claimed they couldn't live without whisky, were unable to get the stuff except in small quantities at preposterous prices. The struggle resolved itself very simply into whether they were going to use their money to purchase food or purchase liquor. The instinct of self-preservation won every time. There are men alive now who would have drunk themselves to death if they had not been captured by the Nips. After their liberation, I suppose their psychological bias toward liquor reasserted itself. They are probably again on their way to a wet but merry death.

Similarly, drug addiction was no problem in O'Donnell and Cabanatuan during the first year. Fear of impending death from starvation weighed too heavily upon addicts to make their efforts for procuring drugs anything but cursory. More important was the fact that morphine, codeine, and sedatives like Luminal were not available in any large amounts until the Red Cross supplies arrived. When they did, the picture changed. There were probably a dozen drug addicts in Cabanatuan while I was imprisoned there. I don't know how they got their narcotics. I'm sure the drugs were sold or given to them by some medics who stole them from the wards where they were being dispensed or from the medical supply depot. Ward surgeons kept their narcotics on their persons. Still, some leaked out to the addicts who would sell their souls for the dope.

Tobacco addiction had almost as great a hold on the behavior of prisoners as drug addiction, in many instances. Prisoners hired themselves out to their mates as servants ("Dog robbers" we called them), dish and clothes washers to procure a daily ration of tobacco. Tobacco addiction had so great a hold on some men that they traded off their pitiful allowance of food for tobacco. They perished.

The sex drive ran a very poor race against the drive for self-preservation during our miserable years of incarceration. We talked food, we argued interminably about the best way food should be cooked. We collected recipes. We waited impatiently for our next meal. We dreamed about food. It haunted us in our waking hours and plagued us in our sleep. Even when the food situation improved so that we could assuage our hunger with enough rice, mongo beans, and vegetables, we were still food crazy. Nightly we sat about in our bahais almost sadistically tormenting each other with descriptions of bountiful meals we had eaten: oysters à la Rockefeller, New England broiled lobster, thick Kansas City steaks smothered in mushrooms, white bread, Idaho potatoes, Brunswick stew, apple pie and ice cream, blueberry pies, watermelons, and oranges. Our mouths drooled.

We dreamed pornographic dreams. They seemed unreal even in the dream state. We hooted and whistled in a halfhearted manner at Filipinos who walked down the road near the camp. For most of us, the sex drive slowly ceased beating on our consciousness. I could understand for the first time how men entering the Catholic Church could undertake the vows of celibacy.

The homosexuals in camp (of whom we had about a dozen) found their sex drive shrivel into impotency during the first year of starvation. Sex cannot compete with food privation. Men like Queenie wanted food, not sex stimulation. After they had recovered from their illnesses and after the food setup improved drastically, they found themselves in a pervert's seventh heaven. They had no competition from female chippies. They had no fear of punishment. Colonel Beecher, recognizing the problem, requested permission to isolate them. The Nips refused. Our own psychopathic ward was too small to house them. They drifted loose in the camp—notorious prostitutes.

Sex indulgence was still possible for those darlings of the Japs, the American prisoner truck drivers and mechanics. Wherever the Japs went they established houses of prostitution. In Cabanatuan there were rows of Filipino cribs which they frequented, both privates and officers. In Manila, in addition to the local stock of trollops, they imported large numbers of prostitutes from Japan who were housed in the Dakota Street district. On their runs into town, the Nip guards stopped off for a bit of sex excitation. It wasn't long before the truck drivers wangled permission from them to do the same. One of the drivers, a hard-boiled, long hombre from Texas, told me of repeated visits he had made to the cribs. On one of them, this scene transpired:

"Rosita," he said to a slim-hipped dalaga (girl) lounging in the Nipa shack, "how about a little action? I haven't much time."

"Joe," she replied, shaking her head, "you must sleep with Carmelita today."

"Like hell, I will. I want you," he growled.

"But, Joe," she whispered, "I am sick. I have the clap." "That's a damn shame. I'm sorry you're in trouble. Why don't you quit working and cure yourself?"

"No, Joe. I must make many Japs sick. They killed my two brothers in O'Donnell prison," she said softly.

There's more than one way of fighting a war!

From the very beginning of their imprisonment, men desperately sought means of maintaining their sanity while their physical lives were disintegrating under the impact of disease and starvation. For a while talking was an outlet. They talked about their war experiences; they described food they were going to eat when they were free; they cursed the Nips; they bitched about the work details they were on; they described their homes, families, and peacetime occupations; they related all the stories they had ever heard. Suddenly they found they had talked themselves out. They had nothing new to say, merely a repetition of what they had already said a dozen times. They knew the lives, prejudices, hopes and fears of their immediate neighbors. They became somewhat maniacal when their friends again began the same old baloney of who they were and what they had done.

Out of sheer desperation and boredom they began playing games. They carved chess and checker sets out of scraps of wood. They made acey-deucey sets out of scraps of cloth. They made Monopoly games out of scraps of paper. They carved dice out of bits of carabao horn. Dog-eared decks of cards appeared. Men played poker all night by the light of a flickering oil wick—"on the cuff."

Then they became bored with games. They didn't want to talk or play with anybody. Making a knife blade out of scrap metal, they ground a fine edge on it and fitted it with a wooden handle wrapped with a bit of scrap wire. They carved pipes in wood, dog tags in leather and carabao horn. They wrote poetry, music, and short stories. They worked in metal, making their own dies to ornament scraps of flattened iron and aluminum. They read and re-read the few books and magazines that found their way into camp. They did anything they could to be by themselves, to avoid going insane.

As they gradually adjusted themselves to suffering and hardship, the desire for companionship again reasserted itself. They yearned to be members of a social group. They yearned for music and entertainment. To help them help themselves was the job of Colonel O. O. Wilson, or "Zero" Wilson as we called him, a tall, gaunt, bald-headed officer with a delightfully dry sense of humor. After much difficulty he got permission from the Japs to organize our jazz band, of which Lieutenant Henry had informed me upon my arrival in Cabanatuan. A few of the men from Corregidor and Bataan had stumbled into the Cabanatuan Prison with their beloved instruments. The band started with a couple of guitars strummed by sandy-haired Private Chester McClure and happy "Pappy" Harris of Corregidor, and a singing clarinet played by Private First Class Ken Marshall, a Shanghai Marine. Private Kadolf made himself a set of drums out of carabao hide. The band grew as they smuggled instruments into camp from Manila. Hot-lipped Martin Salas played a trumpet. Dignified Lieutenant Parcher seconded him with a cornet. They got a saxophone and flute. Lieutenant Cuncil joined with a sweet muted trombone. A piano was too big to smuggle in. The Nips consented to its open arrival. Private Kratz, a pug-nosed lover of jive, was the leader.

They had no music. They had memories. They remembered, arranged, and wrote the scores of jazz and classical music. They wrote new music which was hot, sweet, and melodious. On Wednesday nights after the sun went down they gave their concerts on a little illuminated stage in the open field between Group 1 and Group 2 areas. For an hour the hot gusts of "St.

Louis Blues" or the sweet strains of the "Blue Danube" swept over the faces of thousands of ragged prisoners sitting on the bare ground, their eyes focused on Kratz's waving baton. For an hour they were lifted out of their misery and transported on the wings of music to a land they loved. Most of these musicians died. The memory of the music they played for us will live a long time.

There were many who could not play but loved to sing. Zero Wilson organized a glee club under the direction of a very elderly gentleman, a Mr. Baugh. He was slight, gray, and very wrinkled. He had lived in the Philippines for years. I believe he had taught music in their schools. He was silent and reserved. I had him in my ward for months but haven't the slightest idea of who or what he was. He loved and knew music. Drawing on his phenomenal memory he wrote the vocal parts for not only Stephen Foster's lovely melodies, but more complicated music like the "Pilgrims' Chorus." The glee club filled a need in our prison community. The vocalists looked forward eagerly to losing themselves in their rehearsals. We looked forward just as eagerly to losing ourselves in the massed voices of their performances.

There were some who could neither sing nor play, but who could act. Zero Wilson organized a theater group which wrote their own scripts, built their own props, and sewed their own costumes, including some lovely evening gowns. They were a happy-go-lucky group of comedians who worked all day on the farm and then spent their evening hours rehearsing for our entertainment. Lieutenant Manning, tall, ex-drama coach from Harvard, and handsome Captain Childers, of the Fifty-seventh Philippine Scouts, were the heavies. Lieutenant Mossel, wisecracking lawyer from Kansas City; toothless, blond-haired Lieutenant Swann, a limey; and Lyle Hughes of the navy were the comedians. Corporal Eddie McEntyre, an infantryman, brought the crowd to their feet when he appeared dressed in a tight-fitting black turban and low-backed, dazzling evening gown. They were hard put to turn out a show every other Saturday night. They did. These are some I remember: *Journey's End, What Price Glory?, Frankenstein,*

Turnabout, Three Men on a Horse, The Champ, Public Enemy No. 1, Trip to Havana, A Christmas Carol.

A regular theatergoer was that champion ratter "Suchow," an English bulldog, mascot of the Shanghai Marines. He had long learned how to get around by himself. He had traveled into the innermost recesses of Shanghai with the Marines before the war. When they decided to square away for an all-night carousal, they called a rickshaw, placed Suchow on the seat, and had him carried back to their barracks. At Cabanatuan he was a favorite character. Caught in dog traps on three occasions (a well established prison practice to obtain meat), he was released by starving prisoners. His owner had sewn a little pillow for him to keep his butt out of the mud. On show nights, pillow balanced on his square head, he trotted to a spot reserved for him in front of the stage. Everybody in camp who could walk or crawl turned out for these performances. In the land of make-believe, they forgot the Nips.

Zero Wilson then reached out into broader fields. His subordinates organized a university in which a host of subjects was taught, ranging from sociology to anatomy. With a Japanese grammar Dr. Takenoshita had given me in O'Donnell, I attempted to teach the elements of conversational Japanese. The camp was coming to life. With their native resiliency, the love of knowledge in these half-starved Americans again reasserted itself. There were few textbooks available. Men drew upon their memories to transmit ideas and information. These classes, held at night after work, were heavily attended.

At the same time, the gregariousness which is an inherent part of Americans made itself evident. The Kiwanians, Knights of Columbus, Knights of Pythias, Masons, and similar organizations held their weekly meetings, usually without refreshments. State clubs were organized to bring together home folks. I was hard put to make a decision when the Massachusetts and Georgia clubs met on the same night.

Suddenly the Nips retracted their permission. No group could meet other than religious groups. Even the chaplains were compelled to submit their sermons for censorship. The university was officially disbanded. Only anatomy and Japanese could be taught; not a very wide choice. We continued to meet secretly with our own kind and teach in smaller groups.

When Red Cross food and medical supplies arrived before the Christmas of 1943, the mental and physical health of the prisoners took a great upswing. They handled their farm work more easily. They still had energy to burn. The recreation officers set up baseball diamonds and volley-ball courts. They passed the boxing gloves around. Men began to feel and act like human beings. Enough money was being smuggled into camp so that one hundred thousand pesos' worth of food was bought monthly in the commissary by that great conniver, Colonel Johnston, although the Nips were paying us only thirty-five thousand pesos a month. He did an incredible job doctoring the figures he used with the Nip noncoms in charge of the commissary.

Everything was looking up. There were no deaths. Thousands of Red Cross books arrived which the Nips released slowly to a library that was set up. Enough shoes for everybody were available. We had an adequate supply of medicine and plenty of hot news.

It was a shot in the arm to learn of the invasion of Tarawa in the Gilberts and the capture of Kwajalein in the Marshalls. Freedom was right around the corner. We cheered the "Ruskies" when they crossed the pre-1939 Polish border in a great winter offensive. The camp went wild with the news of the first great raid on Truk. We expected to be free in the summer of 1944. I almost attacked Willie Perilman when he said we would still be prisoners in the summer of 1945.

In this work of rehabilitation, the reverend and priest played a notable role. It was easier for miserable, starved and diseased prisoners to accept the word of God when we saw these chaplains live His word. By action rather than sermon, they carried on their work of rebuilding a faith in better life. Emaciated Father Curran insisted on working the farm on his day of rest so that those who were ill could remain in their barracks. Chaplain Tiffany denied himself food so that others could eat. Father Mc-Donnell chose the heaviest loads for his bony shoulders so that weaker men would not break down. Older men like Father Talbot and Chaplain Oliver, with his neck (broken by a sadistic Jap guard) swathed in plaster of Paris, visited the sick and the well with kindly words of cheer.

They built chapels out of scrap wood and transformed them by the magic of their words into holy places of worship. Golden-tongued, red-headed Chaplain Taylor, an evangelist, lifted the hearts of his congregation from the mud of a prison camp to the clouds soaring high above them. Men went to church who had never gone before in their lives. They continued to go even after their physical welfare had improved. They loved and trusted these men. On Christmas Eve, before a little stage decorated with greenery, they came by the thousands to see and hear the story of the birth of Jesus celebrated in the solemn High Mass. They left with foreheads smooth and eyes shining.

We Jews had no rabbi. Among those of my faith still alive in camp we found one who could conduct services. Lieutenant Jack Goldberg, pug-nosed ex-amateur pugilist from New York City, assembled us on Friday nights in his galley. In this tumble-down Nipa shack, surrounded by pots and pans, we reaffirmed the faith of our fathers. On Yom Kippur we met near the little entertainment stage in the open field before the sun went down.

In camp we had an elderly American Jew of Polish descent named Kliatchko. He had spent his adolescent years in a rabbinical seminary in Warsaw. Forced to flee for his life during a raging pogrom, he migrated to the States. He worked there for years until our entry into World War I. He volunteered, was shipped overseas, and fought in the Argonne Forest with the engineers. He stayed in the service for years; eventually he landed in the Philippines where he retired. He married a Filipino girl and settled down peacefully to grow rice and raise a family. I don't know how successful a farmer he was. He raised thirteen children. When the Nips overran the central plain of Luzon after their landings at Lingayen Bay, he was cut off in the province of Bulacan, north of Manila. Leaving his wife and family in the care of neighbors, he sailed down the west coast in a banca at night to reach Bataan. At the ripe old age of sixty-two he again volunteered for service in an engineering outfit to fight for his country. He served throughout the Bataan campaign. After his capture he eventually arrived in Cabanatuan Prison. The Nips put him in charge of the carabao herd. Gnarled stick in hand, he took them out to graze, singing old Hebrew melodies he had thought he had long forgotten.

Of the several hundreds of Jews who started prison life in Cabanatuan, there were less than eighty still alive in the closing days of 1943. We straggled toward our house of worship under heaven's roof from all parts of camp: Americans from New York and San Francisco, refugees from Vienna and Berlin who had volunteered for service at the outbreak of the war. Old Kliatchko appeared before us as the broiling-hot sun dipped toward the serrated edge of the Sierra Madre Range which overlooked the camp. He wore his old-type campaign hat with its wide floppy brim, a sun-bleached khaki shirt with its tails hanging free over neatly patched shorts, and a pair of wooden skivvies. He threw a shredded white-silk tallith (praying shawl) with its fringe of tassels over his bowed shoulders. The deep bronze of his high cheekbones, separated by a powerful nose, was heightened by the massive, curly white beard that flowed over his chest. He raised his sunken brown eyes heavenward and began the haunting Hebrew melody and prayer Kol Nidre.

"'Bless the Lord, O my soul, and forget not all his benefits; Who forgiveth all my iniquity; who healeth all my disease; Who redeemth my life from destruction; Who encompasseth me with loving kindness and tender mercy.'"

The Nip in the guard tower leaned on his rifle, watching us curiously. Ragged G.I.'s strolled back and forth along the path leading to their barracks near our assembly.

"'Inspire with courage all who wait for Thee, hasten the day that will bring gladness to all the dwellers on earth and victory of the spirit to those who bear witness to Thy unity. Then shall iniquity be made dumb and all wickedness shall vanish like smoke, for the reign of evil shall have passed away from the earth.'"

The red ball of the sun dropped behind the purple mountain. In the fast-falling twilight, little white ricebirds wheeled and turned.

"'As now too, my dear ones gather around me at this sacred time and place, I realize how closely welded are the links of love in the circle of the family. Not for myself alone but for all the members of my household do I beseech Thy mercy.'"

Eyes blurred with mist, the scene before me faded. I saw the synagogue in which my family were gathered in prayer and supplication; its high vaulted ceiling with doves of peace flitting about the painted billowing clouds; the colonnaded ark of the covenant with its red-velvet drapery and Ten Commandments of Moses embroidered in white silk; the golden eagle with its outspread wings surmounting it; the painting of the Wailing Wall of the Temple on the wall behind it; the crouching snarling lions of Judah, tails lashing, hovering protectively over it; the silken flags flanking it; on the right, the American; on the left, the flag of Zion with its two horizontal sky-blue stripes and its three broader white ones, the blue six-pointed star of David flaming in the center. I saw my father standing at the tabernacle, his blue eyes fixed on the Bible. I saw a little old gray-haired woman in the balcony turning the pages of her prayer book salted down with the tears that dropped from her cheeks while she dreamed of her son ten thousand miles away.

The sunset sent streamers of orange and purple far-flung into heaven. Kliatchko's deep vibrant voice rose to meet them. Beating his chest with clenched, gnarled fist at the end of each sentence, he prayed for forgiveness:

"'For the sin which we have sinned against Thee under stress or through choice;

For the sin which we have sinned against Thee openly or in secret;

For the sin which we have sinned against Thee in stubbornness or in error;

For the sin which we have sinned against Thee by abuse of power;

For all these sins, O God of Forgiveness, bear with us, pardon us, forgive us.'"

By the light of the flickering stars and the quarter-moon, I looked at the intent faces of my neighbors: stubby Captain Berkelheimer, the medic detachment commander; the razor-faced Lenk brothers, refugees from Czechoslovakia; stalwart Ben Hessenberger, carabao driver, refugee from Germany; sway-backed Captain Bennison. They didn't know it, but they were attending their last Yom Kippur service on this earth.

Old man Kliatchko raised a curved carabao horn to his pursed lips and blew a long piercing blast. We straggled back to our Nipa shacks.

CHAPTER 11.
Bon Voyage On The China Sea

"AL," SAID COLONEL CRAIG, OUR chief medical officer at Cabanatuan, crossing his long, thin legs, "how are you feeling?"

"Swell, Colonel. I just finished a course of carbasone my good friend smuggled in to me from Manila for my amoebic dysentery. I've had a hard stool for the first time in two years. How's your arm?"

"Getting better every day," he said, flexing and extending his fingers. "That Red Cross vitamin we got in Christmas is swell stuff for beriberi. We're using it in large doses on the men with 'hot feet.' You know the intractable pain they have in their heels and the soles of their feet in dry beriberi?"

"Yeah," I said drily. "Nothing like having it yourself to appreciate the misery men go through while they have it."

"And Major Warren Wilson, who is giving it to his forty partially blind men, says it has stopped the destruction of the nerves of the eyes. In fact, some of them are getting better."

"That's swell, Colonel. This camp certainly has taken a turn for the better. Plenty of medicine, fair Nips issue chow, Red Cross food and 'hot' news. That raid on Truk in February, 1943, looks to me as if Nimitz is getting ready to hop around it and go for the Philippines. What do you think?"

"The two-day shellacking Truk got with the high-level bombers, dive bombers, and shelling by the navy must have almost completely neutralized that island base," he said, scratching his nose.

"I'm keeping my fingers crossed. If anybody were to ask you, I'm expecting to be recaptured right here in Cabanatuan this summer," I said.

He went on: "It's hard to say whether the Nips will let any of us go. They have sent thousands of prisoners to Japan from the Philippines during the last four months. Do you know how many we have left in camp now?"

"No, I don't."

"There are about fifteen hundred men in Group 3, all chronic amoebic-dysentery carriers; about fifteen hundred in Group 2, mostly officers and old-timers; and three hundred in the hospital. In three days there will be two hundred more leaving for Japan."

"That so?" I asked, interested. "Who's going?"

"Fifty doctors and dentists and a hundred and fifty medics."

"Oh, oh," I said, the light beginning to dawn. "What's the dope?"

"Well," he said, grinning wryly, "they all go to Japan on the same detail. When they arrive…"

If they arrive, I said to myself. We knew what the Yank subs were doing to Nip shipping between here and Japan.

He continued: "When the medical group arrives they will be divided into four sections which will set up hospitals for P.O.W.'s in Japan: one in the island of Kyushu, one in Osaka, one in Tokyo, and the last in the northern island of Hokkaido."

"Where do I fit in, Colonel?" I asked sourly.

"Well, Al," he said, rubbing his chin, "I have to send one surgeon with each group. I'm sending Captain Roland, Captain Barshop, one navy surgeon, and I wanted to send Lieutenant Colonel Blank of the air corps."

"And?"

"He says he has a sore back from doing some lifting," he replied shortly.

"I saw him walking about as big as life yesterday," I said. He was a tall, well built officer with a sour puss.

"Yes, I know. He was in here talking to me today. He had the brass to suggest that I go in his place."

"What are you going to do about it, Colonel?"

"There's nothing I can do. I can't court-martial him for refusal to obey orders, and I don't want to turn him over to the Nips," he said perplexed.

"I suppose that makes me 'Mickie'?" I asked, heart pounding.

"I'm afraid so, Al. It sounds like a good detail," he added, encouragingly. "It's the first time they have sent a complete medical group. You can't tell about these things."

You certainly can't tell about "these things"! That was the last time I saw Colonel Craig alive.

I was packing my belongings the next day when Private First Class Liebert pushed open the bahai door.

"Doc, I hear you're going to Japan," he said excitedly.

"Yup, Liebert, I am. I'm not crazy about the idea. At best, I'm a lousy sailor. I hoped the next trip I was going to take would be in an American boat."

"If you're going, I'm going," he said abruptly.

"Don't be a fool, Liebert. Everything is in the groove in this camp. You can't tell what kind of a hellhole you'll land in in Japan. You can't tell if you'll ever get to Japan. Moreover, your name isn't even on the alerted list."

"I'm going," he said stubbornly. He saw Colonel Craig immediately and had himself put on the list of medics scheduled to leave.

I turned over the Carabao Wallow to tall, dark-haired Captain John Wallace of Illinois. I said good-bye to Lieutenant Henry, my genial ex-barrack leader. He had been working the farm for months and was as brown as a walnut.

"How about a camping trip in West Virginia when we get home, Doc?" he suggested.

I saw Colonel Ball with his floppy straw hat shading his boiled-lobster face. He gave me some marigold and zinnia flower seeds to take along to Japan.

I shook hands with Lieutenant Schwartz. "They can't do that to you," he said, his mobile mouth twisted with disgust.

I had my last bull session with Ensign Jack Gordon of Atlanta. We joked about the many unsuccessful attempts we had made to cook Brunswick stew with scrawny native chickens, mongo beans, and scrap carabao meat. I kidded lantern-jawed Chaplain Tiffany about his prolonged correspondence with his lovely confederate, "Highpockets," in Manila. Pappy Kiser gave me another banana pie with its patented peppermint tooth-powder frosting. That king of the hobos was the only survivor of this group of men.

The next day the Nips released some of the mountain of Red Cross mail that had been accumulating in camp for months. I received two letters from my folks and a radiogram from Mrs. Walter Rich of Atlanta: the first mail in two years of imprisonment. Sister Marion wrote:

> **In our next letter I'll try to send you some pictures of the children to keep you in touch with the family. Joan is eight now and Leonard is five. Paul, who was not yet born when you left, is now two and a half. He will recognize you because we show him your picture. We write every week, and send a package of food and medicine every month. We pray for your safe return. God bless you.**

This was the only mail I received from my folks throughout my imprisonment. I received only one food parcel. It had been thoroughly pilfered by the Nips.

I wrote a last note:

HANNA, DARLING:

> **When you receive this I'll be on my way to Japan. Give my best to your folks and Fred. Be ever so careful in your work. I have your locket sewn into my shirt. If things get dismal in Japan, I'll have it to cheer me. I still have the red socks you knitted. They're too precious to wear. When the sun goes down in Manila, think of me in Japan. I'll do the same thing. Maybe we'll make con-**

tact. You and I will sail into a peaceful harbor. You must believe it. I must believe it. Wait for me.

At four P.M. we fell in on the gravel road separating the work camp from the Nip area. The stars shone peacefully overhead while sullen-faced, bandy-legged Nip guards with fixed bayonets herded us on the waiting trucks.

"*Kura, bakero!*" they bellowed. (Get along, you son of a bitch!) They drove the butts of their rifles in the backs of those waiting to load. We piled in without duffel bags, thirty to a truck. We stood about for half an hour while the slopeheads counted and recounted. Finally, the order to depart was given. The heavily laden trucks groaned down the road, their flickering headlights feebly illuminating the clouds of dust thrown up by the rolling vehicles. Through the silent fields into the still-sleeping city of Cabanatuan we rolled as the half-moon sailed overhead, illuminating the bare plaza near the railroad station. A rooster crowed sleepily in the distance. We hustled from the trucks to a line of coaches waiting on the tracks.

"Jesus Christ," Liebert grinned, dumping my luggage in the aisle, "what a break! Truck ride to Cabanatuan! Coach ride to Manila! Maybe these slopeheads have decided they're losin' the war and are gonna give us a break."

The steam whistle screeched. The wood-burning engine slowly picked up speed. The coach jerked and shuffled along. There was no doubt that we were getting better treatment on this trip. It was a lot easier to take than the ride to Cabanatuan Prison in tightly packed, airless freight cars a year and a half ago. The dark night lifted slowly as we rumbled through desolate rice fields with their stubble of parched stalks. As the sky brightened, the moving train flushed hundreds of tiny white ricebirds who had settled down for an early breakfast. The sun's rays, reflected from a bare-faced cliff high up in the somber mass of Mount Aryat, illuminated a winding road that curled about its base. It grew hot and then hotter in the tiny coach with its sealed windows. The train crawled over a trestle bridge high above the Pampanga

River. Since we had last seen it more than a year ago, it had been repaired and rebuilt with wooden trusses replacing the steel ones blown up by our demolition units on their retreat from Lingayen Bay. We came to a lurching stop at Biga, north of San Fernando, sixty miles from Manila.

A Nip guard approached a black-shawled food vendor, an elderly woman with wrinkled face and snarled hands.

"Ikutsuka," he asked, pointing to the bananas. (How much) *"Mai ni-ju sen,"* she replied. (Twenty centavos each) He bought a dozen, paying her two pesos, forty centavos.

I sent Liebert over to get a dozen. When he received them, he paid her a similar amount. She returned one peso, eighty centavos, saying, "They are only five centavos for Americans."

We lurched through San Fernando with its warehouses burned to the ground and its shattered churches staring at us blindly. For hours the train crawled down the tracks, heading southward for Manila past little streams where long-haired Filipinos were pounding their clothes on flat rocks, while their bare-bottomed children drove huge Carabaos into the mud for their midday wallow.

In the smoke-begrimed railroad station of Manila, we unloaded quickly, were counted again by the Nips, and marched down dusty, sun-swept streets. The city was not impressive after a two-year absence. Piles of rubbish and garbage littered the gutters. Escarraga Street, formerly filled with flashy American autos and tooting yellow taxis, was empty except for an occasional calesa pony driven by its moody cochero. We could see no trucks. Pushcarts and renovated auto chassis were being pulled by skinny, sweating Filipinos. Pedicabs, little homemade vehicles trundled by a bicycle rider, carried their burden of passengers. Occasionally an army auto, flying its Nip flag, scooted by. Most of the stores were closed and boarded. Those that were open sold no food except fruits. The air of desolation was thick enough to cut. As we marched toward them, Filipinos rubbed their cheeks with widespread fingers, making the "V" sign winking significantly.

The gates of Bilibid Prison clanged open. We marched in. They clanged shut again ominously. This was an actual prison formerly used to house offenders against the peace in Manila. It was built like a wheel with the rim represented by a twenty-foot-high cement wall surmounted by a fringe of charged electric wires. Along every sixty-degree arc of the wheel was a blockhouse with its Nip guard and machine gun. The spokes of the wheel were represented by solidly constructed cement barracks, now medical wards. Its hub was the Nip guardhouse which we saluted as we passed. On we trudged past groups of gray-faced, tattered patients into a two-story cement building, still incomplete, with wide-open spaces in its walls for windows.

"These are your quarters until you leave for Japan," said an eagle-beaked American Navy lieutenant who had joined our shambling group as we entered. "There are no cots and no mattresses available. I'm sorry, but you'll have to sleep on the concrete floors. We have four hundred prisoners who work in the port area. They live upstairs and sleep on concrete after a hard day's work unloading freight. Make the best of it while you're here. This isn't Cabanatuan. This is Bilibid, the worst of the worst. Be careful. Salute the guards who will be coming through here every hour to check on you or you'll get kicked in the nuts. Many of them understand some English, so go easy on the war news. You may think you're tough, but they have cute little tricks they can play to find out where you're getting any dope about the war. You're lucky you're just passing through. I wish I was going with you," he ended wistfully.

I took a turn about the compound. Its walls were lined with hundreds of graves. Some of them were recent, with freshly turned dirt. The wards were of solidly constructed masonry. They were packed with metal cots and wooden frames covered with canvas. Listless faces stared at the ceiling dully. They heard my footsteps but didn't care who was around. I fled out into the open, past sheds housing wash racks, showers, and latrines. Lack of water was not responsible for the heavy cloud of despair that hung over Bilibid.

Rounding the corner, I ran headlong into Colonel Frank Adamo. His hair had turned to silver. His thin ascetic face was a sickly greenish-tan. Through his shabby shirt and shorts stuck his spindly arms and legs. Almost two years had elapsed since he left Little Baguio for Corregidor.

"You sure look swell, Al," he said softly. I looked like a mountain beside him.

"What's new with you, Frank?" I asked.

He shrugged his shoulders. "One day is the same as the next. The weeks drift by and then the months. Nothing happens except that we get weaker steadily. If the Yanks don't get here soon, we'll all be dead."

"How's the chow?"

"Pretty slim. You'll find out soon enough."

"What happened to you after you left Little Baguio, Frank?"

"After I left Little Baguio I went to Corregidor. When Corregidor surrendered, the Nips brought me here. It was plenty rough for a while. Then the Red Cross supplies came in, about December, 1942. Things picked up. Deaths from beriberi dwindled. We got a fair ration of rice, mongo beans, and some fish. We didn't gain weight but we didn't lose any. We were able to buy some food from a canteen. The boys on the outside work detail smuggled in more from friendly Filipinos."

"Why does everybody look as if they're going to kick the bucket, Frank?"

"Well, Al," he said, stroking his white hair, "about three months ago we got a new Nip C.O. The rations were cut sharply to about two-thirds of what we had been getting. A week later, one of the prisoners working on an outside detail was caught smuggling in some chow. As a warning to everybody in Bilibid, the Nip C.O. closed the food canteen. It's been opened again this week. Previously, we could buy forty pesos' worth of food a month. Now we can buy three pesos' worth. With bananas twenty centavos each, you can figure out how much food we can buy."

"What about medicine, Frank? Can you get all you need for your patients?"

He led me into a barrack that was filled to the rafters with hundreds of cases of Red Cross medicine. "Here it is. Tons of it. Vitamin pills by the hundreds of thousands. They don't take the place of bread, meat, jam, butter, and vegetables. You remember Pharmacist Mate Jones, don't you, Al, your medic on the gas-gangrene ward?"

I nodded.

"He's partially blind from beriberi. One eye is all shot. The other is not much better. He's taking plenty of vitamins now. He doesn't show any improvement."

"That's tough luck. Jones was a great surgical technician."

"There are plenty like him among the doctors as well as the patients," Colonel Adamo said slowly.

"Here's hoping the Yanks land in the Philippines this summer," I said encouragingly. "The news is hot. Have you heard about the raid on Truk and the pounding Ponape is getting in the Carolines?"

He nodded, smiling. "Not so loud, Al, you're not in Cabanatuan. The news coverage here is excellent. We get the Nip-controlled Manila Tribune smuggled in daily.

"More important is the news the prisoners get who work in the refinery at Pandakan. They get news through their short-wave sets and hand it on to us. There are plenty of Filipinos working there who are sabotaging the Nips. Gasoline comes in from Java. It is refined and put into fifty-five-gallon drums. The Filipinos put a shot of sugar in each drum or punch a hole in the bottom with an ice pick or screw the cap on lightly so that the gasoline will evaporate."

I continued on my rounds looking for old faces. I found Lieutenant Nelson, a navy surgeon who also had worked in Little Baguio. He weighed a hundred and ten pounds, including his wispy blond, pointed beard. I saw Sergeant Abraham of the Carabao Wallow. His muscles had shrunk. His asthma was as bad as ever. I chatted with frosty-faced Max Blouse, whose gnarled left hand was beginning to come to life. Colonel Schock and Colonel Duckworth had adjoining cots in the main building. Each had dropped about fifty pounds in weight since I had last seen them. It was especially noticeable in the Duck when I examined the huge ventral hernia that had developed in his appendiceal scar. He was still as tough and crusty as ever, in spite of starvation and disability.

"The ball is rolling, Captain," he said, his sharp eyes boring into mine, "and it's going to crush the Nips like this." He pressed the nail of his thumb on a bedbug crawling on the iron framework of his cot. "I don't know whether I'll be alive when it happens, but it's inevitable." He was a tough soldier who never quit.

Life dragged interminably during our two weeks in Bilibid. We fell in for roll call morning and night. We remained in our formation until the count was declared correct.

The diet was simple: lugao for breakfast, three spoonfuls of cracked corn and a watery vegetable soup for lunch, steamed rice and barley with an occasional piece of dried fish for supper. Hunger was with us from early morning until bedtime. For some reason unknown to me, our group of transient docs and medics were each permitted to buy forty pesos worth of food in the canteen: mongo beans, peanuts, bananas, and papayas. That night our quarters resembled Rich's bargain basement during a post-holiday clearance sale. Patient-prisoners by the hundreds tottered and limped into our quarters on crutches. Faces pinched with hunger, they offered to trade their store of clothing for a handful of peanuts or mongo beans.

The blond aviator who had finally decided to have his foot amputated in Little Baguio limped in on his homemade peg leg with an old sweater in his hand. Another patient from the gas-gangrene ward had a belt he wanted to trade. Some of the expert traders among the patients acted as middlemen for their friends. They got their cut of the proceeds. Red Cross wool shirts and trousers, socks knitted from unraveled sweaters, wool navy watch caps and pea jackets were offered and eagerly accepted by the transients who were on their way to the ice and snow of Japan after three years in the tropics. The trading was fast and furious. Before "lights out" at nine o'clock, eight thousand pesos' worth of food was in the hands of these starving Americans: either given to them or traded for woolens which were of no use to them in Manila.

We were alerted on two occasions. Still we remained in Bilibid. The details working in the port area brought marrow-chilling news of a convoy of five Jap ships which had left Manila the day before our arrival. Two had been sunk in the China Sea west of Corregidor. The others had limped back, their hulls shattered by torpedoes. It wasn't a bright picture. If we left, we might end up in the briny. If we remained, we would soon look and feel like the others in Bilibid. All in all, the fear of starvation was greater than the fear of drowning.

We heaved a sigh of relief when the gates of Bilibid finally opened for us. Again we trudged into the deserted, dying city. I eagerly scanned the faces of the few white women we passed. I saw only slender Filipinas wearing long black veils of mourning on their way to church for early mass. They slowed down to watch us trudge by with our duffle bags loaded on our shoulders. Ragged, barefooted children trailed behind us, a safe distance from the glowering guards. We turned the corner of Ascarga Street into broad Quezon Boulevard.

The huge doors of famous Quiapo Church, at the foot of Quezon Bridge, gaped wide open. Through its portals flowed the solemn harmony of massed voices which blended with our mood of depression. The column of prisoners halted before a tiny native market in front of the church. An interminable convoy of Jap trucks rolled by. I relaxed against a fruit vendor's cart, idly watching the slowly moving crowd of early morning shoppers on the sidewalk.

A vibrantly whispered "Al!" roused me from my reveries. My sleep-laden eyes popped wide open. On the sidewalk across from the fruit vendor's cart stood Hanna, wedged between three Filipino women. Her face was haggard, deep furrows in her brow, tanned skin drawn tightly over cheekbones, finely chiseled nose pinched. Only her liquid brown eyes were as soft as ever. Masses of wavy brown hair tumbled down over her shoulders, Filipino style. A sun-bleached, patched green dress hung limply over her shrunken body. I had seen it before the war at the Casa Manana when it caressed gently modulated curves. Her collarbones protruded. Her chin had set and squared.

A Nip guard with fixed bayonet strolled toward the vendor's cart. He picked a pomelo and munched it moodily. Reaching into my musette haversack slung over my shoulder, I rummaged frantically until I found the red socks she had sent me in Camp O'Donnell. I wiped the perspiration from my face and neck with them, watching Hanna.

Her lips smiled recognition as tears rolled slowly down her face.

"Kura," growled the guards. (Get along.) We loaded our gear and shuffled along in the center of the boulevard. Hanna followed on the sidewalk, nodding and smiling as I turned my head.

Over Quezon Bridge, across the muddy Pasig River we trudged. Down the lovely boulevard lined with waving palm trees. We could see the outlines of the Army and Navy Club looming in the distance, now Jap headquarters. Near the Manila Hotel, with flashing red poinsettias as a background, Hanna waved farewell to me as we plunged into Intramuros, the Walled City. Through the streets of the port area we walked, enjoying the cool morning breeze blowing in from Manila Bay, until we came to Pier 7, projecting fingerlike into the sea. There was a rusty unpainted freighter of about five thousand tons waiting at the dock. It flew the Japanese maritime flag from its masthead, a black lightninglike zigzag on a white background. There were hundreds of Jap civilians on the forward deck of the ship. Old men wearing American-style clothing and flat-faced women with their children strapped to their backs, Indian-papoose fashion, were being evacuated from the Philippines.

We hustled up the gangplank past the "Chick Sales" lining the rails. We plunged down into the gloom of the aft hold pierced by the glimmer of a dozen thirty-watt bulbs. The hold was lined by a double-decker, wooden framework, covered with crude planks which constituted its floors. With Lieutenant Mohnac and cocky

Captain Kostecki acting as amateur interpreters for a bespectacled Nip noncom, we dumped our luggage and crawled on the planks. There was room enough to lie down with several inches to spare. Major Bahrenberg, our ranking officer, ex-pediatrician from Ohio, was the first to learn the honeymoon was over. He had his unlit, unfilled briar pipe knocked from his gentle face by a slant-eyed Nip guard.

"*Tobako dame daro,*" he bellowed. (No smoking except near the water bucket.) He pointed to a half-filled pail of water in the center of the hold.

The ship pulled away from the dock slowly. It anchored in the North Channel near Corregidor. This island lay with its shoulders humped in the sea, waiting patiently to receive American paratroopers who were to land on it within a year. There were a dozen ships at anchor in the bay, a part of our convoy. They were all riding high in the water. There was no more loot to transport to Japan from pillaged, starving Luzon. That night the anchor lifted, the propellers thrashed, the ship vibrated. We were on our way across the submarine-infested waters of the China Sea, sailing seventeen hundred miles for the Land of the Rising Sun.

"*Benjo yoroshi Ka,*" I asked the sleepy-eyed guard, sitting on the deck near the hatch, rifle across his knees. (How about my going to the latrine?)

"*Ush,*" he mumbled sleepily. (O.K.)

The stars were twinkling brightly. The Southern Cross inclined toward the horizon as if carried on the shoulders of a weary man. By the light of the half-moon, I counted sixteen vessels, of which one looked like a heavy cruiser, and two destroyers. The land mass of Luzon slowly faded away while we zigzagged due west toward the coast of China. Squatting on my heels in the latrine, I brooded over the chances of two hundred men getting out of a single hatchway if we were hit by a torpedo. Hanna's beautiful, pitifully starved face appeared before me. I smoothed the wrinkles from her brow and kissed her parched, bloodless lips. Two years of life in the crucible of Jap-occupied Manila had changed her from a gay adolescent, filled with the juice of life, into a mature, haggard woman. How had she known I was in Bilibid? How did she know when we were to leave Bilibid?

I stumbled down the stairs, wrapped a blanket about my head and shoulders. Head nestled on a life preserver filled with kapok, I dreamed hideous nightmares of sinking ships and drowning men.

Life on board ship was dull and excessively uncomfortable. Yet it was a luxury trip compared with the experience of prisoners in subsequent prison ships. We had only enough water for drinking. We could go to the latrines on deck at fixed intervals. Lieutenant Mohnac got permission to hold setting-up exercises on deck for a fifteen-minute period daily. Our own G.I.'s cooked our food in the Nip galley and dished it out hot from wooden buckets. The meals were standard: a mess kit full of steamed rice three times a day, with watery soup made of vegetables of pork-fat scraps, twice a day. We stayed hungry throughout the trip. Mornings and afternoons were spent playing bridge, poker, or shooting craps. In the evening, Lieutenant Tarzan Tucker organized variety shows with our medics putting on the acts. They strummed guitars, sang hillbilly and cowboy songs, tap-danced, and put on comic skits. "Bellbottom Trousers" will forever be identified with this voyage. These medics were a spirited, happy-go-lucky group of tough hombres whose lust for life two years of imprisonment could not destroy. I played bridge daily with Lieutenant "Maw" Kelly of Atlanta, Lieutenant Don Smith, and Lieutenant Alex Mohnac until I fell sick with a combination of fever and dysentery, intensified by my usual seasickness. Private First Class Liebert buzzed about me constantly like an overgrown hen clucking to a sick chick.

"Jesus Christ, Doc," he said anxiously, "between pukin' and crappin' there won't be much left of you when we git to Japan."

We had been permitted by the Japs to take along two small cases of medicine. With the help of sulfadiazine, the diarrhea and fever were finally controlled. The seasickness continued.

"Doc," Liebert asked, "I think I can make a deal. Have you got any jewelry left?"

"A ring," I answered indifferently. Aged Mr. Goldin of Atlanta had given me a Masonic ring which I had carefully sewed into my belt before the fall of Bataan. The Nips never found it. Throughout the long, hectic months at O'Donnell, I had refused to sell it. It gave me one point of contact with the paradisaical past, as I felt its pressure against my side.

"Give it to me, Doc," he pleaded. "One of the Nip cooks said he'd fix up some chow for you if you paid off." I handed him the belt.

He came back with the ugliest, dirtiest Nip I have ever seen. He was less than five feet tall. He walked with a crouch, long arms reaching down to bandy knees. There was a dirty dishrag wrapped like a halo around his bald head. An even dirtier loin-cloth was tied about his middle in the form of a G-string. His eyes, nose, and mouth greeted each other in the center of a flat face. When he smiled, which was often, his bare red gums, flanked by broken canine teeth, said "Hello." In his hands he carried two heavenly, ripe tangerines. My friend "Joe-Joe," half man, half ape, kept me alive throughout the remainder of the trip with fruit, an occasional egg, dried bananas preserved in sugar, a mush made of rice flour ground with soybeans and milk, and ten cans of papaya juice he purchased in Takao, Formosa, when we anchored in that harbor. He came to visit, face beaming, to watch the progress of my convalescence. He understood no English. I couldn't understand his tongue-tied Japanese. He was ugly. I will remember him for his kindness when my handsome-faced acquaintances have slipped from memory.

Two nights before we landed in Takao, there was a submarine alarm. We were hustled from the deck. The hatches were battened down. We waited tensely in darkness, listening to the depth charges dropped in the distance. The next morning we looked for the heavy cruiser that had been escorting us. A Nip told us it had been sunk.

We beat our way slowly, under an airplane escort, into landlocked Takao Harbor, Nip naval base on the south-west corner of Formosa. The harbor was long and narrow, protected on the sea side by a low-lying island on which a huge Jap Army cantonment was built. The huge city fringed the water's edge with its factories belching black smoke. Oil reservoirs, wharves, and warehouses packed together, magnificent bombing targets. Hundreds of squat, flat-nosed Korean women came aboard from lighters loaded with sacks of sugar. They cleared the planks from the central area of our aft hold, clambered nimbly down into the well of the ship, and went to work. For twelve hours a day they labored, using small steel baling hooks in each hand. They worked dexterously, piling two-hundred pound sacks of sugar neatly against the steel ribs of the ship.

Once under way again, it was not long before our men broke into the hold to get some sugar. It was white crystalline cane. It tasted like ice cream to us. We ate it by the handful. The yearning for sweetness assuaged, we filled our socks and shoes with it. We hid the booty in our duffle bags. I found it was great stuff for seasickness.

We zigzagged onward through the Straits of Formosa into the East China Sea. We passed a series of isolated, truncated peaks rising in loneliness out of the ocean. We sighted the land mass of Okinawa. Between Korea and the southernmost of the three main islands of Japan we moved, buffeted by a miniature typhoon. Through the Straits of Shimonoseki, between Kyushu and Honshu, the major island of Japan, we steamed to land in the great railroad terminus and seaport of Moji, on the northern tip of Kyushu, not far from the city of Nagasaki. We disembarked in a yard filled with miniature, lightweight tanks.

Customs officials pawed through our belongings. They stole some packages of Red Cross cigarettes. They didn't spot our sugar. We were hustled to a far-flung railroad yard a half mile away, where we loaded into standard-gauge coaches waiting on a siding.

We left one party of ten doctors and fifty corpsmen behind. The train took off into a recently completed tunnel which plunged below the depths of the Straits of Shimonoseki, connecting the islands of Kyushu and Honshu. The Nip noncom in charge, Sugaharo, was a lance corporal who spoke meticulous English with an Oxford accent. He was a neatly dressed, pleas-ant-voiced, Christian Jap who had been educated at an American mission school in Japan. During the many transfers we made, he never lost his temper or raised his voice. He was a good Jap. We stopped off for further transportation at a large warehouse in Osaka, where we were joined by two Nip doctors. One was a reg-ular-featured, hard-jawed, loud-mouthed slope-head who spent hours teaching our navy group of doctors and medics military commands and marching maneuvers in Japanese. We were glad to hear his rasping voice drift out of the building when he finally departed with his group of medics.

Our group was taken over by the second Nip, Dr. Tokuda, apparently an angel compared with his confrere. He wore horn-rimmed glasses on a nubbin of a nose and baggy britches draped about a pair of bowed legs. He knew some English and German. He was curious to learn about our previous medical training. When he found out that Captain "Penoche" Saldivar had spent years in Mexico, he was just as curious to learn about sex life south of the border. We entrained for the last leg of our two-day trip to Tokyo. Our hopes soared high as Dr. Tokuda told us about the prisoner of war hospital we were to staff: good chow, plenty of fish and milk, a canteen packed with edibles, hot baths, running water, and stores of Red Cross medicine.

Al Mohnac nudged me: "What a break. No more shacks, open latrines, and bedbugs. It sure looks as if we hit the jackpot. I'll bet we can get permission to visit some of the big hospitals in Tokyo and buy some of the latest medical journals."

"It sounds O.K. to me," I said, smiling happily, envisioning an operating pavilion with a tile floor and operating lights sus-pended from the ceiling.

Refreshed by our last meal, served on the train in little wood-en boxes filled with steamed rice, seaweed, and pickled dikons (similar to huge white turnips), we got off at Shinagawa Station in Tokyo. The high-pitched voice of a woman train announcer tore at our eardrums constantly.

The platform was filled with Japanese men and women who eyed us curiously. The men were clothed uniformly in black or brown shoddy unpressed suits topped by a dark felt hat. The women wore dark blouses tucked into baggy trousers tied at the ankles. On their feet they wore white socks with a split toe fitting into stilt-like wood sandals. Most of them were mothers who carried babies on their backs under padded, blanket-like, silk-covered kimonos, giving them a hideous, hunch-backed appearance. There seemed to be no adults working in the station; the ticket takers were chubby-faced high-school girls wearing tightly woven pigtails, blue blouses with white trimmings, and baggy pants. Clusters of schoolboys did a poor job of keeping the station clean.

We trudged down a steep flight of concrete stairs leading to the street, which was lined on both sides with broken-down abandoned cars. It looked like a vast auto-wrecking yard. There were innumerable air-raid shelters dug in the sidewalks. Apparently the populace expected the Yanks to drop powder puffs. These dugouts were shallow, about four feet deep, covered with scrap wood and camouflaged by flowerpots. We turned off the main highway. We followed a winding graveled street in a light rain which had begun to fall. The neighborhood grew more and more shabby with ramshackle, two-story unpainted tenements and single-story clapboard hovels. As the rain fell and the landscape took on the appearance of a Stateside jungle town, our spirits sank. We splashed through puddles of muddy water silently. The dismal gray colored our hearts.

Chapter 12.
Shinagawa, Tokyo:
The Spider Does Research

THE UNPAINTED, ROTTING GATES CREAKED open. We trudged wearily into a compound fifty yards square, crowded with a half dozen shabby, ramshackle, single-story wooden buildings. In the narrow street stood Major Ed Kagy, whom I had last seen in Cabanatuan a year and a half ago. He was dressed in an oversized Canadian G.I. uniform which hung limply on his tall, gaunt frame. His finely chiseled features had shriveled so that the skin was tightly drawn over his ascetic nose and prominent cheekbones.

"Welcome to hell," he grinned sardonically.

It looked like a gray dismal hell to us coming from the lush green of Cabanatuan with a view of majestic Mount Aryat on one side and the rolling mountains of the Sierra Madre Range on the other.

The compound was a tiny man-made island enclosed by a ten-foot-high wooden fence surrounded on all sides by foul-smelling drainage canals. The wards, three on each side of a narrow company street, were about the size of a modest six-room apartment. Of tinderbox construction, without floors or running water, they housed shallow, open latrines, three hundred sick and dying Allied prisoners, innumerable rats, bedbugs, flies, fleas, body and head lice.

We stood about in the cold drizzle waiting for the customary inspection of luggage and for the explosion that would ensue when our concealed sugar would be unearthed. We must have had at least four hundred pounds of the "take," as it was referred to for safety's sake, hidden on our persons and in our gear. Fortunately it was too gusty and wet for the hardy Nips to expose themselves. They herded the forty of us into two tiny rooms, our sleeping quarters, about twenty by twelve feet. We hurriedly unloaded and concealed our precious hoard in the latrine. Then we spread out our belongings in a more leisurely fashion. The inspection was cursory.

The next morning, after a restless night, unable to sleep because of the cold wind whistling through the walls of the room and the broken windowpanes, we were still awake when Major Kagy visited us.

"Ed," we asked, "what's happened since you left Cabanatuan in the early part of 1943? Why are you so thin? We had an idea that you men who had gotten to Japan, and to Tokyo especially, would be living off the fat of the land right next to the Swiss Consulate and the Red Cross representatives."

He smiled wryly. "We had a pretty good trip with fair chow and not too much sickness aboard. We lost only eleven during the twenty-day trip. In the eyes of the Nips, that trip made a master surgeon out of me in one easy lesson. One of the G.I.'s came down with acute appendicitis. Doc Proff and I had to tackle it. As you know, both of us are trained only in internal medicine. We had a hell of a time, using a razor blade for a scalpel, a few hemostats, no drapes or gowns, and a couple of planks as an improvised operating table. As luck would have it, our patient pulled through all right."

"We eventually landed in this stinkpot, which was then a combined headquarters camp for the Tokyo area and a work camp with about six hundred Allied prisoners. There was damn little medicine and even less food, except for what the men could swipe on the job. The Philippines was a bit of heaven compared with this flophouse. We had two Nip doctors in our hair all the time, one of whom you've already had the misfortune of meeting. Dr. Tokuda is a rat. His superior, Dr. Fugi, is a bigger one."

"Is that so!" we interjected, surprised. "Tokuda seemed harmless enough on the trip to us. As a matter of fact, we thought he was a lot more pleasant than the other Nip doc with him."

"You'll learn," Kagy said grimly. "He's a stinker and a big one."

"So is the C.O. of this camp, Colonel Sezuki, a middle-aged ex-line officer who considers himself a pretty good amateur doctor. Did you ever hear of the 'Moksa' treatment of disease?" he asked suddenly.

"No," we all shook our heads blankly.

"It's an example of Nip medicine at its finest before it became adulterated with Occidental ideas. Medical faddists in the States are dyed-in-the-wool conservatives compared with the Moksa artists. According to them, you don't have to know anything about the germ theory of disease or worry your head over vitamins to cure any kind of illness. According to them, physiology is baloney and pathology is applesauce. All you need is some incense powder and a sharp needle, preferably carried about in a dirty pocket."

"You remember the trouble beriberi patients had with paralysis of the legs and 'hot feet' in Cabanatuan?" he queried.

We nodded.

"We had the same problems," he continued, "but in Japan we were not permitted to treat them with vitamin B1. Oh, no. Colonel Sezuki ordered: 'All patients, including those with beriberi, must receive Moksa treatment twice a week under the direct supervision of Nipponese doctors or Nipponese medical orderlies.'"

We stirred uneasily. "What was the treatment like?"

"It was very simple. The Moksa 'witch' doctors came in. They instructed the Nip and our medical orderlies. They brought with them some dried powder endowed with healing qualities. It was made of the skin of a snake, musk, and the tooth of a lion. A pinch of this was placed on the patient's skin and ignited. The patient was held down forcibly while he writhed and howled with pain. Simple, isn't it? If he had pneumonia, a series of these burns were inflicted on either side of the backbone from the neck to the loin. If he was urinating blood because of scurvy, the skin over the kidneys was 'Moksarized'. The boys with the 'hot feet', of course, got a series of burns over their shanks. If that didn't help, the needle came into action. It was plunged into the legs, aimed at one of the large nerve trunks, and then wiggled around. I guess the idea was to make a hole in the nerve and let the bad 'humors' out. I don't know what the idea was. Fantastic," he muttered, "fantastic."

"How long did this hocus-pocus last?"

"Officially, it has never terminated," he answered. "The Nip medical orderlies, shiftless as they are, stopped doing it themselves. They passed the work to our medics who kept cutting down the dose of the powder. Finally they ceased using it entirely. Mind you, this order applied to the whole Tokyo area with its ten thousand white prisoners. I don't know what the setup still is at other camps. All these burns inflicted on starved skin, of course, became septic. Some of the men got joint infections. They have permanently stiff legs. After one bloke died of septicemia following a Moksa burn, the Nip doctors here winked their eyes at our side-stepping the order."

During our stay at Shinagawa I had occasion to examine hundreds of patients, many of whom had old healed Moksa scars on their bodies, arms, and legs. They told me that those who refused treatment were beaten. They had accepted this novel approach to disease as stoically as possible.

We got the word that Dr. Fugi had arrived in camp and wished to see the new doctors. As did all Nip doctors we saw, he sported a two-handled samurai sword of which he was inordinately proud. The Nip doctors we met in the Philippines and Japan were, first and foremost, officers in the worst sense of the word—proud of their brass, resentful of any possible slight to their rank, domineering and insulting to their subordinates, even to the extent of physically whipping them. Secondly, they were

Nips—irritable, given to sudden fluctuations of emotion, ranging from frothing rage to unexpected gentility; untrustworthy in their promises, dishonest and easily bought off with trifles, petty chiselers of the cheapest type. Finally, they were doctors of a mediocre variety. They had learned some basic science, especially anatomy and pathology, but were primitive in their knowledge of physiology, pharmacology, and biochemistry. They were sadly lacking in the knowledge of the elements of physical diagnosis. The relationship of signs and symptoms of illness to disease itself, the logical thought processes that must take place to eliminate false diagnosis and establish a proper one, were beyond their capabilities. In our experience, they were not given to logical reasoning. Their medical training had done little to remedy this basic fault. To them, swollen legs meant beriberi, as a quick snap diagnosis. The alternate diagnosis of heart or kidney disease, hypoproteinemia, filariasis, or varicose veins did not occur to their illogical flashy poopheads. I'll have more to say about their surgery later on.

Fugi was slim, short, and pasty-faced, with the usual closely clipped hair. He had delicately molded cheekbones, shifty eyes, and a loose slobbering mouth with lips constantly wet. The lack of flesh on him, his nervousness, and the tremor of his hands reminded me of some hop-heads I had seen at the Grady Hospital before the war. I later learned he wasn't a snowbird but a chronic alcoholic. He was returning from a week-end spree. He still had a hangover of the genial variety. He spoke English and German fairly well. We found him quite gracious, smiling, in fact, almost charming.

"How was the trip? Were you crowded? How do you feel? How was the chow on board ship?" he asked, smirking.

Our answers were all guarded.

"Yes," he added, "I am happy to have you in Shinagawa. Unfortunately, there are many prisoners who are ill. Your help is needed to cure them. I am so sorry that Americans who were notorious meat-eaters have so much trouble with a rice and barley diet. Maybe if they are prisoners long enough, their bodies will become adjusted to the Nipponese dietary," he finished.

We silently but fervently prayed the Yanks would save them from this adjustment.

"Of course, the war will last many years, at least ten. You must work hard to keep your brother prisoners alive. Where were you trained?"

University of Pennsylvania, Cornell, Western Reserve, Harvard, he was told.

"Oh, yes, I know those schools. Very good, but not as good as Japanese medical schools."

Finally the harangue was over. We were dismissed.

"Weinstein remain," Dr. Fugi said. Throughout our imprisonment, the Japs never called us by our professional titles or army rank. At first we were resentful. Later we became accustomed to this omission as well as being referred to as bakero (fool), and robero (thief). We never became accustomed to being whipped.

"Weinstein," he said, "I am told you are a surgeon." "I've had some training in surgery," I responded.

"Ah, so ka? I shall be a great surgeon. Are these not surgeon's hands?" he smirked with nauseating humility, extending two quivering trembling paws.

"No doubt. No doubt."

"I shall now extend you the honor of accompanying me while I see surgical cases."

I followed him to the surgical ward. I saw what he had to exhibit: two patients with fractures of the thigh bones caused by accidents months ago. Both had been operated on by a Nip orthopedic specialist brought in from the Imperial University Medical School. Both patients had extensive osteomyelitis (infection of the bone), with limbs as straight as a hound dog's hind leg. We saw several patients with back injuries unsupported by slings, traction or fracture beds. They lay curled up on the straw-covered floor. To his comments on the excellence of the results, I made polite but noncommittal replies. Fugi was either an ignoramus or an idiot.

While I was examining a patient with a suspected acute abdominal ailment, we carried on a casual conversation.

"Yes," he said in answer to my query, "I have gone to medical school in Tokyo. I passed my examination and was licensed before the war."

"Are you a doctor in the regular army?" I asked.

"Oh, no, by no means. Regular army doctors are very poor physicians. I am a good doctor. I had a private practice until the Imperial Nipponese Government called all loyal Japanese doctors into service," he said proudly. "Are you in the regular army?"

"No, Dr. Fugi. I also was doing private practice in Atlanta, Georgia, before the war."

"Why did you leave your practice?" he asked.

"In 1940, when our President declared a state of emergency, I, in the company of millions of Americans, responded and joined the army," said I, bending over the patient, my back to Fugi.

Wham! I got a clout on the ear that knocked me sprawling. Dazed from having rammed my head against the wall when I went flying, I picked myself up and turned around. *Crack!* This time across the face.

"You have insulted me," dancing up and down. "You have insulted my Bushido, my fighting warrior spirit," howling with rage. *Wham!* "You are insolent and arrogant!" *Wham!* "You must be disciplined! I shall kill you!" *Wham! Wham! Wham!* And so it went for half an hour, with me flopping on, over, and around my future patients while he wound up one haymaker after another. Finally the storm subsided. He ordered me to stand at attention outside the building in the driving icy rain for two hours.

I stood there, breathing heavily as the cold water caressed my bruised and swollen face, confused, enraged, and thwarted. One habit that many prisoners of war picked up during their incarceration was that of talking to themselves. I don't know why it was so gratifying. Maybe it was because we became so deathly weary of the sound of our neighbors' voices in our close confinement.

Maybe it was because it was easier to analyze our own thoughts when heard as well as thought.

I soliloquized: "Well, Al, old boy, you've got yours at long last. You've often wondered how long you'd remain a virgin. How do you like it?"

"No God damn good."

"What did you say to make that bastard fly off the handle?"

"I'll be switched if I know."

"You're too damn smart, shooting your mouth off about what a loyal American you are. If you had any brain you could have been a loyal American in Camp Blanding, Florida. Instead you volunteer to go to the Philippines."

"Aw, shut up! I'm miserable enough without you rubbing it in. You know I wanted to see a little of the world while I was in the army."

"You got your wish!"

"You haven't heard me bellyaching, have you?"

"No, I haven't yet. But watch your step with this sonovabitch or you will. He's tricky and he's high-strung. Kid him along or you won't be able to do any good in this stinking hole. Swallow your pride and keep your mouth shut. You'll have to be a bigger liar, thief, and soft-soaper in Japan than you were in the Philippines to get anything out of the Nips for your patients and save yourself more whippings. Don't lose your head because you got a smack in the face."

"O.K. O.K."

I was finally ordered indoors. I came down with a cough and raging fever that lasted a week.

Life for us in Shinagawa Prison began, appropriately, on April Fool's Day, 1944. It had a macabre, musical-comedy quality to it with characters flitting on and off the stage in their dances of life and death. During the four months I was there, we officers and medics played a game with the Nips in which we matched cunning, soft soap, thievery, and an insight into Jap psychology against their stupidity, power, chiseling, and abysmal indifference to the fate of patients in this hospital. Each Nip in camp had to be played differently. Certain approaches were of no value. It was a waste of time to appeal to them on the basis of human sympathy. Such terms as the brotherhood of man had no significance to them. They had been too deeply inculcated with the dogma of Shintoism which taught them that the culture and innate intelligence of the Nipponese was superior to all other races. It was a waste of time to appeal to them as physicians who were brothers in the science and art of healing.

To Dr. Tokuda and Dr. Fugi we were prisoners, first and always. We had to obey their orders concerning the treatment of patients or be punished. As physicians, we were of interest to them only in so far as we could impart our knowledge and technique. In the very process of doing so, their hatred for us increased. Dr. Tokuda was a young man of twenty-eight, son of wealthy parents in the moving-picture industry, a recent graduate of a Tokyo university and medical school. He had not yet submitted a medical thesis and was not licensed to practice medicine other than in the Army. He was short, slight, with shaven head, sloping forehead, and receding chin. His shifty eyes never focused on your face. He waddled about in glittering riding boots and baggy britches, the crotch of which almost reached the back of his knees. We called him "Dung in Britches." His bowlegged gait and beetle head also earned him the pseudonym of the "Spider."

Prisoner-patients were experimental animals to be used in furthering his knowledge of medicine and surgery. He had a monkeylike curiosity about medicine. He had an overpowering desire to become a great physician and surgeon in eight easy lessons. He was torn by psychological conflict. He wanted to learn from us. At the same time he wanted to impress us with his superior knowledge. He wanted to learn from us. Yet he hated us for teaching him. Association with us increased his knowledge and inferiority complex simultaneously. He was proud of the improvement we made in the hospital in so far as it reflected on his professional standing in the eyes of his confreres in Nip headquarters in Omori, Tokyo. We had to play on this broad streak of vanity to procure equipment, medicine, and food for emaciated diseased prisoners.

"Dr. Tokuda," we said, "all Allied governments will be interested in your magnificent administration of this fine hospital when the war comes to an end. They will be grateful to you for your efforts in curing their countrymen. You will be a great person in their eyes."

He beamed. We got some of the things we needed.

If we tried the reverse approach, insisting upon the proper care of prisoners under the Geneva Convention and implying that he would be punished for his misdemeanors, he glared in rage and broke out into wild tirades. We got nothing. We ate humble pie, passively resisting him in his less dangerous experimentation and fighting him openly when the health and life of patients were at stake. We played a bitter, painful, losing game which had few compensating humorous elements. Few prisoner-doctors and medics lasted long at Shinagawa in this uneven battle because they tried bucking him.

From the day of the establishment of this prison hospital late in 1942, a long line of physicians and surgeons entered and left Shinagawa: pallid Commander Van Peenan, captured in Guam; Oxford-trained Dr. Whitfield, taken in Hong Kong; anemic Major Ed Kagy; gentle-voiced Major Behrenberg of Ohio; smiling Captain Penoche Saldivar of Texas; Mephistopheles-bearded, Australian Major John Woodward, captured in Singapore; tiny, peppery, toothless missionary Dr. Price, taken in China, young Lieutenants Robinson, Kelly, Smith, Palermo, and myself. They flattered, connived, protested, and fought Dr. Tokuda for the lives of their patients. They were eventually farmed out to the minor leagues or sent out to Omori Prison for punishment.

Al Mohnac and I moved into Lieutenant Jim Davis's quarters, a corner room, ten by ten feet, covered with tatami (straw mats). We sorted out our handful of patched clothes on an overhead shelf and sat on the straw Japanese fashion, with feet tucked under butt. It was uncomfortable at first. It became second nature after the muscles and ligaments of the legs were stretched out properly. In addition to its three tenants, the room housed sixty dog-eared books (the hospital library), a collection of pamphlets depicting the beauty and culture of Japan, three Red Cross baseball mitts, an indoor baseball, a tiny wooden table and bench, a wheezy phonograph with a handful of records, a volley ball and net, and thousands of fleas and bedbugs.

We were separated from the adjacent hospital room by a thin clapboard wall which swarmed with bedbugs. We played a game with the inmates of the adjacent room. By spraying the wall with oil stolen from the garage we drove the bedbugs into their rooms. By dousing the wall with hot water, the patients drove them back into ours. The only result of these maneuvers was that the bedbugs became violently vicious. The fleas preferred the straw mats. I constructed a collapsible wooden frame with a canvas stretched across it to get away from their bloodsucking proclivities. It helped until Dr. Tokuda declared all such claptrap makeshift beds illegal. When in Japan, we were to sleep on straw like the Japanese—or else.

Lieutenant Jim Davis had been in this prison since late 1942. He was a painfully slim, thin-boned officer with flashing black eyes, sharp nose, and chin. I believe he was raised in New England by his devoted widowed mother. With her Irish love of family, she had educated her children by the sweat of her brow. Jim was a brilliant student. He was admitted to the Naval Academy at Annapolis where he was a topflight performer. Further training in Rensselaer Institute equipped him for naval engineering. Following the destruction of Cavite Navy Yard in the Philippines where he was assistant superintendent, he went to Cebu, in the Philippines, to help set up a navy base.

He was captured and brought to Shinagawa. Here he continued to behave like a man and an officer who felt his responsibilities to his subordinate prisoner Americans. At the first sign of trouble, he was up on his feet protesting beatings that were prevalent in this camp when it was opened. He cajoled and argued with the Nip guards and noncoms in charge of the hospital. He physically intervened between men being beaten and guards doing the beating. He finally won their respect. The beatings dwindled away. The administrative noncom Tserumi Gocho (corporal), a fairly decent Nip as Nips go, practically let him run the camp.

Jim was a devoted family man with a wife and child living in Altadena, California. He had a tiny snapshot of them over his little work desk which he studied for hours, face drawn, eyes misty. He made Al Mohnac and me welcome in his tiny home. He filled it with warmth and kindness. Here we plotted our campaigns against Tokuda and analyzed the newspapers smuggled in from the outside. Here we argued interminably about the course of the war in Europe and in the South Pacific. Dr. Tokuda once called Jim in to discuss the differences between Nipponese culture and Western philosophy. In his usual straightforward manner, Jim did so. Tokuda replied by knocking him down. Thereafter Tokuda asked for no more lessons and Jim offered no more instruction.

Jim was responsible for the maintenance of the camp and the proper discipline of about three hundred patients. Half of this mixed lot were American G.I.'s and gobs. The others were a conglomeration of Britishers, Canadians, Chinese, South Africans, and Javanese Dutchmen, ranging from white to blackest black. Some of the Dutch were solid citizens. Many of them did not bear close inspection. When they decided they wanted to die, there was no stopping them.

I asked one of them, huddled on the floor wrapped in a threadbare blanket, "Allan, why don't you eat your bread?" pointing to a hunk of half-baked rice-wheat bread covered with green mold.

"Sir, I want to see Our Father," he mumbled.

He did a few days later.

The diet in this camp was worse than in any previous prison camp, except Bilibid. We had lugoa cooked with cabbage or leeks for breakfast; a watery vegetable soup with some bits of boiled eggplant, cabbage, leeks, carrots or dikons for lunch and supper. With each of these two meals we had a loaf of green moldy bread about three by three inches. When the local bakery ceased functioning, this was replaced by a meager ration of steamed rice, barley or red millet (like bird seed). Occasionally, we got some cow's stomach, intestines, liver, lungs, and bones from the local slaughterhouse to add to the soup. After the bones had been boiled and reboiled, they were issued by lottery to the patients, who splintered and chewed them. There weren't many left for poor Chocolate.

Chocolate was a brown setter who was also struggling to keep body and soul together. A patient had brought him in a year ago, a young frolicking puppy with a shaggy tail bigger than his body. To perfect his imperfectible surgical technique, Dr. Tokuda had done an enterostomy on him so that his fecal stream was diverted from his intestines through an opening in his abdominal wall rather than flowing normally into his rectum. Chocolate survived this experience. He learned other quaint Nip customs from the guards who, grasping him by the tail, heaved him on the sharply sloping tin roofs of the wards. They roared with laughter as he tried frantically to dig in. Slipping and sliding down the pitched roof, he fell in a tangled heap on the ground. He bore a charmed life. On three occasions the Japs tied him into a rice sack and tossed him into the drainage canal. Chocolate learned to hate the Nips and avoided them like the plague. He learned to differentiate between a slopehead, a Chinaman, a Filipino, and a full-blooded Javanese.

To live, he completely reversed his normal sleep cycle. When the sun rose, he quietly slunk off to one of his many hiding places. After evening tenko (roll call) the Nips took off to their quarters. Chocolate came strutting from his hideout, flag waving gaily, to visit his friends, have his ears rubbed, and eat his daily ration of rice the prisoners saved for him out of their meager allowance. We talked to him about our problems, grumbled about the grub, and told him the latest dope about the war. Resting on the floor, his liquid brown eyes focused on our faces, he took it all in, drooping his head when we sounded forlorn, growling when we uttered the phrase "God damn Jap," and thumping his tail approvingly when we gleefully told him of the latest licking the Nips were getting in the New Guinea sector.

Chocolate, our loyal devoted friend and voluntary prisoner, was killed by the Japs.

Our patient's bone-grinding apparatus was not as efficient as Chocolate's. Several of the bone eaters developed intestinal obstruction due to fecal impaction (a hard ball of feces in the rectum). On rectal examination, the examining finger felt as if it had rammed into a porcupine. Spicules of bone incorporated in the fecal mass presented their needlelike points in all directions. We had only two pairs of priceless, patched rubber gloves. It was necessary to remove these fecal impactions with bare fingers.

In reply to our protests concerning this inadequate diet, Dr. Tokuda said viciously: "These patients are not working. They are entitled to only two-thirds of a working prisoner's ration."

"How are they to be cured of beriberi without food?"

He shrugged his shoulders indifferently. "Give them rice polishings."

He made a list of persons permanently disabled: about fifteen patients with bone deformities due to improper surgical treatment of fractures incurred while at work. He included forty patients with tuberculosis. He put these men on a special ration: two-thirds of what the temporarily disabled patients received.

Although prisoner-officers received forty yen a month ($10) there was no commissary in which to spend this money. About once a month apples or a few sweet rice cakes came in which we purchased for the whole camp, as well as some very bum Nip cigarettes. There was no way of stealing food on the outside because there were no prisoner work details living at the hospital. With starvation rampant, it was necessary to bury garbage immediately to prevent hungry men from dipping into it. It was necessary to maintain the closest watch on the galley to prevent chiseling. This was one of Al Mohnac's jobs which he handled with consummate skill. He practically lived in the galley to stop leaks.

"Folks," he said to Jim and me one day, "the 'Eyeties' are again trading their clothes for food with the Nip noncoms in charge of the kitchen. We're losing about one hundred loaves of bread a week."

Jim flared up. "The no-good bastards. We comfort them, cut them in on the news, and they steal our chow."

"What are you going to do, Al?" I asked.

"I don't know. The last time I complained to the Spider, he said he had no control over the Nip noncoms in the kitchen. He's a God damn liar. He won't do anything."

"What do you think about my speaking to Arigawa?" I asked.

"Sure. It won't do any harm."

We had ten Italians in Shinagawa. Eight of them were merchant mariners who had been arrested in Yokohama Bay when Mussolini had been given the bum's rush after the surrender of Italy in September, 1943. With the capitulation of General Badoglio, several Italian ships had been scuttled by their crews in Shanghai. At this time the commander of the Italian Fleet in China waters, Captain Praili, and Commander Bernanti, his executive officer, were resting peacefully in the Grand Hotel in Tokyo. The Kempeitei (secret police) threw them into a civilian prison and then into Ofuna, the questioning and torture camp run by the Jap Navy for Allied prisoners. There they were beaten and banged around for months.

They were accused of having ordered the scuttling of the Italian ships in Shanghai. They denied any complicity. Although Japan was not at war with Italy they were imprisoned in Shinagawa. Captain Praili was a short, stocky, rosy-cheeked officer with a shock of close-clipped white hair. Vivacious, gesticulating with his arms and shoulders, he described Nip mentality in one word, "Fantastic." Commander Bernanti was a taller, slim fellow with black hair, glasses, and an inquisitive nose. He was rather on the oily side. Both spoke English fluently. The Japs warned us to keep away from the Italian prisoners. In defiance of these orders we made it our business to see them and transmit the news when we got it through the grapevine. Later, when we did physical labor together, they were frequent visitors in our hut. We played bridge with them frequently during the evening before nine o'clock ten-ko.

The most Oriental Mr. Onishi, No. 1 interpreter at Omori Headquarters Camp, was a frequent visitor at Shinagawa. He put pressure on the "Eyeties" to reaffirm their allegiance to Mussolini. They succumbed one by one to his blandishments and promises of release from prison—all except Captain Praili. The Nips were especially anxious to get him because of his rank of admiral. It would have been fine propaganda to publish a statement from him in the Nip press in which he affirmed his allegiance to Mussolini and offered his services to Japan.

"Sign the paper and you are a free man," Onishi wheedled.

"I cannot do so," Captain Praili answered politely.

"Good food, good quarters," Onishi sang.

"When I entered the Italian Navy I took an oath of allegiance to King Victor Emmanuel. I cannot forswear this oath," Captain Praili persisted stubbornly.

Like our fifty-five-year-old Filipino mess attendant, Sergeant Moreno in O'Donnell Prison, Praili's conscience was stronger than his hunger pangs.

In spite of having resworn their allegiance to Mussolini, the Italians were still detained in Shinagawa. These Italians had entered camp with huge piles of luggage filled with towels, linen, shirts, and personal effects. As the bonds of hunger tightened about them in camp they began trading clothes for extra chow with the Nip noncoms in charge of the kitchen. We pointed out to Captain Praili that they were, in effect, stealing this chow from us since all food came from the same storeroom. He did his best to control his compatriots. Hunger was too much for them. They again began their chiseling.

I hunted for our interpreter, aged Mr. Arigawa. He was tiny; about four feet nine. He weighed about ninety pounds. His face was a mass of wrinkles, his eyes shaded by monkeylike pouches. A pair of horn-rimmed glasses was constantly sliding down the bannister of his nubbin-like nose. Before my arrival there had been a second Jap interpreter, the spitting image of him.

They were called "Tweedledum" and "Tweedledee." Mr. Arigawa had been a commission agent importing lumber from Seattle before the war. He spoke English with some difficulty, pursing his heavy lips. During the summer months he wore white trousers and shirt topped off by a white jockey cap with startling effect. In spite of his hoary age he got about the same pushing around by the military Nips in camp as we did. I got to know him well during my first month at Shinagawa. It was evident, after many talks, that he had some softening of the brain due to hardening of the arteries. He was absent-minded and forgetful. But when he got an idea fixed in his mush brain, nothing could change it.

I fell ill again with fever and diarrhea. He was concerned. My eyes popped when he brought me some real white wheat bread and a thermos bottle filled with some honest-to-God sweetened cow's milk. It tasted better than champagne. Until I was on my feet again he brought this chow to me wrapped in the daily Nip paper which I welcomed almost as much as the food. I gave him a civilian shirt and a handsome green-silk tie to show my appreciation. For some reason this stamped me as a son of very wealthy parents. By some twisted thought process the tie, which had a Filene's Department Store label on it, identified me as a member of the wealthy family which controlled this organization.

"Weinstein," he said, "I must plan to go into business soon."

"Yes?" I said, interested. "What business?"

"The lumber-importing business," he replied, pursing his lips. "I want to make much money, money, money," moving his mouth like a child eagerly sucking a nipple.

"Where can you get lumber during the war?"

"There will be a great naval battle during the fall of 1944," he predicted. "Regardless of who wins, the war will come to an end soon after. Japan will need much lumber for construction. There has been no building for eight years. I shall make a million dollars," he said caressing the words, "and you shall make a million."

"I'm a doctor, not a businessman," I said puzzled.

"Ah, yes, you can continue to practice surgery, but you must return to the Philippines, buy up large forest reserves, set up sawmills, and ship the lumber to me for sale."

I had frequently spoken to him about the large tracts of virgin timber throughout the Philippine archipelago.

"What will I use for money, Mr. Arigawa? Peanuts?"

He smiled secretively: "I know your parents are very wealthy. They will give you the money."

I laughed incredulously. "My parents? They did well to raise and educate their six children. They haven't any money."

"You are very modest, Doctor. I know they own a department store," he said, wagging his head.

"The only connection I ever had with a department store was when I sold Red Cross seals in one during the Christmas of 1921."

"Yes, yes, of course," he smiled, unconvinced. "In America, wealthy families train their children in works of charity when they are very young."

I gave it up as a bad job. During the rest of my stay in Shinagawa, he buzzed my ear deaf with talk of my wealth and the profits involved in postwar lumbering.

I nabbed him drifting about the compound, aimlessly kicking a pebble around like a schoolboy on a holiday.

"Mr. Arigawa," I said, drawing him behind a building, "I had a dream last night."

"About money, money, money?" fluttering his protuberant lips.

"No, about the Italians. I dreamed they were trading clothes for bread from the gunso (sergeant) in charge of the galley."

"They are destroying his honesty by bribes," he spluttered, hopping up and down like a sparrow in distress. "I shall put an end to their attempts to undermine his character."

Our bread losses ceased.

We used Mr. Arigawa to good advantage in the case of a white Dutch prisoner whose name I don't remember. I'll call him Van Puyten. He was a tall, thin, wiry fellow with sharp, hard eyes and thin lips he licked constantly. He had a tense manner. Son of wealthy parents, he had traveled and studied extensively in the States. In the Dutch camp from which he came, he had the reputation of being a crook and a stool pigeon. A week before he entered Shinagawa, he mangled his right hand and forearm badly in some machinery. Some said this was done deliberately. He was feverish, toxic, and delirious. Most of the skin had been ripped away from the hand and flexor surface of the forearm. He had gangrene of the ring and little finger. The elbow was fixed in contracture. Forearm and arm were swollen to the size of a rubber inner tube with streptococcus infection. We pumped him full of sulfanilamide until the streptococcus septicemia and extensive infection of the arm subsided slowly.

In the face of the extensive mutilation of the hand, the next step in the procedure would have justifiably been amputation of the arm below the elbow. We decided to attempt to save part of the hand. The gangrenous ring and little fingers were removed. The middle finger had osteomyelitis in the terminal phalanx. This was removed and the end of the finger covered with a skin flap prepared from its palmar surface. After infection of the hand and forearm had subsided, their raw surfaces were covered with many skin grafts from the thighs and abdomen. The bent, contracted elbow was gradually straightened by massage. He was left with a forearm, thumb and index fingers which were ugly but serviceable. We did eight plastic operations on him over a period of three months.

He repaid us for saving his life and arm by becoming a stool pigeon for the Nips.

Shinagawa was a clearinghouse for news and rumors. Sergeant Bersted, a silent, sad-faced American prisoner working in Omori Headquarters Camp, brought news to Jim Davis when he carried supplies into Shinagawa. He was one of the first noncoms captured in the Philippines who knew about radar and the Japs suspected it; but they could not beat the information out of him. We got some news from Jap newspapers. Tap-dancing Private First Class Johnson, one of our medics who worked in the Nip administration building, stole the papers from their files. We had a Chinese prisoner who could read Kongi idiographs (picture writing) but could speak no English. We had Dr. Dossett-Grove, British Naval Reserve, captured in Hong Kong, who could speak Chinese. Jim Davis could read Katakana and Hira Gana (a kind of shorthand). Between the three they unraveled the news in the Jap newspapers after hours of cussing and head-scratching. We also got notes from all other camps in the Tokyo area containing digests of war news, personnel items, and information of local interest.

An incoming patient was caught by a Jap guard with a very damaging note in his possession. It contained news of shipping in Yokohama Bay. A Nip convoy had attempted to leave the harbor on three occasions. It eventually made a run for it but limped back with four ships sunk and several others smashed. The Nips were convinced they had uncovered a spy ring in Shinagawa which was sending information about shipping to American submarines encircling Japan. The Kempei Tei (secret police) raided Shinagawa in full force. They ripped up the floor boards and walls of our quarters looking for a secret sending radio. They searched for diaries and incriminating documents. They shook us down and roughed us up. The hospital was a shambles when they finished. They found a few notes on our patients whom they questioned and threatened day after day. Thereafter Van Puyten was seen leaving the questioning rooms nightly with a loaf of bread tucked under his arm. While he was under anesthesia for another plastic operation on his arm, we searched his personal effects. Among them we found a rough copy of a letter. It read:

DEAR DR. TOKUDA:

I know how the prisoners get news into camp. I hate them. I want to help you. I can show you how they get information and where they hide their diaries, letters, and maps, if you give me some extra bread and sugar.

VAN PUYTEN

We decided to say nothing to Van Puyten. We passed the word among the prisoners to be careful of their speech when he was snooping.

I went to see Mr. Arigawa, who frequently questioned Van Puyten.

"Mr. Arigawa," I said, "I want to give you some advice."

"What is it?" he asked, pursing his lips.

"When Van Puyten is in your office, always have somebody else in there with you."

"What for?" he asked alarmed, his little eyes blinking.

"To protect you. I think he is crazy. He thinks the whole world is against him, including the Japanese. I advise you to search his clothes. You will find he has been making sharp knives. He may attack you."

I had seen Van Puyten making some crude knives from bits of scrap metal, as many patients did.

Mr. Arigawa hurriedly got a guard and checked Van Puyten's belongings. They found the sharp-pointed instruments. The nightly conferences ceased. Shortly thereafter we were able to convince the Japs that the Dutchman was fit for duty. He was sent back to his work camp.

Operating at Shinagawa was a nightmare. Several nights after my arrival in April, 1944, Dr. Fugi found us examining a submariner named Landrum, a tall, thin lad from Richmond, Virginia. He had been sent in from one of the work camps for a suspected acute inflammation of the appendix.

Dr. Fugi was half drunk. "Prepare the operating room. I will do this operation," he slobbered.

"But Dr. Fugi," we protested, "this man does not have the signs and symptoms of appendicitis. His temperature and pulse are normal. His physical examination is negative. His white-blood-cell count is normal. He has mild diarrhea."

"I shall operate," Dr. Fugi stormed, his face darkening.

We carried Landrum into the operating room, a cubicle about ten by seven feet in size. It was heated by a small potbellied, coal-burning stove. It was bitter cold. We had one dim electric bulb for light. The same torn rubber gloves, gowns, instruments, and wooden table used for autopsies were used for operating. The tiny room was crowded with curious Jap guards watching the fun. After Al Mohnac gave the spinal anesthesia, Dr. Fugi clumsily slashed through the abdominal wall over the region of the appendix. He searched for it fruitlessly for thirty minutes. He finally let us find it for him. He cut the appendical artery and was unable to control the bleeding. We did. He ripped the normal appendix out by its roots, tearing a hole in the large bowel to which it was attached. Feces oozed through the hole. He spread the feces liberally throughout the operative field with his clumsy hands. Unable to witness any more of this butchery we took the instruments from him and finished the operation. It had taken two-and-a-half hours to remove a normal appendix. Landrum developed peritonitis, intestinal obstruction, jaundice, and bilateral broncho pneumonia. The wings of the Angel of Death fluttered about him for two weeks. He finally made the grade.

This hospital was used for patients from all work camps in the Tokyo area, which had ten thousand white prisoners. We pleaded time and again with the Spider for more equipment and surgical instruments.

"I cannot get them. We have enough," he exploded angrily. He hated suggestions and hated me for offering them.

He finally consented to the use of a larger room in the Nip headquarters building for an operating room. Private First Class Liebert stole white paint somewhere and coated its walls.

I spoke to Jim Davis about constructing a spotlight whose rays would focus two feet from its source. He spent hours covering pads of paper with long lines of algebraic calculations. He came out with the theoretical answer. We had a Norwegian ship's carpenter in camp who had been captured by a German raider in the Indian Ocean and brought to Japan. Petersen had thin blond hair, bright blue eyes in a pale face, and a bright red ulcer in the duodenum. We presented him with the practical problem. He went to work. He cut up a tin-plated soybean oil can into parabolic strips and soldered them together into a reflector. An

Australian carpenter built a wooden stand for it, with an inge-
nious three-way control joint, out of scrap wood so that it could
be angulated in all directions.

I wanted an electric water bath to sterilize instruments. Jim
figured out the details. Petersen built it, using plates from flattened metal cans. He sunk these plates in a water bath so that
they acted as a resistance mechanism to boil the water. Our
white-haired Australian carpenter built the wooden container. I needed a steam sterilizer for towels, sheets, and gauze. Jim
calculated the electrical resistance necessary for this larger unit.
Petersen constructed a unit similar to the instrument sterilizer
which he soldered to the bottom of a large tin receptacle. This
contained the dry goods used in operations. Steam generated in
the lower unit circulated through the upper and was led back
again to the lower. We could find no container strong enough to
build a steam-pressure sterilizer. To check whether the steam generated in our unit penetrated the center of the bundle of sheets,
we placed a raw potato in the bundle. If it was uncooked after
one hour we figured the pack was not adequately sterilized and
was still full of bacteria. Back into the sterilizer it went. If it was
cooked we went ahead with the operation. I ate the potato. That
was my cut.

We delayed operations until we could make the instruments
we needed. Al Mohnac also made himself a set of dental instruments. Before we could operate on several patients with osteomyelitis of the thigh bone Petersen made me some bone chisels out
of scrap metal which he tempered in boiling soybean oil he stole
from the Nip kitchen. He made a very effective bone saw out of
the steel strapping of a Red Cross parcel. He cut the teeth with a
homemade chisel. He filed and set them, and fitted the saw to a
wooden handle with a frame of a steel rod stolen from our sliding
doors. The finished product looked like a butcher's bone saw. It
worked.

Kendall, a redheaded American prisoner, developed empyema, a collection of thick pus in the chest, following lobar pneumonia. We had no rib periosteal elevator or rib cutter. Petersen

made a rib elevator by taking a scissors apart and filing off half of the steel oval through which the thumb slips. I made a rib cutter with three steel guitar strings I had brought with me from the Carabao Wallow. I braided them into a Gigli saw. The Gigli saw had little loops at its ends through which steel-handled grips would be attached. Petersen made them. Under local anesthesia we cut through the periosteum (covering) of a rib overlying the empyema. We stripped it back with Petersen's scissors-periosteum elevator, exposing the bare rib. We threaded the braided guitar-string Gigli saw under one end of the rib and attached the steel handles. By grasping both handles and making tension on the braided steel, it pulled taut under the rib. Pulled back and forth with both bands, the braided wires cut through the rib. After a repeat job on the upper end of the rib, a piece of rib about two inches long came away clean. We got about a pint of thick creamy pus. We made a modified "Wangenstein" irrigation-suction apparatus and some "blow" bottles to help him expand his lung. Kendall recovered.

The Australian made a series of wooden splints for our bone cases: Thomas splints for leg fractures, adjustable walking calipers, canes and crutches for the convalescents. An Australian prisoner named Gorman entered the hospital with a broken back. We did not have enough plaster of Paris to make a body cast for him. We built a fracture bed. We sewed a sling out of burlap bags to immobilize his body suspended above the floor. Dr. Groves wanted a pneumothorax machine to collapse the lungs of his tuberculosis patients. Petersen made one with accurate calibrations. Captain Keschner, boisterous pathologist from New York City, wanted an incubator. Petersen made it. He never used it because Dr. Tokuda wouldn't get the media necessary to grow and identify bacteria. Bearded Australian Major Woodward wanted a machine to test for early destruction of the nerves of the eye from beriberi. Our Australian carpenter made it. Jim Davis figured out an accurate chart to test visual acuity. One of the British medical corpsmen made a huge chart out of black-out curtains to test for blind spots in the visual field caused by beriberi. With the help of these men and Liebert's capacity to steal essential surgical supplies from the Jap storeroom, a fairly adequate operating pavilion came into being.

Although our surgical setup improved, our problems concerning the treatment of patients who needed surgery became more complicated. Dr. Tokuda was not interested in the proper treatment of disease by surgery. He was interested only in perfecting himself in the technique of surgery. According to black-haired Pharmacist Mate Valois, captured in Guam, Tokuda had killed one patient on whom he had operated for appendicitis prior to my arrival. This did not deter this embryonic surgeon. He insisted on operating on all patients who required surgery and many who did not need the knife to cure them of their ailments. With practice, he became worse rather than better. He had no diagnostic ability and less manual dexterity. I have timed him when he attempted to ligate one clamped blood vessel. It took five minutes.

To keep helpless patients from falling into the hands of this butcher, we had to rely upon guile and cunning. All our efforts were directed toward the end of preventing any surgery from being done at Shinagawa other than that of the most urgent nature. We received patients sent in from work camps with the diagnoses of appendicitis, gall-bladder disease, kidney stone, and hernia. We changed their diagnoses. We hid the patients in medical wards under false ones. If their symptoms subsided, we rested them up and sent them back to their work camps. It was safer for them to take their chances on a recurrence of their illness than to risk death at the hands of the great Spider. If they got worse, they were operated on at night while he was out of camp. This was done in the face of his direct orders forbidding any surgery being done other than by Dr. Tokuda. Black with anger the next morning, he cussed and howled when he found out that a victim had escaped his tender ministration. We told him blandly that it was an emergency and we were unable to reach him. These operations were done on the wards, kneeling on the straw-covered floor.

When Dr. Tokuda left for a three- or four-day tour of inspection, we had a field day operating on patients we had hidden in the medical wards; appendices, incarcerated hernias, and bleeding hemorrhoids. We advised patients with gallstones and peptic ulcer of the stomach to refuse operation if he discovered their ailments. Major surgery of this type performed by him would have been a death sentence. He beat these patients for refusing operation. He sent them back to their work camps to labor.

Certain patients had to be operated on to live. Dr. Tokuda began the operation, and mucked about until we finally took the instruments from him to finish the job. It infuriated him. After Commander Hugh Cleave of the British Navy, captured in Hong Kong, came to Shinagawa, we pulled a brother and sister act on the Spider. Between the two of us, Cleave and I kept him so confused, elbowing him out of the way or holding retractors, that we were able to finish operations before he was able to do any damage. We repaired a double hernia on Italian Commander Bernanti in this manner. The Spider was furious. He couldn't get a lick in.

On the medical side, Captain "Siggie" Clayman, trained in Switzerland; crisp-voiced British Captain Warrick, Dr. Dossett-Grove, specialist in tuberculosis, and Major Behrenberg, had the same trouble with Dr. Tokuda. This Jap doctor examined all patients and prescribed all treatment which he ordered them to carry out, under the threat of punishment for disobedience. They didn't. Pharmacist Mate redheaded "Poogy" Rice, captured in Guam, worked in the medical-supply room. He stole enough medicine of a proper type for these doctors so that they could treat their patients properly. He stole even more for us. When patients went back to their work camps, we gave them a supply of medicine for their American prisoner doctors in these camps. We knew they were short. By an interchange of notes, we learned their most urgent needs and met them.

The Spider was not only a physician and surgeon, but also a great research man, a second Noguchi. He was continually writing papers on studies of malnutrition on our starving patients;

blood studies, gastric analyses, clinical observations on beriberi. These studies had no value. They were poorly planned. The results were incorrectly analyzed. For example, he made a study of blood pressure, both systolic and diastolic, among all beriberi patients. According to his figures, the average blood pressure of the patients in camp was 112/28. The normal diastolic (the lower figure) is usually about 80. We pointed out that this average diastolic pressure was actually the average age of the patients in camp. He had confused two lists of figures: the list of blood pressures and the list of ages.

Soon the Spider busied himself with grim, deadly experimentation. No prisoner-doctor was permitted in the tuberculosis ward. These patients were his experimental animals. He attempted to cure them with bizarre mixtures of infected bile and soybean milk injected intravenously. Many of them died.

Another character in camp we detested almost as much as the Spider was an American prisoner-doctor we called the "Quarterback," or the "Q.B." He was from the Western seaboard. He had thinning brown hair, cold grayish, fishy eyes, and aquiline nose and loose, lascivious lips. He was of medium stature, heavy set and potbellied. His obeisance and servility before the Spider nauseated us.

When we ticked him off for his groveling manner, he flew into a rage, screaming: "There's a buzz saw over our heads. If we don't play ball with Dr. Tokuda, we'll all have our heads cut off." Meaning his own, especially.

He was harsh with the patients, unnecessarily so, when they stepped out of line. His only redeeming feature was a good medical education. He got his nickname by interfering and coaching all other doctors, except Tokuda, in the conduct of their specialties: nose and throat, anesthesia, pathology, surgery, and tuberculosis. He was not dishonest nor was he guilty of malpractice. But he was so filled with fear for his own personal safety that he took no active role in our combined attempts to prevent the Spider from mutilating patients. In his own slimy manner, he was able to get some supplies out of him. But by kowtowing continually to the Spider, we felt he weakened the staff's combined position in combating this notorious Jap.

Patients and doctors made the best of their miserable existence. When the pressure was off, we laughed, joked, played bridge and chess. The phonograph and its records circulated from one ward to another. As the cold weather abated, we organized little outdoor concerts. A cockney squeezed an accordion, a Hawaiian and an American strummed the guitars, a Dutchman drew a soft bow over a sweet-sounding violin.

I planted rows of yellow marigolds, multicolored zinnias, blue strawflowers, red lady's-slippers and tiger canna lilies in front of the wards. The patients put in vegetable gardens in the clam-shell, sandy compound and fertilized them with night soil. We raised a crop. What we didn't steal, the Nips corralled for themselves. We split about fifty-fifty.

We paced back and forth in the narrow company street under the starlit sky discussing the news in whispers. Without it we would have gone off the deep end. It was our bread and meat, our sustenance, our beacon of redemption. We gloated with sadistic glee when the Nip newspaper announced that their garrisons in Hollandia and Biak New Guinea had died to the last man for the glory of the emperor. We trembled with excitement when Saipan and Guam were invaded in June, 1944. The big push was on. We stilled our hunger pangs with hopes of recapture. The Nips reported a great naval victory prior to these landings. We were thrilled to hear about it. We always interpreted their claims in reverse. We were unhappy only if there was no news of naval fighting. Everything was looking up.

Rome was recaptured. The Russians smashed into Rumania and Poland. When the news broke that we had landed in Normandy, France, in June, 1944, our joy was hard to stifle. Dying patients forced themselves to eat. By sheer strength of mind, they willed to live.

I had it all figured out. Germany would surrender in September and Japan by December. Christmas, 1944, would see me free. I tossed restlessly on the flea-infested, straw-covered floor, thinking of reunion in Manila.

The lilt of Hanna's gay laughter filled my ears. I was conscious of the smell of her hair, the flash of her smiling brown eyes, the rustle of her sheer white evening gown, the warmth of her body as my arms engulfed her and my lips sought out hers. Swept by passion for the first time in years of imprisonment, I clung to this dream world.

The moon flooded Manila Bay, sending up shimmering waves of reflected light as we strolled down Taft Avenue into the Keg Room of Jai Alai. The bartender, gaily clad in green and white, took our orders for champagne cocktails. We edged our way through the crowds into the Sky Room where the lovely strains of "Tales from the Vienna Woods" filled the air-conditioned night club. Seated at a table for two in this lovely room high above the city, we nibbled at oysters a la Rockefeller, sipped piping-hot turtle soup, savored of lapu-lapu en papillote, teased ourselves with choice morsels of lobster Thermidor, and cooled ourselves in flaming baked Alaska. As the hours of the night flowed, we danced to the rhythmic beat of the languorous Argentine orchestra.

Murky dawn broke over Shinagawa. I still tossed on the flea-infested straw-covered floor.

Our treatment got worse rather than better. The chow was cut down to such an extent that we coached the patients to tell the Spider they were cured when he examined them for discharge. Sick as they were, their chances for survival were better while laboring at their work camps rather than resting and starving in Shinagawa. All prisoner-doctors were forced to sign a statement saying they willingly volunteered for physical labor. Refusal to do so meant no chow. We were put to work digging trenches and air-raid shelters for the Nip guards and medical personnel. We christened one of them "Fort Tokuda."

Allied prisoner-doctors entered and left Shinagawa. One of these was Captain Nelson Kaufman of the Thirty-first Infantry in the Philippines. He was a brown-haired, brown-eyed, olive-skinned handsome officer who had been doctoring at a work camp in Yokohama since late in 1942. His men worshipped him.

He was fearless, cunning, and capable. By badgering the Nip C.O. in charge of his camp, he was frequently taken into Tokyo and permitted to buy medicine for his patients on the open market. During the severe winter of 1943, only four prisoners died in his camp. Working hand in hand with Commander Birchell, a Canadian flight officer, he brought the Nip guards under control. These two prisoners howled about the chow, threatening to lodge complaints with the Nip headquarters camp in Tokyo. Rations were increased. The prisoners in this camp who worked in Nip shipyards were instructed to "slow down" if the company didn't feed them properly at their noonday meal. It worked. As was true of so many prisoner-doctors in Japan, Nelson was finally sent away from his camp for bucking the Nips in his attempt to procure more medicine and food for the sick and less work for the well. He landed up in Shinagawa Hospital en route to Omori Headquarters Camp for punishment.

The long expected and dreaded blowup with the Spider took place with the arrival of a French-Canadian, Private First Class LeBell. He had suffered from nausea, vomiting, and gripping abdominal pain of two days' duration. Tall and gaunt, his black fever-brightened eyes were sunk deep in their orbital cavities; nostrils flared back and forth with air hunger, lips were dry and cracked. His bony nose reared up like a promontory in his haggard face, and his abdomen was tense, distended, and painful throughout. There was a ragged scar from a previous operation for a ruptured appendix. His pulse was rapid. It was evident to even a neophyte that some surgical catastrophe was taking place.

I went to see the Spider: "Dr. Tokuda, we have a patient who must be operated on immediately."

He blinked his slit eyes behind his thick glasses. "What's wrong with him?"

"I don't know. It's something quite complicated technically. Maybe peritonitis, perforated peptic ulcer of the stomach or intestinal obstruction. He is very sick. He will die if he is not operated on."

"Prepare the operating room," he said sourly.

We gave LeBell two liters of saline solution subcutaneously, two blood-plasma transfusions, and a third during the operation. Private First Class Liebert prepared and sterilized the necessary linen and instruments. Al Mohnac gave his usual smooth spinal anesthesia. We flopped LeBell over on his back, painted his belly with iodine, and draped it with sheets, leaving exposed a long narrow strip of iodine-tinted skin. Dr. Fugi, Nip guards and non-coms crowded into the room to watch the show. Adenoid-voiced Hugh Cleave and I were scrubbed and gloved. We waited until the great Tokuda made his appearance. We set to work before he could lay his clumsy hands on the instruments. I made a long right rectus incision (almost in the midline) and went through the abdominal wall quickly.

"How's he doing, Al?" I asked, working.

"O.K. Blood pressure kind of low. About 90/60. Shall I give him some caffeine and adrenalin?"

"Yes. Keep the plasmas going if that bottle runs dry before we're finished."

The abdomen was filled with a blood-tinged fluid. Through the twelve-inch exploratory incision could be seen a loop of small bowel distended to the size of an inner tube. Instead of being pink, it was a dark reddish-purple. I traced the loop down. There was a tough fibrous band, a relic of a previous attack of a rup-tured appendix that extended from the inner side of an old op-erative scar to the depths of the abdominal cavity. Four feet of bowel had looped about it in such a manner as to interfere with its own blood supply. I cut the band of adhesions and untwisted the bowel.

Hands pawing in the abdominal wound, the Spider peered at it and at me.

"That loop of bowel is dead. Cut it out and connect up the ends of the intestine," he said curtly.

"Let's put the injured loop of bowel back in the warmth of the abdominal cavity and wait a few minutes until it has a chance to regain its circulation," I suggested.

"No! Cut it off!" he stormed.

I put the bowel back in the abdominal cavity and closed the edge of the wound with some towel clips. I waited ten minutes by the clock while the Spider fussed and fumed, insisting that the operation proceed. I removed the towel clips and drew out the loop of the gut again. The purple color had faded. It was a bright brick red. I examined it carefully. There was no evidence of any perforation or necrosis of bowel wall.

"This bowel looks O.K. to me," I said. "What do you think, Hugh?"

"Looks all right, Al."

"What do you think, Keschner?"

"Leave it in, Al," he growled.

"I order you to cut it out," the Spider stormed. Apparently he had never seen an intestinal resection in his life and wanted to observe the technique of this operation. My brain twisted and turned.

LeBell is going to die anyway. Why antagonize the Spider?

How the hell do you know he's going to die?

Do what you are ordered. Let him die. If you are sent out of camp, other patients who are still here will suffer because you won't be around to operate on them.

That's a lot of eyewash. Hugh Cleave is just as good a surgeon and scrapper as you are.

Why should I stick my chin out? I've had my share of misery.

You're a no-good yellow bastard. LeBell is in no shape to have an unnecessary intestinal resection, sick as he is with beriberi. If you do it, you'll kill him. You'll have his blood on your conscience as long as you live.

"I won't do it," I said to the Spider.

He flew into a rage and stomped out of the room followed by Dr. Fugi. Hugh and I closed the belly.

LeBell was critically ill for a week with postoperative bronchopneumonia and paralytic ileus (nonfunctioning bowels). He made the grade by a hair's breadth. I heard subsequently through the grapevine that he was eventually discharged from the hospital and returned to work.

During this week, the Spider's face turned black with thunder every time he saw me. He finally called me to his office.

Voice dripping venom, he said: "You are a prisoner. I am a Japanese officer. You have refused to obey my orders. I shall send you to Omori Camp for punishment. You will never forget me."

He was right, I never will.

CHAPTER 13.
Camp Omori:
The Wily Bird
Beats Out a Tune

DOWN THE LAST HUNDRED YARDS of winding street Captain Kaufman and I trudged, soaked with perspiration and streaked with dirt. We turned the last corner and could see a stretch of canal separating the low-lying manmade island on which Omori Headquarters Camp rested. We stopped at the foot of a rickety, humpbacked, wooden footbridge which spanned this canal.

"*Yasume Ka?*" we asked the guard. (May we rest?)

"*Ush,*" he said, flashing a gaping mouth full of gold-plated teeth at us.

It was a placid scene, far removed from prison life and war. On the right, in the distance, was a forest of chimneys belching black clouds of smoke which floated lazily upward. Interspersed were clusters of flat squat oil reservoirs and larger gas tanks. Behind was a gently swelling hill covered with deeply-tinted green towering pine trees through whose spreading branches we could see the sun reflecting from the white walls of a great mansion, the home of one of the members of the royal house. Far off to the left were the huge, rambling two-story barracks of the naval training station filled with thousands of would-be admirals. In the canal, about as wide as a football field, were several small skiffs drifting idly with the tide. One of them near us was filled with four Nip versions of the American Huckleberry Finn. Grasping their poles, they watched their lines to detect the first evidence of a bite. A sudden jerk and up came a flashing silver-gray fingerling. Triumphantly, young Huckleberry Moto rebaited his hook and slouched back on his haunches.

"Owari!" barked the guard. (Finished!) Shouldering our packs again, we shuffled over the footbridge past several acres of garden where pumpkin vines, peanuts, soybeans and eggplants were eking out a stunted, miserable living from the barren, sandy, shell-covered soil. We entered the acre-large compound which housed six hundred Allied prisoners, some of whom passed us silently without a glance of welcome or recognition. We were led to the administration building. There we dropped our luggage in front of the office, more commonly called the "cage," which housed the official disciplinarian, Corporal Watanabi. We learned later to refer to him as the "Bird," "Wily Bird," "Mr. Adam" or the "Animal."

A question we were to hear repeated time and time again among the prisoners in this prison was: "What's the position?"

The reply would be either: "The Animal is in his cage," in which case we all relaxed and breathed easily for a short respite, or: "The Animal is on the prowl," whereupon we buckled down to our work and waited tensely for the Animal to strike.

In the office, ready to greet us, were Cato Chui (Lieutenant Cato), Watanabi, and Nishino San (Mr. Nishino). Lieutenant Cato was camp commandant, a wizened, dark-faced Nip with thick glasses, closely set, shifty eyes, pudgy nose, and loose slobbering lips. Watanabi was a well-built Nip, about five foot seven, with sturdily built shoulders surmounted by a well modeled head and features almost Occidental in type. His face was marred only by a slight cast to the eyes which became intensified when he flew into a rage. Dressed in a white jacket and trousers like an ice-cream salesman, he gazed at us, a wry, sardonic smile on his handsome face. I made a mental note that he didn't look as bad as his reputation. The most obsequious Nishino looked more like the prewar Hollywood version of a Westernized Nip. Slim, slant-eyed, thin-lipped, with long hair well pomaded, he started off the proceedings by interpreting Lieutenant Cato's speech.

"You two have been sent to this camp because you have a bad attitude and are arrogant. Our reports say you have refused to cooperate with the Nipponese authorities and have disobeyed the orders of officers of the Imperial Nipponese Army. You are on our official black list."

Grinning, he added: "It is our duty to teach you discipline and impress upon you that you are prisoners and must obey all orders of the Nipponese even should they emanate from a third class private. We forgive you for your past offenses and hope you will be obedient here. Unfortunately, we have enough doctors in this camp and so you will not do professional work. You will not be treated as doctors. You will do physical labor similar to that done by other prisoner officers. Do you understand?"

"*Hai* (Yes)!" we both shouted in the best Japanese style.

"You will now stand at attention until Corporal Watanabi is ready to inspect your luggage."

We stood at the Nip version of attention, head erect, eyes staring, body stiff, all fingers of hands extended and pressed hard toward the thighs. This began at ten o'clock. The Bird sat in his office in front of us, sneaking a look at us out of his slant eyes from time to time. At noon, a guard approached, leading Private First Class McDermit, one of our medics who had come with us from Manila and was working at Shinagawa prisoner-of-war hospital. Laboring in the supply department as he did, he often made trips to Omori under guard to haul necessities back to the hospital.

The guard had words with the Bird. His face tightened and darkened with anger. Flinging himself out of his chair he dashed out of the building to McDermit.

In pidgin English he demanded: "Why did you leave our supply room to go to the latrine?"

"I wanted to give some pepper and salt to one of my friends here," McDermit answered, stiffening his bony, five-foot-three frame to attention.

"Ah, so ka?" the Bird answered softening. "It is kind and noble of you to share your food with your friend. I admire you, but," face darkening again, "it is against my orders for you to communicate with anyone in this camp."

Lifting a haymaker from the ground, he knocked McDermit cold with his clenched fist, turned on his heel and re-entered his office.

After a few minutes, eyes still glazed, McDermit picked himself up and staggered away.

We continued standing at attention. The Bird ate a leisurely lunch. I pondered over this exhibition of behaviorism. Here evidently was a sample of a high-class Nip. He was the son of a wealthy family; college-bred at one of Tokyo's finest private schools, Waseda University; an athlete; a keen mind and observant personality trained for journalism before the war. He spoke English fairly well unless he was in a rage. I found out later he was fairly conversant in literature and the arts.

To me, he personalized one of the basic characteristics of the Japanese: their emotional instability. For a moment he was filled with kind emotions because of McDermit's generosity. He complimented him. Immediately thereafter, enraged because of the assumed slight to his authority, he knocked him out. There he was again, placidly eating his lunch: a gamut of emotions experienced in less than five minutes; hair-trigger, unpredictable responses; rattlesnake with the power to mutilate and kill. I shuddered to think of life in the States under the domination of such personalities. I was overcome with a feeling of thwarted rage, tension, and physical fear which came close to making a nervous wreck out of me before I left this camp.

About one o'clock, this business of rigid attention began to play hell with us. Proper blood circulation of the brain in the erect position depends in part on muscular activity. The contraction of the muscles of the legs tends to milk the blood in the veins of the legs upward into the general circulation. Without this aid, blood and blood serum tend to puddle in the legs, making so much less available to the brain. Transient blackout and intermittent dizziness set in. Four-legged animals do not have this problem because their head and heart are almost on the same level. I regretted that we had evolved the erect posture from our prehistoric four-legged stance. We found that this lightheadedness could be partially counteracted by alternately contracting and relaxing the muscles of the arms and legs while standing at rigid attention, somewhat on the style of the modified Swedish dynamic exercise.

The joints also catch hell in this, the mildest form of Japanese punishment; especially the lower back and the arches of the feet. The lower back is made up of three bones: two lateral bones and the central keystone bone, the sacrum, which supports the spinal column. The joints between these are held in position dynamically by ligaments and by the pull of muscles above them. These bones don't have the rigidity of an arch of masonry. They gradually give as the weight of the body tends to drive the sacrum downward, spreading its two lateral neighbors. Any woman who has had a baby will recognize the type of pain I am describing: dull, aching, gnawing, radiating across the back and down the legs.

The feet swell, sweat, heat, and flatten out until it would seem that the skin about them would burst. We learned it was advisable to wear a couple of pairs of wool socks and extra-large laced shoes when taking this form of punishment.

The Bird finally broke down and came out to check our baggage. Notes, notebooks (blank and filled), pictures, mail from home already censored and stamped with the Nip censor "chop," Phi Beta Kappa key, wallet and contents were confiscated.

When I protested the loss of the censored letter, he answered, his face darkening: "You must not complain; you must obey. You are here to be disciplined. If you disobey, you will be punished. If you obey, you will also be punished—but not so much. *Wakata?*" (Do you understand?)

With these pregnant words, he turned us over to a Lieutenant Martindale for further instructions.

Camp Omori was laid out in a quadrangle. We walked through a short company street flanked on both sides with double-decker wooden barracks, each housing about a hundred men. At the far end was the kitchen; at the near end the Bird's office. The street was under his constant surveillance. Behind the barracks or billets, as the British called them, were the latrines, the nature of whose construction I was to learn more intimately in the very near future.

Lieutenant Martindale, as I recall, was an American aviator shot down in the South Pacific. He was slim, soft-spoken, and kind-faced. As prisoner officer of the day, he was responsible for teaching us the regulations of the camp. If we were poor students, we would get slugged. He also would get whipped. He led us to our room at the end of the billet, a fair-sized closet seven by five feet in dimension, in which Nelson and I were to live and sleep.

"The Bird is a bastard," he said as a starter, "and as Nips go, a clever bastard, much more observant than the average run of slopeheads. I'll give you as much dope as I can on how he'll try to trip you up. It may not help much because you're both 'hot' now. He'll continue to lay for you until some new prisoner comes in for punishment. Not until then will he lay off you. When he enters the room, somebody yell '*Kiotski* (Attention)! *Karay* (Salute)!' Bow, and remain bowed until he returns the salute. Then yell *Naray* (Terminate salute)!' but remain standing at attention until he leaves the room or you'll get walloped.

"Look right at his eyes when he speaks. If they begin to glaze over, watch out. If possible, look neither sullen nor servile. It's damn hard to strike a happy medium, but it's necessary and sometimes possible. Make your answers without hesitation and not too prolonged or you'll get bashed for talking too much. If he's going to work on you, keep your chin down so he won't be able to drive his fist, straight arm or jab fashion, against your Adam's apple. That's a favorite trick of his. It's a lot more comfortable to take it on the chin than to have your windpipe smashed."

"Is there anybody in camp we can protest to if we get roughed up?" Kaufman asked angrily. "Lieutenant Cato just reassured us that if we minded our own business we would be treated as officers—except for physical labor."

Martindale smiled incredulously. He laughed silently.

"Cato," he whispered slowly. "Cato. He's a bigger bastard than the Bird, if that's possible. He's a dyed-in-the-wool sadist. Several months before you arrived, we had a British P.O.W. officer in this camp who had spent fifteen years teaching English in Japan. He was married to a Jap. He spoke the language fluently. It was in Hong Kong, I believe, that he was captured and then brought here. For some reason unknown to me, both the Bird and Cato hated him. They really pushed him around. One day Cato, who is just a bundle of inferiority complexes on bow legs, thought this 'limey' was insolent. He beat him with a scabbard until he couldn't stand. Then he practically kicked his testicles off. It was several weeks before he could walk. Finally, one of the Nip officers, 'Gentleman Jim,' whom you will meet, was able to get him transferred to another camp before Cato murdered him. I'm afraid you won't get much sympathy from Cato."

"How about Colonel Sacaba, who is C.O. of all P.O.W. camps in the Tokyo area?"

"The Bird is his right-hand man and draws his orders directly from him."

"What about the Red Cross and the Swiss representatives?"

"You won't see them around. There's one bloke named Prince Tokagawa, a member of the royal family connected with Red Cross work, who visits here occasionally. We've complained to him on more than one occasion. He says it is impossible for anybody to interfere with the military in their treatment of prisoners—even if they wanted to!"

"Well, to get back to the Bird," said Martindale grimly. "He's suspicious of everybody and everything. He'll hide outside your room and try to listen to what you're saying. Speak in whispers. Don't use real names in conversation. Use only the Bird's nickname and the nicknames of the other Nips in camp."

"The Bird will suddenly burst into your room and shout: *Nan da? Nani hanasu Ka* (What's going on? What the hell are you talking about)?"

"If you're about to have a bull session, always have a previously prepared topic to switch to. Something completely natural, like fishing, music, the folks back home or women. Sex is a good one because he's a real wolf. He's sex crazy like most Nips. Invite him to sit with you. Continue on without hesitation with the prepared topic. Get it?"

"Yeah," I said glumly. "It seems like all this nervous tension would drive a guy nuts in no time."

"Well," Martindale laughed nervously, peering into the corridor, "it's not exactly a rest cure. Most of us are jumpy. But we get by. It was a bit too much for Lieutenant Blank, an engineer captured in Mindanoa. He got permission to work with troops handling freight, just to get away from camp during the day. You can always do that, although the rest of the officers prefer to stick it out rather than let the Nips know they have us licked. Commander Blank, U.S.N., our liaison officer, is as nervous as a bitch in heat. Commander Callahan, U.S.N., has taken a terrific pounding. He is holding on by the skin of his teeth."

He gazed intently at Nelson and myself.

"Yeah," Kaufman said softly. "I guess we ought to be able to string along."

"Swell. One more bit of advice: When you're talking to the slopeheads, don't use the word 'Jap.' They go stark, raving mad when you do. To them, it has the same connotation as 'Dagoes,' 'kikes,' 'boogies,' or 'frogs.' Be damn sure the word you always use is 'Nipponese.'"

We busied ourselves arranging our gear under Martindale's instructions. Everything had to be folded neatly and piled on a tiny shelf: winter clothing on the bottom, and summer stuff on top, a detailed un-modifiable arrangement over which we sweated for an hour until Martindale thought it would pass inspection. Try folding jackets, towels, handkerchiefs, long drawers, and sweaters, so that the presenting edge is exactly twelve inches in width. Then try stacking them so they won't lean and tumble. It takes patience and experience. If I learned anything as a P.O.W.

it was clothes-folding. To make a living I can always fall back on this training and hire out as a clothes-folder to the ladies.

The next day was "weight day." Everybody in camp trooped down to the dispensary to get weighed. This weighing business exemplified another peculiarity of the Nips. They loved to collect figures and draw brightly colored charts to show weight loss or gain. (That is, we collected the figures and drew the charts for them.) Unfortunately, the interpretation of data and conclusions drawn from the charts never, in my experience, modified or increased the food handout. Whenever there was an announcement that the food ration was being increased we buckled our belts. It was usually cut. The vegetable issue might be increased, but the rice, barley or millet would be simultaneously cut. Potatoes might come into camp, but would be issued in place of rice. Since a pound of rice has three times as much food value as a pound of potatoes, the results were self-evident. Instead of being hungry, we were ravenous.

As Nelson and I were leaving the building, the Bird came strolling down the hallway. We both saluted briskly and moved out into the compound when a roar of rage froze us in our tracks. Turning quickly, we saw him charging at us, face turgid with wrath, fist clenched, arm outstretched, straight-arm fashion. I drew my chin down, but not quickly enough. The full violence of the blow landed on my Adam's apple. Down I went, choking and spewing. I scrambled to my feet to avoid his boots. Retreating again, he pulled the same Nip trick on Nelson, bellowing in a hodgepodge of English and Japanese.

"You are insolent! You are disobedient! You do not salute properly! I will teach you! I will give you Japanese military education! *Kiotski* (Attention)!"

Twisting his body and arm as far back as he could, he let fly a haymaker which landed flush on the jaw. The timing was excellent and the blow was clean, to avoid bruising his knuckles. Balanced as my feet were on wooden clogs, it was impossible not to be knocked down. This performance went on for about fifteen minutes. First Nelson hit the dust, and then I did. Over and over again with deadly, painful monotony. He was evidently a one-punch man, using the same timing and right cross. After a few wallops, by watching his eyes closely, we could tell when he was about to let fly. We then learned to roll imperceptibly with the punch just as it landed before flying into the dirt. At the expense of a few chipped teeth, we also learned to keep our jaws tightly clenched.

Puffing and blowing, he said finally: "You must remember my instructions. Salutation is very important. You must not insult me. Now, you must practice saluting this tree," pointing to one near his office, which we did for about three hours, taking turns bellowing, *"Kiotski! Karay! Naray!"*

This was the first real licking I had received since the trimming I got from a redheaded Italian kid named Gabriel in a sandlot fight in grammar-school days. I learned several lessons: I learned how much punishment could be avoided by rolling with the punch; I learned I was more revolted and torn down when I was forced to watch a fellow prisoner beaten than when I was licked myself; and I learned that, when it was uncertain whether the Bird was going to go off the deep end or merely continue to bellow, there was a peculiar sense of relief when he began flailing about.

"Well, Nelson, how's the jaw?" I asked, pointing to his face ballooned out like a cantaloupe.

"O.K., Al," he grinned wryly. "You're not exactly a Barrymore yourself. That shiner is going to be a pip tomorrow."

It is curious how tissue in two people will react differently to the same injury. For three and one-half months, Nelson's jaw inflated and deflated, while my left eye sported a halo of purple, red and yellow of varying intensities. He never acquired a peeper. I never acquired a swollen jaw. Maybe the Bird was landing a little higher on me than on him.

"Chow down" sounded. We hurried into our billet. There were six officers eating in our mess. Among them was Lieutenant Blank, a tall, thin, bespectacled Texan, captured at Corregidor. He was distinctly unpopular because of his smirking, fawning behavior toward the Japs. Lieutenant Ries was a South African engineer; sandy-haired, short and wizened, captured in Malaya. He had an especially tough job. He was in charge of the leather shop and attempted to protect the P.O.W.'s working in it from being batted around. In spite of his tense and high-strung manner, he often took the rap for others.

Across the table was Captain Garrett, U.S.A.C. flight officer, shot down over Tarawa. He was a tough turkey. Blondish, clean-cut, square-jawed, stalwart in bearing, he made no bones about how he felt about the Japs. In a crash landing over Tarawa, he had broken his right thigh. He lay in a miserable hovel in his own excrement, unwashed and starved, while his captors attempted to pump him for information which he steadfastly refused to give. They did not understand his curses and his pleading to be put out of his misery. They understood him well when he spit in their faces if they came too close to him. Eventually, gangrene set in. He had his leg amputated above the knee and without anesthesia. He slowly recovered. Apparently, the Japs were convinced he had valuable information. They flew him to Japan for further questioning. According to Garrett, a number of other American aviator-prisoners were slaughtered by the Japs before the Yanks invaded the island of Tarawa.

It was good to see again Captain Shmayla, M.C., of O'Donnell Prison. He had been sent to a small camp west of Tokyo where, as usual, prisoners were being overworked, underfed, and dying for lack of proper food and medical care. By dint of guile, persuasion, flattery, and threats of reporting conditions to the Tokyo Headquarters Camp, he was able to increase slowly the food ration and the number of prisoners he kept at rest in quarters. He went out to labor himself to keep some ailing prisoner at rest in camp. Finally, he ran into heavy weather, as did so many of the prisoner doctors in Japan. He was sent to Omori for punishment because of "disobedience."

Our lunch, a rice-barley mixture, was brought in wooden buckets. We scooped it out with wooden paddles and carefully divided it into equal portions. We each received about eight to ten ounces, net weight. The side dish was a boiled carrot and a half of a dried fish, about one to two ounces. Cards were cut for the fish. High man had his first choice, a choice which was made carefully and deliberately. This system was in vogue in all prison camps in which I lived. It was the only way of avoiding trouble between the closest of friends. Starvation plays peculiar tricks with human behavior and the human mind. We had seen prisoners of all ranks suddenly fly into a rage, come to blows, and accuse their fellow men of chiseling on the distribution of food. Hard living, disease, and starvation make heroes of few men. More frequently does it make animals of men who, in the normal course of living, would go through life with a clean slate.

There were some chiselers and crooks among the prisoners in all camps. We have often marveled why there were not more. It was our job, as doctors and officers, to keep their numbers down to a minimum. This was not easy for many reasons: we were human ourselves and hungry; it was not easy to turn down offers of extra chow made to us by fellow prisoner cooks who were the kings of the prison camps; it would have been easy to rationalize that the health of the doctor was vital to the wellbeing of the whole camp. However, it would have been impossible to raise hell with others attempting to chisel or sell food if our own noses were dirty. Most of us played the game clean by choice. Some men died because they insisted on a clean conscience.

When it came to stealing from the Nips' kitchen or from the Nip civilians outside the camp, there were no holds barred. We encouraged it, provided it could be done without getting the whole camp into trouble. It brought extra chow into camp. It saved lives. Many of us, including myself, lived because we became master crooks.

There was good *esprit de corps* in most camps. Our unutterable hatred of the Nips fused us into unity, regardless of nationality, religion or rank. Morale was especially high at Omori, both among the G.I.'s and the officers. Nelson and I saw evidence of it at our first meal. As part of our punishment, the C.O. had told us we would be on two-thirds rations. At the risk of their own necks, these officers insisted upon all sharing alike. Aside from the fact that the cut in their own rations was ill advised in the face of their own precarious health, they knew they would be beaten if the Japs found out we were getting more than the ordered two-thirds ration. To avoid exposure, Nelson and I hid part of our rice-barley mix until we had downed some of it. Then we put the rest on our plates. It was a wise precaution. Just as the chow was dished out, the Bird slammed open the sliding door to check on our ration. Everything being in order, he left, grinning maliciously when he found his orders were being carried out. So did we as we patted our bellies.

Having "knocked back" (English Army slang for having finished or eaten) our sumptuous repast, the talk turned to news and news coverage. Although there was no secret short-wave radio in this camp, news from several sources was plentiful: Jap newspapers, radio digests from civilians, and scuttlebutt picked up by men at various work projects. Radio news came from an embittered Korean truck driver at the Yokohama docks. He had lived in Japan for twenty years. Before the war he had built up a successful trucking business. With the outbreak of hostilities, his fleet of twelve trucks had been commandeered by the government. With customary Nipponese magnanimity, he was offered a job driving one of his own trucks. Since refusal to work would have put him in jeopardy and resulted in the loss of his ration card, he accepted.

With the little English he knew and the pidgin Japanese the P.O.W.'s picked up, he was able to transmit digests of the news from his short-wave set. He had a maniacal hatred of the Nips. He gloatingly related the pounding they were taking in the New Guinea and Central Pacific theaters. This news, unfortunately, was not entirely reliable because it was sometimes garbled in transmission by the G.I.'s who were the go-betweens. Almost daily we got the Tokyo Times printed in English and other Tokyo papers printed in Japanese. These were brought in by P.O.W.'s who worked on the docks unloading sugar. We called them Mitsubishi "sugar barons." They paid off Jap civilians for these newspapers with sugar they stole on the job.

In spite of their much vaunted fighting spirit and loyalty to country, the Nips were easy to bribe, provided no other Nips were around to squeal on them. Many were petty chiselers of the cheapest type. One contact worked in this manner. Joe Blow, Private First Class, and a slopehead working together would get to know each other well. They would exchange pictures of their families. They grumbled about the food and long hours of labor. After an *entente cordiale* was established, conversation would ensue, if no other Nips were about.

Joe: "*Senso dame daro* (War is bad. I think)."

Slopehead: "*So desu, kimona nai, tabemono nai, boom-boom takusan* (Yes, that's right: no clothes, no food, plenty of fighting)."

Joe: "*Mo sikoshi, senso owari, omo imasu ka* (Do you think the war will be over soon)?"

Slopehead (Sucking wind between his teeth and shaking his head sadly): "*Wakarimasen, Nozomi masu. Senso dai ichi ban dame* (I don't know. I hope so. War is number-one disaster)."

Joe: "*Shinbun wo yoroshi kaki masuka* (Does the paper write things are well)?"

Slopehead: "*Shinbun dai ichi ban bagero* (The papers are God damn liars)."

Joe (Cautiously) : "*Shinbun suki masu. Mo ichi aru koto go dekimasuka* (I like newspapers. Can you get one for me)?"

Slopehead (Tilting his head and sucking more wind): "*Taihen Abunai. Keredemo tabun desyo, Nanda* (It is very dangerous. Maybe. What's the deal)?"

Joe: "*Sato arimasu* (I've got some sugar)."

Slopehead (Flashing a mouthful of ugly gold teeth): "*Ah so desu* (Now you're talking). *Ikitsu ka* (How much)?"

Joe: "*Ichi shinbun, hanban hanban kilo sato* (One paper, a half kilo of sugar)."

Slopehead: "*Taihen sukoshi* (That's damn little)."

Joe: *"Tabun ato de mo sukoski agette imasu* (I may be able to increase the ante later on)."

Slopehead: *"Ush* (O.K.)."

A hiding place was chosen—a pile of rubbish, an abandoned rowboat, a hole in the ground or a secret panel in the latrine—in which a half canteen cup of sugar was placed. When the coast was clear the sugar was picked up by the Nip and a paper left in its place. This was then tucked in the lining of a sleeve and carried into camp. If the Nips in camp were raising hell, shaking down all incoming details, as they did frequently, it was torn up into pieces and carried boldly in trouser pockets: benjo (toilet paper), of course. Overwhelmed as the Nips were with the sense of their intelligence and wisdom, they never saw through this simple ruse. The papers were then usually delivered to Commander Blynn, U.S.N., and Commander Hurt, submariner, for study and analysis.

Dave Hurt was a tall gray-haired officer. The G.I.'s loved him for his kindness. His brother officers respected him for his failure to crack up under beatings and torture at the Ofuna Navel Questioning Camp. Rank to him meant responsibility, not privilege.

On Sunday mornings he got out his shears and clippers to cut our hair while he quietly told us the news. Blynnie was made of the same stuff. Sallow, gray, and hungry, he maintained his happy spirit and infectious confidence in our early recapture. From them we learned of the breakthrough of the First and Third American armies in July, 1944, and their smashing drive through France, culminating in the liberation of Paris. We heard of the landing in southern France, the capture of Marseilles, and the triumphant march up the Rhone Valley to the Swiss border. We chortled with glee when Hitler announced an unsuccessful attempt to assassinate him. They told us of the surrender of Rumania, Bulgaria, and Finland to Russia in September, 1944. We learned of the first crossing of Russian troops into Germany. The German forces were folding up like an accordion all over Europe. We could smell victory twelve thousand miles away.

After our daily whippings, Nelson and I went to bed on the wooden floor, hugging this news to our bosoms. We repeated each batch of information over and over again like devout Catholics reciting the Rosary.

Before the war, Hanna and I had frequently visited Nelson in his cozy apartment in Manila.

"Al," he said, with a smile in his voice, "it looks as if wedding bells will ring sooner than you expected."

That night Nelson and I fell asleep on the floor of our filthy straw-covered, lice-ridden cubicle. I had a dream.

I was in an immense foundry with sulphur fumes and acrid smoke which cut like a knife into my eyes and lungs. The clashing, grinding gears of mammoth cranes overhead deafened my ears. High in the vaulted roof they moved back and forth, illuminated by a sudden blinding glare from open-hearth blast furnaces. Freight cars loaded with scrap metal rumbled over their tracks. A low-slung freight car pulled up before an open furnace. It was loaded with bells. Three gnomelike Japs clothed in loincloths and a patina of sweat and dirt clambered aboard. Grinning and chattering they motioned to me to follow. I stumbled about the mass of metal, bruising my shins. In the intermittent flaring of eye-searing light, I saw temple bells of India and China covered with dragons and Buddhas; the massive bell from Harvard Memorial hall, the cracked Liberty Bell, the jingling bells of the calesa ponies in Manila. Thousands of wedding bells lay piled one on top of the other. Each had a name inscribed on it. Grunting and straining, the Japs lifted the bells, showed them to me, and tossed them into the glowing furnace shimmering with molten metal. I read the inscriptions: Captain Lemire, Ben Hessenberger, Pilar Campos, Captain Brewer, Lieutenant McCaffrey, Captain Bennison. The pile of wedding bells shrank rapidly.

Laughing uproariously, the Nips shoved another wedding bell into my face. Heart pounding, I read my name on it. Swinging at them with clenched fist, I screamed "Daichi ban Bagero (You God damn fools! Take your filthy hands off that one. It belongs to me)!"

We fought until I was knocked down. Chest heaving with terror, blood streaming from my mouth, they carried me to the open furnace, still clinging to my bell.

The Japs chanted "Waeensutaeen shinde masyo (Weinstein shall die. No marriage ceremony for him)!"

They swung me like a pendulum ready to let fly into the caldron filled with molten metal when a burly American Marine appeared.

He tapped the Nips on the shoulder, saying briskly: "O.K., Joe. I'll take over."

"Are you all right?" Nelson asked anxiously.

"I'm O.K.," I said slowly. "Why?"

"You were screaming," he answered, looking at my face dripping perspiration.

The Nip papers reported the war in Europe fairly accurately, magnifying Allied losses and minimizing our advances. In the Pacific, the Nip news reports were regularly fallacious and sometimes ridiculous. When they eventually reported the loss of an island, they compared it to a cigarette butt that a smoker would throw away. He had extracted all the value out of the cigarette. The butt was therefore useless. They reported our attempted landing on Leyte in the Philippines in October, 1944, as a desperate, futile gesture to pacify public demand in the States for action in the Pacific. Our landing forces were, of course, wiped out. They offered the news of the series of naval battles in Philippine waters as stupendous naval victories for themselves. To substantiate their claims, they declared a three-day national holiday for their own sullen, incredulous public. Flags waved and thousands marched in honor of the valor of the Japanese Navy. Japanese civilians laboring beside American prisoners told them they had long ceased to believe newspaper reports of naval victories.

"Mo sukoski senso Owari," they grumbled. (Pretty soon Japan will surrender.) They were sick of the war, sick of the short rations and long hours of labor. In the Mitsubishi Shipyards, slowdown and sit-down strikes took place as a protest against further cuts in the daily rice ration. Many of these civilian workers had

their heads chopped off by the Kempei Tei (secret police). The slowdown process continued. In other plants it was not necessary. Supplies of raw materials, especially iron, steel, and coal, had dried up to such an extent that production dwindled. These summer months of 1944 were thrilling ones for us after two years of prison life. The prospects of recapture became imminent. We dreamed vividly and constantly of home.

In this camp, there were about one hundred American G.I.'s, three hundred Britons captured in Hong Kong, about forty American, British, and Australian officers, and a handful of Norwegian sailors who had been picked up by German raiders in the Indian Ocean and dumped in Tokyo. They lived in double-decker barracks with a central aisle. They slept on vermin-infested, rice straw, mat-covered wooden floors. There were shallow pit latrines in the rear, housed in shanties where Commander Blynn and Commander Hurt studied their contraband Nip newspapers while squatting on their haunches.

These prisoners were divided into groups of a hundred. Under guard, they left at eight o'clock for work. They returned at five o'clock. Most of them worked as stevedores at freight terminals and shipyards in Tokyo and Yokohama. They were a rugged, hard-boiled group of men, survivors of two years of Japanese confinement and cruelty. The physically and mentally unfit among them had been weeded out by privation and disease. We called them "weak sisters." The physically strong and mentally cunning still lived. In spite of their limited rations they were able to outwork the Jap civilians laboring beside them. They took a hard day's work grimly. They returned to camp unwhipped, cleaned up at the wooden wash troughs, and relaxed. They played poker and bridge, shot crap, and told stories. They tumbled and wrestled with each other. Occasionally they fought with bare knuckles. Many of them loved to sing. Voices massed and blended, they made the rafters of their barracks vibrate, roaring their defiance to the Japs in melody.

Except for those of us who were on punishment rations, the chow issue at Omori was better than at Shinagawa Hospital: a heaping mess kit full of rice or barley three times a day; a fairly thick vegetable soup; a piece of dried salted fish three times a week; an occasional dish of boiled soybeans. Not very appetizing, but enough to support life and replace burned-out muscle. The good health and high spirits of the Omori prisoners were not due to this diet alone. They had become past masters at the art of petty larceny. Handling freight, they frequently handled food stores: rice, dried fish, and canned goods which they brought in concealed in false pockets of their shirts and overcoats. They were regularly shaken down by the company guards and camp guards. In spite of constant surveillance, stolen food continued to come into camp, sometimes in a trickle, sometimes in a flood. From time to time they were caught, beaten, and given extra physical labor as punishment. They continued to steal to live. We officers who worked in camp had no such opportunities. Although we were still receiving about $10 a month, there was nothing to buy in our canteen except Japanese tooth powder, ersatz pepper, spices, and salt. We were glad to buy any food that was stolen.

A tall, lean Scotsman entered our little cubicle and shut the sliding door behind him. In his thick brogue he asked: "Doc, can you use some dried fish?"

"I sure can, Jock. What have you got today?"

He wriggled his right arm. A two-foot-long, smoked red salmon slipped slowly out of the sleeve of his overcoat.

He shook the left. A bag of rice noodles tumbled to the floor. From his trouser leg he drew a handful of small cakes of hard-pressed sugar. From the tail of his overcoat he drew a bundle of cured tobacco leaves. He topped things off by selling me his canteen filled with grain alcohol.

Sugar-stealing was the specialty of the Mitsubishi Shipyard Sugar Barons as they unloaded freighters coming from Formosa. They were organized under a Nip guard we called the "Mad Man." He had been a pimp, ex-pugilist, and a small-time racketeer on the Yokohama waterfront before the war. He was tall and slim for a Nip, and walked with a careless grace, his rifle slung over his shoulder. He had dark, flashing eyes without the usual

Oriental slant. His face was graced with a clean-cut nose and smiling lips. He hated the Nip military system which had forced him into three years of warfare in China. The other Nip guards feared him. He was free with his fists. I once saw him lift a guard off his feet with a haymaker. He organized a full-fledged racket among the Sugar Barons a la Capone: an initiation fee of forty yen, monthly "protection" dues of twenty yen, 50 per cent cut on sugar stolen. The prisoners were transported by truck to the shipyards ten miles away. While hustling sacks of sugar from the holds of ships, they filled spare stockings with it, each sock holding about four pounds. During their lunch hour they secreted their yield in secret panels in their rest room.

At the end of their day's work they lined up and were searched by the company guards. They waited in formation for the trucks to bring them back to camp. The Jap truck drivers, who were also cut in on the racket, purposefully came a half-hour to an hour late. After waiting a while, the prisoners obtained permission from the company guards to return to the rest rooms to await the truck's arrival. With the help of "Rube Goldberg" contraptions, they suspended their socks of sugar in their sleeves and trousers, under their armpits and crotches. They slipped smaller sacks into oversized shoes they wore. They lashed socks filled with sugar to the backs of their necks under their turtle-roll sweaters. They strapped them to the flat of their abdomens. They were walking sugar warehouses. When the trucks arrived, the Mad Man shooed away the company guards and loaded his P.O.W. charges. Back to camp they went to conceal their precious hoards. Sugar was currency in camp. They traded it for cigarettes from the Nip guards. They traded with prisoners on other work details for food. A half-canteen of sugar was standard price of an evening's entertainment with the few homosexuals in camp.

The number of officers in camp fluctuated, depending upon how many were sent in for punishment and how many arrived with the new batches of prisoners brought up from the Philippines. Captured submarine and air-corps officers endured months of torture, first at the Ofuna Naval Questioning Camp. Thereafter they came to Omori Prison for a final polishing.

The prisoner-officer in nominal charge of the Americans was Commander Mayer. An emaciated, broken-voiced, broken-spirited sick man, captured when our destroyers were sunk in the Java Sea battle in 1942. He was responsible for transmitting orders from the Japs to us. He helped keep their records. A handful of prisoner-officers worked in the galley, the sewing room, and the leather shop. The rest did physical labor. They dug up almost every foot of sandy soil in the compound and outside the fence with pick and shovel. They fertilized this poverty-stricken soil with buckets of benjo (night soil). They planted tomatoes, dikons, carrots, pumpkins, leeks, and eggplants. They weeded and watered them by hand. Before the stunted crops came to maturity, they were harvested by order of the Japs. The soil was then refilled for a second crop. When there was no work for us in the fields, we made compost piles out of rice-straw sacks and night soil, treading the piles down with our bare feet. Colonel Pike, professional football player from the Middle West who had been shot down over China, was in charge of the garden detail under the Bird. Six-foot-three, lithe as a panther, he stood passively at attention while the Bird beat on him when he was displeased with the work of this garden group. Another group of officers worked in the leather shop sewing tiny bits of dog and goat leather into patterns which were used to cover Japanese field equipment.

Nelson Kaufman and I received special work assignments from the Bird. From seven A.M. to eight A.M. we swept the prison yard with brooms improvised from twigs tied to a branch. The Bird inspected our work. If he disapproved, we got another beating. After a hasty breakfast we spent the rest of the day loading night soil from the pit latrines into wooden buckets. Suspending them on a bamboo pole, we toted them outside the prison compound and dumped them into a pit near the drainage canal which surrounded the camp. The Bird spied on us constantly. If we were walking too slowly, we got whipped. If the buckets were not loaded heavily enough to suit his fancy, we got whipped. If there was no fault to find, we got whipped. He enjoyed the exercise of his power over us. He enjoyed knocking us down. Ordinarily he used his fists while we stood at attention. We steeled ourselves for the crash in the face and prepared to roll with the punch. When in an especially violent rage, he preferred to lash us with a heavy leather belt or a two-handed kendo (stick) made of bamboo. On one occasion he caught me across the neck with it, fracturing and dislocating my windpipe. Spewing and coughing blood, I reduced the dislocation myself to prevent strangulation. The next day I could feel air bubbles under the skin of my neck where air had leaked into the tissues from the windpipe. I loaded up with sulfathiazole to avoid the dreaded complication of mediastinitis (infection of the root of the neck that spreads down into the chest). I still have a partial paralysis of vocal cords from that wallop.

We usually finished off our lickings by standing at attention in the broiling sun for hours or by practicing bowing to a pumpkin until in our confused minds it bobbed back to us. Following a hasty supper, we spent several hours compulsorily washing clothes, usually the Bird's or some other Nip's. We had no soap. Yet the clothes had to be spotless to pass his inspection the next morning or another whipping was in order. He awakened us at night to inspect our cubicles, the clothes arrangement, its cleanliness. He searched us for contraband diaries and food. We lived in a constant state of physical exhaustion and nervous tension under the shadow of the Bird hovering over us ready to strike.

We did other odd jobs: washing windows, scrubbing floors, shifting one-hundred-and-fifty-pound sacks of rice and other stores in the kitchen. The latter job we rather enjoyed, because it paid dividends. While Nelson kept a sharp lookout, I greedily filled my mouth with sugar. It tasted better than champagne. Dry rice noodles used by the Nips came in foot-square wooden boxes which shattered easily when dropped. In between kitchen chores, we stuffed our bellies full of them. Washed down with a little water they were effective in stifling hunger pangs.

Nelson and I were tottering out of the guard gate carrying a heavy loaded bucket of benjo suspended from a bamboo pole. It was hot. The pole had cut a deep groove in our shoulders. The Bird appeared out of nowhere. He inspected the size of the load. No complaint on that score.

"How many buckets an hour are you dipping?" he asked angrily.

"We haven't timed ourselves," I replied. "Maybe the guard at the gate can tell you," pointing to the slopehead standing at attention, his rifle at present arms. They jabbered back and forth. From what I could gather, the Bird was being assured that we were working steadily.

"Where are you dumping the benjo today?" he asked, mollified.

"In that hole near the canal retaining wall."

He looked at it. "It is a very small hole. There is little benjo in it. You have been lazy!" he whooped, working himself into a rage.

"Yes, it is small, but very deep," I replied politely.

He picked up some rocks and squatted on his heels. He plopped the rocks into the pit, studying the height of the geysers of night soil he created.

"*Ush,*" he said. They were high enough to suit his royal highness. We went back to work again.

An especially backbreaking job was the ration run. Trucks brought in sacks of vegetables, rice, barley, and coal weighing from one hundred to two hundred pounds. The narrow footpath leading from the mainland to the little man-made island on which Omori rested was not wide enough to carry a truck. Piled on our backs, we carried these sacks a distance of three hundred yards over the humpbacked rickety bridge, across the island, through the prison compound into the galley. Neck, back, feet, and heart took a pounding in this occupation. At the end of it, we were so nauseatingly exhausted we couldn't eat our meager rations.

A job I liked was going into Tokyo for charcoal, ice or fresh fish for the Nip galley with a mousy, flat-chested Nip named

Fukajima. (We pronounced his name a little differently.) I took a two-wheeled pushcart with me to easy my burden. I liked the job because it was such a great relief to get away from the bamboo pole of the snooping, slamming Bird even for several hours. Fukajima was all right as long as he was flattered. When cajoled, he didn't rush me with my loads.

I could see Tokyo was being evacuated by thousands of people who crowded the railroad stations with their piles of bedding and swarms of flat-faced children with their Dutch-clip haircuts. Crowds of grade- and high-school children, stripped to the waist, were wrecking wooden buildings, creating street-wide fire lanes that extended as far as the eye could see. These ran parallel with each other. They were intersected at regular intervals by similar lanes. All tenement houses along the railroad lines leading in and out of the city had been pulled down.

Other than a few aged fire engines, Tokyo relied on hand pumps, bucket brigades, and these fire lanes to protect against the spread of fire by bombings which the government was warning its population would take place in the near future. The narrow, winding streets of Tokyo were filled with paper and wooden shacks piled one on the other. These were to be the scene of merry bonfires in December, 1944. When I saw them in the summer of that year, almost all of the stores were boarded up or presented for sale cheap toys and kitchen utensils made of wood and bamboo. Grocery and clothing stores and restaurants were all closed. Everything was rationed from central warehouses.

In camp we were constantly warned that the civilian population was enraged at the Americans. The Nip prison administration said they were our "guardians." I never encountered an enraged citizen. On the other hand, I met several who went out of their way to make my lot more bearable at the risk of their own safety. The civilians I met merely went through the motions of expediting the war effort. They had a bellyful of war.

As new arrivals came into camp, the pressure eased up on Nelson and me. The Bird was too busy whipping other "disobedient, arrogant prisoner-doctors" to beat us with any regularity.

Unfortunately, he still associated us. When he whipped Nelson for an alleged insult, he called for me and let me have it. It also worked in reverse. Eventually, he had more benjo carriers than he needed. He assigned Nelson and me to the leather shop where thirty permanently disabled and convalescent patients and officers worked. Sitting on workbenches, we busily sewed bits of leather together when the Bird was around. When he left we loafed and discussed food we were going to eat at the end of the war. The finished patterns of leather were piled on a shelf about two feet from the floor. The Nips had some hens which they permitted loose in the compound to scratch for a living. Some of them wandering into the leather shop found these soft piles of fur comfortable nests in which to lay their eggs. All work ceased when "Lady Jane," a regular contributor, sauntered in, flapped her wings, and fluttered on a pile near Lieutenant "Sedgie" Henson, an American aviator from Mississippi. She smoothed her feathers and settled down to the business of laying her daily egg. Just as the act of parturition was completed, Sedgie seized the surprised hen by the wings. Disgusted, she found herself hurled out of an adjacent window before she could announce to the world, and especially to the Nips, that she had given birth to an offspring. We drew lots for the warm egg and swallowed the evidence on the spot. In spite of her rough treatment, Lady Jane returned daily to deposit new contributions.

In other prison camps I had met most of the American doctors who were arriving at Omori for punishment. Major Berry had been in charge of one of our hospitals in O'Donnell Prison in the Philippines. He was tall and slim. He had a prematurely aged face, steady, hard eyes and tightly compressed lips. In Japan he was in charge of the medical work in a large prison camp in Hakodate, steel and shipping center at the tip of the main island of Hokkaido. He fought the Nips when they attempted to force sick men to go to work. He put continuous pressure on the Japs to improve the quality and quantity of the rations. He protested to the Nip C.O. about the beatings prisoners were receiving. He got beaten himself. He continued to protest. Working conditions and the health of the prisoners in Hakodate Prison slowly improved as a result of his efforts. Finally, after a last blowout, the Nip C.O. sent this solid citizen to Omori for punishment.

The stories told by peppery Dr. Price, captured in China; flatnosed Captain Shmayla, Lieutenant Robinson, whom I knew in the Philippines; and Australian Major Woodward fitted into the same general pattern, with different settings and different Nip C.O.'s. These doctors retained their mental equilibrium and their feeling of responsibility as physicians toward their fellow prisoners when it would have been easy and understandable to quit. They were whipped and beaten at Omori. Yet, when they were sent out again to do professional work, they continued to fight the Japs in their attempt to heal or protect the sick.

As more prisoners arrived from the Philippines after harrowing voyages in crowded prison ships, the size of the camp increased to seven hundred. One of the new arrivals was Captain D'Amor, a gentle-faced, bespectacled American doctor captured in Mindanao. When the Bird inspected his luggage, he found a poem in which the words "slant-eyed Jap" were written. In a towering rage, he beat D'Amor almost into insensibility. After that, D'Amor was a marked man, destined for the most exhausting, degrading physical labor and daily beatings. We pitied him. There was nothing we could do other than offer our sympathy. Our American and British prisoner administrative officers repeatedly protested to Colonel Sezuki, former chief of Omori, and leonine-faced, dumpy Colonel Sacaba, the present incumbent. The beatings continued. We prisoners receiving punishment could do no more than pray for the early arrival of the Yanks in Japan.

Another arrival was my old friend Captain Dan Golenternik of El Paso, Texas. I had left him in Cabanatuan Prison eight months ago, working on the farm with many other doctors. At that time, he was solid muscle and bone with well filled-out shoulders and arms.

I looked at him, eyes popping: "For Christ sake, Dan, what's happened to you?"

A slow smile drifted across his haggard face. His eyes were sunken, his Groucho Marx mustache a black smudge across his upper lip. Arms were spindly, abdomen and legs bloated with beriberi.

"After you left, Al, Cabanatuan went to hell quickly. The Nips got rougher and tougher. The chow for the workers was cut in half. Patients in the hospital got even less. You remember the old 'Dixie Action,' don't you, Al?"

I nodded. If prisoner Joe Blow wanted an extra day of rest, he paid one of his buddies 5 pesos ($2.50) to fall into the work detail in his place.

"Well," Dan smiled grimly, "the Dixie Action went into reverse. On our day of rest we got the same starvation ration as hospital patients, instead of a worker's ration. We actually paid five pesos to take the place of men who were scheduled to go out to work so that we could get a worker's ration.

"The Nips closed the commissary. We weren't able to buy any extra chow. They tightened up on the guards. It was practically impossible to smuggle in any food. The little that did come into the black market sold for impossible prices: one egg, banana or coconut went for a hundred pesos; a chicken sold for a thousand pesos.

"We ran out of medicine. Everybody developed beriberi."

"Were you able to keep in contact with the Manila underground, Dan?"

"For a while," Dan smiled grimly. "Then the Kempei Tei shook down the carabao drivers and found some notes on Threatt, the civilian. You remember him, don't you?" I nodded.

"Hell broke loose after that. They threw all men in contact with the underground into the brig: ex-Governor Rogers of Mindanao; Colonel Jack Schwartz of the hospital; Colonel Mack; your buddy, Chaplain Tiffany; Captain Jack LeMire of Little Baguio, and a number of others. The Nips thought they had discovered a spy ring. These Americans were beaten regularly. For months they slept on the floor without mosquito nets and blankets. They were given little water and less rice. They were still in the brig when this detail left Cabanatuan for Japan. We were glad to get out of that hellhole."

"What happened to the underground in Manila?"

"The Japs made a clean sweep, Al," he said grimly. "Father Budenbrook died in Fort Santiago dungeon. Lovely Pilar Campos and Screwball No. 1 and No. 3 were killed. Tony Escoda and his beloved wife had their heads cut off. Ramon Amusatagui and Mr. Joaquin Mencarini and his wife were murdered. High Pockets and Mrs. Utinsky are still alive in jail."

"What about Hanna?" I asked, heart pounding.

"I don't know what's happened to her, Al," he said slowly. "The Japs are on her trail."

"Is she alive?" I begged.

"I don't know."

I don't know. I don't know. I don't know. The words repeated themselves with maddening monotony.

A mother bent anxiously over her baby lying comatose on a hospital bed. It breathed jerkily, blowing bubbles of saliva through its parted lips. The door opened slowly as the doctor entered.

"Is my baby going to live?" she pleaded in a dry, husky voice.

He looked at the child. He looked at the mother gravely. "I don't know," he muttered.

A little, dried-up old lady was propped up in bed. Deep furrows of age lined her forehead, partially concealed by a straggling lock of gray hair. The left side of her face was ballooned out, paralyzed. Her left arm drooped limply on the coverlet, also paralyzed.

"I know I'm going to die," she whispered thickly through the right side of her face. "My husband died the same day he had a stroke. I'm not afraid. What I want to know is: Will I see my husband again after I die?"

She looked questioningly at the pastor of her church. He sat moodily, chin cupped in hand, staring at the floor. "I don't know," he muttered.

Hanna was young and resilient, filled with her love of life and my love for her. The memory of beatings, starvation, and fear would fade away. A new life in a new world was waiting to be born. Why should a rose be frosted in the bud? Why should a blade of grass be uprooted by a snarling dog digging for a bone? Why should her vibrant body be buried in the dhobie clay of the Philippines?

"Is she alive?" I asked Dan.

"I don't know," he muttered.

I don't know. I don't know. I don't know. The refrain repeated itself with maddening monotony.

For the first time since the surrender at Little Baguio, I heard news of my medic, Sergeant Joe Robertson, ex-trapper from Wyoming. He had escaped to Corregidor. Following the surrender of this island he went to work in Pasay Manila, the prison camp for the bone-breaking Nichols Field detail where hundreds of American prisoners had been worked to death building an airport under the broiling sun. For half a year there were two medics in that detail but no doctors or dentists. Robbie was one of them. He pulled teeth and filled cavities. He wangled small amounts of medical and surgical supplies from the visiting Jap doctor. He made ointments out of vaseline and cod-liver-oil pills. He stole bandages and gauze dressings. He improvised a stomach tube to feed powdered quinine to men comatose with cerebral malaria. He ground charcoal to make anti-diarrhea medicine. He gradually won the confidence of the Jap doctor and was permitted to keep from one hundred to one hundred and fifty prisoners resting in quarters.

Corporal Gorkowitz of D Battery, Two Hundredth Anti-aircraft, developed extensive infection of the leg and thigh. The Jap doctor wanted him transferred to the Japanese military hospital to have his leg amputated. Robbie talked him out of it. At night, without anesthesia or proper instruments, he operated on the leg. He made a first incision near the Achilles tendon. Ounces of thick yellow pus oozed out. Several parallel incisions in the calf of the leg yielded the same septic fluid. He nursed and dressed and coddled that leg. It healed after two months of constant treatment. The Nips finally sent a prisoner-doctor, Major Phillip Bress, into this camp. They beat and pistol-whipped him for demanding medicine for the sick. He was eventually killed.

At Omori the medical and dental setup wasn't bad.

Captain Goad, a pale-faced, long-suffering, much-beaten American had been doctoring in this camp for a couple of years. He took orders from a sadistic Nip medical orderly and from the Bird. This animal passed on all patients who Goad thought should be rested in quarters or hospitalized in a little shanty. With the right proportion of cunning, adroitness, and soft soap, he usually wheedled the necessary permission. If the proportion wasn't right, he and his patients got whipped. On alternate days, Major Berry ran the sick call while Goad did physical labor on the farm detail and vice versa.

There was plenty of Red Cross medicine in camp. The major problem was to get the Nips to release it. With Red Cross medicine and stolen food supplementing the Nip ration, the health of this camp remained unusually good.

We had a library made up of books brought in by the men and officers on their arrival, supplemented later on by Red Cross books. It was a blessing to be able to lose one's self in the adventures of Captain Hornblower and Oliver Wiswell.

The Britishers from Hong Kong had their musical instruments. There was a tall, sad-faced limey warrant officer who directed a little jazz band in the open, under the starlit sky. Hot trumpets blew, guitars strummed, and violins took up the melody while weary prisoners relaxed and dreamed of home and freedom. The Red Cross sent in an especially good electric phonograph with a fine collection of records, both jazz and classical. If the Bird was in a good humor, we got permission to play it. Some of the records that I heard for the first time in October, 1944, were "Queenie, the Strip-Tease," "Don't Sit Under the Apple Tree," and some harmony by the Andrews Sisters and Bing Crosby.

Two chaplains came into camp: kindly-faced, elderly Father Braun, who had been missionary to the Indians for twenty years before the war in Mescalero, New Mexico, and bald-headed young Father Bauman, a recent graduate of a seminary. When they were not doing physical labor or being beaten by the Bird, they held mass for Catholics and heavily attended nonsectarian services for the rest of us.

Our evening entertainment was cut short by roll call which took place at eight o'clock when the Jap officer of the day and his noncom inspected the barracks and counted noses. Some of these officers were all right. They went through the ceremony in a rapid, efficient manner. One whom we all admired was called "Gentleman Jim." Tall for a Nip, with finely molded features, straight nose and clear, unslanted brown eyes, he gravely listened to our reports and passed on to the next barrack. Our officers frequently protested to him against the abuse they received from the Bird. Spreading his hands helplessly, he pointed out that this animal received direct permission from Colonel Sacaba to punish prisoners as he saw fit. There was nothing he could do. Another whom we welcomed as O.D. was the "Marionette," a tiny, monkeylike Nip who walked and talked like a wooden puppet. He was always drunk on his night duty. He stumbled about, tripping on his long, two-handed sword. If he was especially drunk, he passed out cigars.

When the Bird took the duty, we all squared away for action. We scrubbed our hands and fingernails, put on our least tattered shirts and shorts and checked on our buttons. Hearts pounding, we waited for the storm to break. The officers in each barrack stood in one formation. The G.I.'s sat in their barrack on the first deck, hands spread on their knees, staring straight ahead, while a second row kneeled on the floor behind them. The Bird steamed into the building yelling, "Tenko (Roll Call)!"

"*Kyotski* (Attention)!" yelled our barrack leader, who bowed to the Bird and then barked rapidly: "*Soin roku mei* (Six men to be accounted for)."

"Jinko ni mei (Two men absent)." *"Ginsayen shi mei* (Four men present)." *"Bango* (Count off)!" We did, in Japanese. *"Jiko ichi mei shushin* (One man sick)." *"Jiko ichi mei shigoto* (One man working)." *"Ijo arimasen* (All present or accounted for)."

The Bird prowled about us, inspecting. He then went into the barrack where the G.I.'s went through the same procedure. Before he had checked all the barracks, hell usually broke loose. He had men standing at attention for hours; others he put to bowing to trees or sounding off in unison in Japanese. He personally whipped several before the evening was over. The camp sounded and looked as if it housed seven hundred crazy men.

In their usual superficial manner, the Nips had stringent orders for the prevention of fire, which they enforced cruelly.

On one hand, they had a great fear of fire; on the other hand, their building regulations permitted the erection of the flimsiest claptrap shacks piled one on top of the other. In Tokyo, electric wires, improperly insulated, were strung across the streets into paper-bamboo huts. They had few automatic pumping engines and even fewer water mains that could be tapped. To improve fire-fighting efficiency, home owners were compelled to organize into amateur fire-fighting units, using hand pumps, leaking hoses, and large wooden tubs as their main source of supply of water.

In prison camp, there were long pages of fire regulations which we had to memorize. Each barrack had a wooden tub holding about fifty gallons of water. Beside it were straw mats and mops with long bamboo handles. In case of fire, these were soaked in water and applied to a burning building. We drilled with a portable hand pump that had only a hundred feet of hose.

Fearing that we would burn the barracks, the Nips neither gave nor sold us any matches. Some of the prisoners rigged up little electric lighters which they plugged into the electric circuit. Others made flint and tinder sets, using an oily rag to catch the spark scraped from a bit of scrap metal by striking it with a rock. We were permitted to smoke only near a homemade ash tray which had some water in it.

Commander Blynn left his hut to procure a light. On his way back, he bumped into the Bird.

"You are smoking in the hallway!" he bellowed, his face darkening with anger.

"I've just got a light from a neighboring barrack, Mr. Watanabi," Blynnie said politely. "I'm on my way back to my hut to smoke."

Wham! Blynnie toppled to the ground, hit on the jaw by a haymaker. He struggled quickly to attention.

"You are disobedient!" the Bird shrieked, pounding Blynnie on the face steadily for fifteen minutes.

Puffing with exertion, he finally barked: "I want to see all officers!"

The dreaded shout, "Everybody out!" resounded through the compound. To us it had a blood-curdling quality because it meant that the Bird was on a rampage. We dreaded it. It meant group punishment or it meant being compelled to stand by helplessly while a brother officer was beaten to his knees. There is a peculiarly nauseating, infuriating quality about watching a beating, which is worse than being beaten.

We tumbled out on the double to arrange ourselves at attention in columns of four in front of the Bird's cage. He was sitting in it scowling.

"You have responded to the summons too slowly," he shouted, beating his desk with his fist. "Fall out until I summon you again."

We did. We came streaking out of our huts when the dreaded shout sounded through the air.

The Bird came out, face twitching with wrath. "I am sick and tired of your disobedience," he screamed. "You are insolent. You are arrogant. You are my prisoners. I am your disciplinarian. I shall kill you all if you disobey me again. Do you understand?"

"Hai!" we all shouted at the top of our lungs in the best Japanese military manner.

He walked up and down through our ranks, looking for a victim. Back and forth he prowled behind me. The hair prickled on the back of my neck. Standing stiffly, eyes staring ahead, hands pressed flat to our thighs, we waited for the "Bird" to spring and claw.

"Captain James!" the blood-curdling, furious words re-sounded. "Come forward."

An elderly British officer stepped out of the ranks, approached him, and saluted. He was thin, haggard, and white haired. He had spent many years in Japan in the import-export business. He knew the language and the customs of the Japs. He had retired to England about 1935 and had volunteered for service at the outbreak of the war. It was in Singapore that he had been captured.

Wham! James reeled to the ground as if he had been struck by lightning. "You did not have your hands pressed to your sides."

James struggled to his feet. "I thought—" he began.

Wham! "I do not care what you thought," the Bird screamed. He beat James until his face was a mass of bruised, torn flesh. There he lay on the ground, bleeding from ears and nose.

"Take him to the guardhouse, where he will stand at attention all night," he ordered.

We were finally permitted to break ranks about midnight. Sick with the horror of the spectacle, I was unable to sleep.

The next day Lieutenant Hankin of San Francisco, prisoner duty officer, came into the leather shop where I was working.

"Al," he said, "the Bird wants you on the double." Steeling myself for another whipping, I hurried to his office.

"How do you like this camp?" he said cunningly. I had seen him work this trap on others before. I knew the answers.

"It is clean and cool near the ocean," I answered politely.

"Would you like to go to another camp?" he queried, watching my face closely.

"I have many friends in this camp, Mr. Watanabi."

"Tonight you leave Camp Omori," he said.

Heart pounding, mad with joy, I packed my few belongings into a duffle bag.

CHAPTER 14
Mitsushima:
The Wily Bird Takes a Cure

I MADE THE ROUNDS SAYING good-bye to my friends. They gave me a rousing send-off.

"What a break, Al," Captain Nelson Kaufman, my fellow sufferer said wistfully. "I wish I was going with you."

They all would have given their right arm to get out of Omori.

I asked the Bird: "May I have my trunk with winter clothes that arrived here from Shinagawa?"

"No," he replied curtly, "you have enough."

"What about the pictures of my family and the censored Red Cross mail you took three months ago?"

"You will not need them," he said scowling. "Do not complain. I give you my last word of advice. If you are sent back from Mitsushima Prison because of arrogance or disobedience, you will not leave Omori alive."

I bowed and beat a hasty retreat.

Two Nip guards who had arrived from Mitsushima picked me up after supper. I left Omori dressed in a sun-bleached khaki shirt patched and repatched with its own sleeves and tails. I had a pair of G.I. khaki trousers trimmed down to shorts. The trouser legs were used to reinforce the seat. I had purchased these clothes in Manila in the spring of 1941. I wore a patched cotton flight jacket with a wool-cloth lining. I got this windfall from a Filipino patient in O'Donnell Prison in 1942 when he cut his throat with a mess-kit knife. On my head was a relic of Cabanatuan, a khaki fatigue cap with a new crown I had sewn with cloth from my trouser legs. On my stubby nose rested a pair of steel-rimmed glasses Hanna had smuggled into Cabanatuan before I left the Philippines. I was especially proud of a sturdy pair of Red Cross leather shoes with rubber soles I got during the Christmas of 1943.

I made a last trip to the latrine, passing the wooden night-soil dipper which I had learned to wield so expertly. With duffle bag on my shoulder, flanked by the two Jap guards, I walked out of Omori's wooden gates. As soon as they closed, the larger of the two Nips generously placed his huge bundle on my shoulders. I didn't give a damn. My heart sang its song of joy as we trudged through the deserted streets of Tokyo under the light of the full moon. My brain, battered by concussion in Bataan, the fall in O'Donnell when I broke my arm, and the Bird's clubbing in Omori confusedly repeated the same refrain: You're leaving Omori. No more whippings, no more night soil, no more leather shop, no more clothes washing, no more nerve-wracking mental torture, no more Bird!

The big Jap was Hiromatsui. I learned to know him as "Big Glass Eye" or the "Big Optic." In a China campaign he had lost an eye which was replaced with a poorly matched glass substitute. He was as tall as I, about five feet ten, with hard, clean-cut features masked by horn-rimmed glasses. He was muscularly built with powerful shoulders and arms. At Mitsushima he became steadily more vicious as the war progressed, beating prisoners with his fists at the slightest provocation. The little Nip was Nishi Gaki or the "Boy Scout" as we called him. After two years in the army, he was retired because of active tuberculosis of the lungs. He was tiny, with a little head drawn toward his shoulders, turtle fashion. He walked with his arms folded behind his back, little beady eyes darting about as he sized me up. I talked my pidgin Japanese, which put them in a good humor. I pumped them for information, cagily asking few direct questions to avoid arousing their suspicious natures.

"Mitsushima has the reputation of being a very efficient camp," I offered.

They beamed: "Yes, the two hundred American and British prisoners are well disciplined. They work very hard building dams and tunnels."

"They have very few accidents," I said.

"Very few," Nishi Gaki lied. He was in charge of the medical work in Mitsushima. "We had a very good Japanese doctor at the company hospital near the camp but he has been called to the army."

"And now the American prisoner doctor does the surgery," I added.

"He is not an American and he is not a surgeon. That is why you are being sent to us from Omori."

The light began to dawn in my rice brain. Cause and effect: a Jap doctor leaves Mitsushima for the army; I leave Omori for Mitsushima.

About midnight we took the steam train which moved southward from Tokyo toward the metropolis of Nagoya. It was packed with frowsy, blue-pantalooned women, with flat-faced babies strapped to their backs. There were elderly men dressed in black shabby clothes bearing enormous bundles of house furnishings. By military order, the nonessential population of Tokyo was being evacuated. Through the starlit night we rode. I held the guards' rifles while they nestled their heads on my shoulders and fell fast asleep. As dawn broke, we transferred to a narrow-gauge electric railroad that left the coastal plain twenty miles north of Nagoya and headed west into the mountains. While my mouth watered, the Japs breakfasted on some steamed rice balls the size of an indoor baseball. The Boy Scout broke down finally. He gave me his unfinished portion wrapped in that day's Japanese newspaper. I wolfed the rice greedily and folded the newspaper, putting it in my pocket.

"Toilet paper," I said. They nodded.

The air grew colder as we wove through the mountain gorges, following the course of a river which narrowed as we climbed.

The scenery resembled the North Georgia Mountains with towering evergreen firs and pines and hardwood trees gaily colored with their autumnal foliage. It was rugged country, cold country. I shivered in my shorts. The train stopped at dreary little villages with their conglomeration of unpainted houses that had no chimneys. I learned later that in peacetime these huts were heated by tiny charcoal-burning braziers. During the war, however, they remained unheated. Only enough charcoal was issued to expedite cooking. Troops of schoolboys dressed in semi-military clothing boarded the train. They crowded in, chattering gaily until they spotted the guards. Then they came stiffly to attention and saluted, hissing "Oss" between their teeth (Most honorable greetings). The train sounded as if it were full of snakes.

The mountain slopes grew steeper. We left the winding river. We headed west through an interminable series of tunnels and over trestle bridges which crossed breathtaking canyons, until we reached another winding river. The train crawled along its narrow roadbed gouged out of sheer cliffs, the silvery stream far below. It came to a slow halt at a railroad station cut into the slope of the mountain. The station sign read "Mitsushima."

The village was a cluster of single and double-story wooden shacks fronting a narrow unpaved street which wound about the face of a mountain heavily coated with evergreens. Most of the stores were closed. The few that were open sold no clothes or food. Only a barbershop with trousered women barbers was doing a rushing business. A long queue of weary-faced women waited passively before a warehouse to receive their monthly issue of rice, barley, millet, and soybeans. They bowed humbly to the police officers guarding the warehouse before they departed, clattering down the streets in their high, stilt-like wooden sandals. A crowd of snotty-nosed children in cotton-padded, silk-covered coats which reached to their knees gazed at me curiously, pointing to my Red Cross brassard and identification tag which gave my name and nationality in Kata Kana (Japanese script). They mouthed the strange-sounding name written in phonetics: *"Waeensutaeen,"* nodding to each other happily when I told them they were correct. It was exciting to see the smiling faces of children after a lapse of more than two years.

Far below the village on the banks of the river was a narrow strip of man-made sandy land as long as a football field and half as wide. It was crowded with buildings: four standard-size, two-decker wooden barracks with broken glass windows; the Jap administration building with its "Fried Egg" flag waving in the breeze; a shack from which a wisp of smoke plumed (the galley); two open latrines, and a small building which the Jap guards said was the dispensary. These buildings were surrounded by a ten-foot-high clapboard fence.

"Not much room to move around in," I thought.

There was a hundred-yard-long suspension bridge which crossed the swirling river adjacent to it. On the opposite slope was a sheer concrete facing through which the exits of two huge tunnels stared blindly. We eased our way down a steep ramp that descended from the station to the camp below, stepping on the wooden ties of a railroad track it supported.

I was brought in to see the camp commandant, Lieutenant Kubo. He was a short Jap with close-clipped hair, slightly slanted eyes, and a deadpan face. I learned later that he was a university graduate who had worked as a lawyer in the Tokyo city government. After several years of fighting in China he received a serious chest wound. Shortly before my arrival, the Jap military assigned him for duty to the prison camp. With him was the camp interpreter, Mr. Machida, the "Goon," born and raised in Sacramento, California. He was a sneaky, round-faced Nip who groveled. One of his eyes was blind and deviated laterally.

After studying my dossier, Lieutenant Kubo said: "You have been sent from Omori where you were held for refusing to cooperate with the Japanese military authority. What has happened in the past is no affair of mine. You will do professional work with Dr. Whitfield, the British doctor in this camp. Do your best to maintain the health of your brother prisoners. That is all."

"Sounds like a good Nip," I said to myself as I bowed my way out.

He was. Dr. Whitfield and I had many conferences with him concerning the health of our men. We always found him receptive to suggestions. He often helped. When he didn't, we knew his hands were tied by the Japanese prison authorities in Tokyo. I never saw him cuss a prisoner or beat him. He was scrupulously honest in the distribution of Red Cross food parcels that came into camp before Christmas, 1944. He made every effort to get us Red Cross medicine from Shinagawa; usually unsuccessfully. He disapproved of corporal punishment. He helped us when we protested the beatings men were receiving from the guards.

There were two especially vicious customers in camp, the "Snake" and "Buick," the latter so-called because he wore an emblem on his hat that looked like the Buick auto emblem. The Snake was wiry and hyperactive; almost white skinned with deeply sunken eyes and thin nose. The prisoners were supposed to dress themselves completely before they went to the latrine. During the winter, for some reason I still don't understand, we found it necessary to urinate four to ten times a night. Undoubtedly this bladder irritability was caused by the deficiency of one or several vitamins. Obviously it wasn't practicable to dress or undress from soup to nuts all night and get any sleep. The Snake hid out behind the barracks when he was night guard to apprehend any partially dressed prisoners. He caught plenty of fish, whipped them with his fists or a bamboo pole, and stood them at attention in the bitter cold for hours.

Buick was another hero cut from the same cloth. He was painfully ugly with hooded slit eyes, flat nose, protuberant lips and splay feet. During the winter it was cold: ten to twenty degrees below freezing. There was no heat in the clapboard barracks through which the wind whistled shrilly. We slept in four shoddy cotton blankets which we made into a bedroll. There were two types, folded in different patterns. We referred to them as the "French whore" and the "Russian whore." I've seen prisoners come to blows arguing the heating virtues of one over the other. We slept on the wooden floor, through which a cold draft poured. To avoid frostbite, men pooled their blankets to make a pallet for two or three. It really made a difference. But it didn't appeal to Buick, who sneaked through the barracks when he was on night duty, checking on bedding. Screaming at the top of his lungs, he beat and pounded the culprits who were huddled together for warmth. This brave man fainted when he came into the dispensary one day to have a bruised finger dressed. Amidst the roaring laughter of prisoners and Japs, we carried him back to his quarters on our homemade bamboo and straw-rope litter.

I met Dr. Richard Whitfield, British Naval Reserve, captured in Hong Kong. He was a tall slender man with thin hair, over-hanging bushy eyebrows, large, soft brown eyes, and a long, delicately modeled nose with a fine pointed tip which wriggled like a rabbit's when he was deep in thought. Oxford graduate, captain of the crew, graduate of Saint Mary's Hospital in London, he was a splendid physician, a leader of men, and a student of Nipponese psychology. He was one of the first Allied prisoners in Japan. For a year he fought Colonel Sezuki, commandant of all prisoners in the Tokyo area. He fought Dr. Tokuda in Shinagawa. By direct protest, written and verbal, flattery, passive resistance, and active thievery, he was able to procure some medicine for his sick and dying brother prisoners—but not enough. More than two hundred died in Shinagawa during the first year of captivity. After a strongly worded letter of protest to Colonel Sezuki, he was made to apologize for his "arrogance." He was then railroaded to Mitsushima.

I told Dick of my experiences with the Spider and the Bird. He told me of the merry-go-round he had been on.

"Before I came to this camp," he said in his crisp British accent, "there were a hundred British and a hundred Chinese prisoners in Mitsushima, all captured in Singapore. They were building a huge hydroelectric dam across the river and blasting two thirty-foot-wide tunnels a mile long which led from the dam site through the base of a mountain to the generating plant erected at the outlets you can see from here. These men had been starved for months in prison camps in Singapore. They were fed almost a pure carbohydrate diet: rice and barley, with little vegetables and less fish. Throughout the winter, clad in ragged clothes and shod in torn tabbies (rubber sneakers with a split toe), they worked in the river, shoveling sand and gravel into toros (flat cars mounted on rails). They pushed them wearily up a grade and dumped them into huge revolving metal barrels which separated the sand from the rock. They blasted those tunnels, clearing the debris with pick and shovel. They mixed cement, concreted the tunnels, and laid the foundations of the dam. With them worked many hundreds of Koreans from early morning to late at night. They were whipped by the guards if they slowed down."

"How often did they get a rest day?" I asked. This sounded like a worse setup than the farm at Cabanatuan.

"Theoretically, one day out of every ten," he replied grimly. "Actually, they worked on this rest day carrying wood and rations from the railroad station, scrubbing the barracks, policing the grounds, enlarging the camp by hauling rocks from the river-bed, delousing and patching their clothing. Then they would have rested if the guards weren't in and out of the barracks badgering or beating them."

"For what?"

"For failing to rise en masse to bow when a guard came in; for smoking several paces from an ash tray; for having no buttons on their shirts and rents in their trousers; for the fun of it," he said thoughtfully, his nose twitching.

"Were there any docs in camp?"

"There was one, a Dutch Javanese half-breed who knew no medicine. He was deathly afraid of the Japs. He was so ignorant that he was even afraid to use the few drugs he had. He had some sulfathiazole pills but the bloody fool didn't use them on his pneumonia cases because he didn't know how. The medical orderlies stole and administered them. Fifty men died of beriberi, starvation, dysentery, pneumonia, and beatings during that first winter," he said slowly.

"How did they get rid of the Dutchman?" I asked.

"An inspection party came from Tokyo. Private First Class Bob Jones, a chunky Welshman whom you'll meet, took one of them into the 'hospital' and showed him the sick and dying. It was even too much for the Japs. The Dutchman and the Nip C.O. got the axe. Lieutenant Kubo and I arrived in camp just about the time the Chinese prisoners living here were sent away. A hundred Americans who had worked themselves to skin and bone in a copper mine up north were sent here for a rest," he smiled, his generous lips spreading across his face.

"Did they get it?"

"By no means. They're doing the same work as the Englishmen who stayed behind."

"Is there much sickness in camp now?" I asked.

"Plenty. After they were captured in Singapore, the British prisoners now in camp worked for a year building a railroad through Thailand to Burma. More than twenty thousand of them died of cholera, malaria, and starvation. The survivors all have recurrent malaria. Most of the Americans in camp have chronic dysentery, probably of the amoebic type," he said, crossing his long legs.

Visions of the O'Donnell Prison stinkpot swept through my mind.

"How are you fixed for medicine, Dick?"

"The little that we have is Jap stuff, which is unstandardized and usually ineffective. We got a little Red Cross medicine which is all gone now. If it wasn't for the Boy Scout we'd be in one hell of a mess. He's temperamental and needs careful handling, but he's kindhearted and industrious. We've taught him a lot about disease. He's my boss and your boss. We can't rest anybody in quarters or put them in the hospital without his permission. If handled carefully he usually strings along with my suggestions and those of Corporal Bullock, our British medical orderly. About once a week he travels to the neighboring city of Eeda to buy medical supplies in the open market: Spranchin for diarrhea, sodium bicarbonate, and ointments. Occasionally, he's able to pick up some vitamins and sulfathiazole pills," he finished.

I laid out all my worldly goods on a little shelf one foot by three feet. I sprawled on the floor in the tiny eight-by-ten-foot room which was to be our home and fell into a sound slumber, shoes tucked under my head, filthy blanket wrapped around my body.

I absorbed the routine of the camp quickly. Our meals came at seven o'clock, noon, and six o'clock, and consisted of an almost indigestible rubbery mass of steamed barley, millet, and a little rice. This combination gave me chronic diarrhea as long as I was at Mitsushima. About twice a week we got a piece of dried fish, herring size, or some soybeans in our barley mix. This was our only source of protein. When Irish potatoes came in, they were substituted by weight for the grain. Since potatoes are two-thirds water, this was the equivalent of cutting our diet by two-thirds. When fresh fish came in, it had deteriorated during transport. We buried it to prevent starving men from eating it. Our vegetables were essentially dikons which were cubed and steamed with the grain. They had a slimy, nauseating taste. For soup we used the bitter green tops of the dikons boiled with mizo (soy-bean paste), which was valuable only because of its high salt content.

During the winter when vegetables were not available, our soups were made of seaweed—shredded or in whole dry leaves—and a pickled fibrous stalk we called "mountain weed." The latter caused so much diarrhea that we also buried it when the Nips issued it from their storeroom. Dikons and pumpkin stored through the winter spoiled so that we had to bury them. We tried feeding them to our two stunted pigs. They weren't interested. Once a month we got seventy pounds of meat and bones which came in from a local slaughterhouse. The Nips stole most of the meat. The bones were covered with a green scum which the cooks scrubbed off with homemade brushes and then soaked overnight in an antiseptic, potassium permanganate, before they boiled them for soup.

After breakfast, Dick and I held sick call for men retained in quarters. We then treated our hospital patients.

They lay huddled in their rags and misery on the straw mat-covered floor. Of two hundred men in camp; between twenty and thirty were seriously ill daily during the winter of 1944 with beriberi, dysentery, malaria, and pneumonia. In addition to these medical cases, there were many accident cases. We cleansed their wounds and covered the lesions with paper which we stuck to the skin with tarlike ointment. Only the most serious injuries received a little of our precious hoard of dressings and gauze bandages.

About ten o'clock, administrative officers Lieutenant John Dunlop and Captain Rhyss, Dick, several light-duty men and I carried the noonday ration out to the work details. The steamed grain was weighed out in buckets which were carried on bamboo poles. In the autumn, when the foliage was turning red and orange, it was a revivifying experience to leave behind the dreary confines of the camp and head out into the mountains without Nip guards. For two hours we felt like free men, swinging along the road cut into the mountain slope, breathing deeply of the crisp invigorating air.

As we passed clusters of men working they straightened their weary backs and asked: "What's the 'point' (ration), Doc? Any news in camp?"

We dropped our buckets at a lean-to where the prisoner work leader carefully extracted the steamed grain from its bucket with a rice paddle. He transferred it to the prisoners' lunch boxes called bentoes, which were little wooden boxes about the size of women's jewelry boxes . While this went on, Dick and I walked through twisting mountain paths beside gurgling brooks, discussing the news or planning a new campaign for more food and less work. Back to camp we strolled, refreshed by our walk, the empty buckets swinging freely from the bamboo pole carried on our shoulders.

The men were scattered about the countryside working on various details known to us by the name of the subcontractors for a hydroelectric construction company, Oiwa, Iwatia, Igarashi, and Kamijo. When the snow fell and the frost settled in the rigors of a mountain winter, I preferred to go to Oiwa on my ration run. There the coke blast furnace burned merrily. There was a small group of Americans working on this detail as machinists, repairing cement mixers and blowers. It was a good detail because the owner. Mr. Oiwa, furnished the prisoners an extra ration of rice and vegetables for their noonday meal. He was a middle-aged, smiling-faced Jap who usually wore a sport jacket. He was probably typical of hundreds of thousands of small-time businessmen ground between the wheels of war. He disapproved of the war and prayed for its early termination.

Patting me on the back he murmured daily: *"Mo sukoshi senso owari* (Soon the war will be over and you will go home)."

As the winter months progressed, more and more of his Jap machinists were called up for service, including dumpy, chubby-faced "Muscle Brain," the twenty-year-old blacksmith. He was a cheerful, happy-go-lucky, stupid youngster who had very little schooling.

He asked Jack Bailey, Shanghai marine: "Why do you call me 'Muscle Brain'?"

Jack replied slyly: "Because your brain is as strong as your muscles."

The Nip beamed. He was never anti-American.

Even sour-pussed "Sugar Boy," the foreman, lost his bushido as the war progressed. He softened up and shined up to the prisoners. "Blinky," the little one-eyed, prematurely aged gnome who worked at the forge, had no love for the Jap military and industrial slavery under which he had lived and labored. Blind socket staring ahead, he told me his troubles in whispers. His father had been a peasant, a rice farmer tilling a little acreage with the help of his wife and children. With heavy taxes, high monopoly prices for fertilizer, and inability to pay the exorbitant interest rates on money borrowed when harvests were poor, his father lost his farm to his mortgager. He became a sharecropper, paying an annual rent of 50 to 60 per cent of his rice yield. Out of his share he had to buy seed, farm tools, fertilizer, and food for his family. Unable to feed and clothe his growing children, he apprenticed his sons to a steel mill. There Blinky worked for years as an indentured laborer-mechanic, receiving only his maintenance until his "training" was completed. He worked as a blacksmith at a lower than subsistence salary, until he was fired after losing an eye and smashing his hands in a factory accident. Two of his sons had been soldiers. They were killed somewhere in the South Pacific. His last boy, a stripling of seventeen, was being called up in January, 1945, to enter the air corps.

His good eye misting, he said: "They will give him a little airplane. He will ride happily through the skies until a B-29 shoots him down."

Blinky was not sullen with the American prisoners because of his losses. He fed the group working in his shop even after he was ordered by the military to cease. He got beaten twice for feeding them. He continued to feed them. He prayed for the defeat of Japan. He prayed for a new Japan where the farmer could buy his own land at reasonable terms from absentee owners; where the mechanic would get a living wage and be permitted to form unions and bargain collectively; where the little businessman like Oiwa would not be driven out of the field by the monopolies of Mitsui and Mitsubishi. He prayed for a democratic Japan.

After lunch Dick and I rested until the men shambled back from work. Then sick call took place. With few exceptions the prisoners who attended sick call would all have been hospital cases by American standards. Seated on either side of the Boy Scout we checked through a long line of sick, emaciated, hungry men. The Boy Scout had a tough job. If he admitted too many men into the hospital, the work sheet submitted monthly to Tokyo would show an alarming drop in the number of man-days lost. He would get torn off a strip (bawled out) by headquarters. If he didn't admit them to the hospital, we raised hell with him. Either way, he couldn't win. He compromised by having patients requiring hospitalization put on a temporary light-duty status in camp doing chores.

On the work sheets they were carried full duty. Where we disagreed, we took the patient's temperature with a phony thermometer which always registered two degrees higher than normal. Like most Japs the Boy Scout placed more dependence on a mechanical means of determining sickness than the prison doctors' diagnostic ability. He then consented to the patient's admission to the hospital.

After sick call was finished we prepared for the second roll call and nose-counting ceremony held in the quadrangle facing the Nipponese headquarters buildings. The morning procedure was cursory; the prisoners had to go to work. The evening one was long, tiring, and dangerous, with the senior Jap "administrators" officiating. Because of physical disability they had been retired from the army and given prison jobs. We feared Tsuchia ("Little Glass Eye"), Hiromatsui ("Big Glass Eye"), Matsuzaki ("Scar-face"), and Komura (the "Punk") in that order. They were the whippers and the sluggers. Senior Sergeant Aria could be handled with flattery. Nishino ("One Arm"), the last of the group of "administrators," was a steady, kindly Nip who always conducted a peaceful roll call. The interpreter Machiria, the Goon, was always present to add to the confusion.

The men lined up in columns of four, in two companies. The officers lined up separately. The Nip duty non-com strutted through from the administration building.

Captain Rhyss spluttered loudly, clacking his false teeth, "*Kyotski* (Attention) !" We stood stiffly, eyes front.

"*Nichoko dono ni karay* (Turn your head and look at the most honorable duty noncommissioned officer)!" Rhyss and the slopehead saluted each other.

Officers and the two enlisted men's barracks then reported those present, those absent, and why they were absent—all in Japanese. Then the fun began with the O.D. inspecting the men.

"Jacket not buttoned." *Wham!*

"Hands not flattened to the sides." *Smack!*

"Chewing tobacco." *Crack!*

"Clothes not washed." *Smash!*

After this came a long speech. Each O.D. had his pet peeve which he expanded upon lengthily while men exhausted from long hours of toil stood shivering in the cold. The Goon did the interpreting.

"Tenko (roll call) is a solemn ceremony. It is a solemn salute to the emperor. When you appear at this formation with clothes unclean, torn, and unbuttoned, you are disrespectful and must be punished." The men had no soap, buttons or patching material. "It has been reported that the men are not saluting properly." Then came a tedious demonstration of a salute. Each Nip saluted differently. "The prisoners do not bow correctly." Another demonstration. "There are too many accidents. Men who have accidents will be punished. Your clothes are not folded neatly in the barracks. Refold them tonight. I shall inspect."

On and on the same phonograph record went for ten months. I learned to repeat these speeches in Japanese and English.

The formation finally ended with a round of salutes. We returned to our quarters to wolf the stingy evening meal which we topped off with some unsweetened black tea we purchased intermittently from the Nips.

We could buy no food or clothes. Officers received $10 a month, noncoms about $8, and G.I.'s $3. Theoretically we received two cigarettes a day. Actually, we were fortunate to get any except through the black market. Occasionally the prisoners were able to buy third-quality Jap cigarettes for ten yen a package from their Jap foremen. When even these were no longer available, we bought pine needles wrapped in cigarette paper. A more economical form of smoking (ten yen for two ounces) was "hair tobacco." This was barley straw chopped up fine and soaked in a tobacco-juice extract. We smoked it in iron pipes something like an opium pipe with a tiny metal bowl.

There was no food to steal on any of the work details except the station detail which handled freight: steel and sacks of cement for the dam, food for Mitsushima Village. The ringleaders were Private First Class Carl Wurtz, a husky Marine from Chicago; R.A.F. Sergeant Fullock, a fighting cock from England; two-fisted Jock Webster of Scotland, and Private First Class Joe Diaz, a Filipino born in Singapore. When rice flour arrived on the freight trains, they stole sacks of it. They transferred the contents into paper cement bags for camouflage. In the center of a huge pile of cement sacks in the warehouse they built a little cave large enough to hold two men and their booty. In it they built an oven and baked rice bread. Heavy as it was without shortening, it was more digestible than the steamed barley mix. They stole rice, using a "shooter," a hollow piece of bamboo sharpened at one end. Angulating it after it was driven into a straw rice sack, the rice grains slithered into containers in a steady stream. They learned this trick from the Jap freight handlers.

In the evening, joined by tall, blond-mustachioed Cambridge graduate Lieutenant John Dunlop, we talked about food, or rather the lack of it; an endless subject of conversation in all prison camps: meals we had eaten, meals we wanted to eat; how best to prepare steak, lobster, and chicken; comparison between British and American food; warm beer versus cold beer; "bitters" versus charged beer. We tortured ourselves masochistically. It was impossible to keep our thoughts away from the subject. Every fiber of our bodies cried out for food.

We talked endlessly about the war. John was an excellent cartographer. With scraps of maps found in a few old history books sent in by the Japanese Y.M.C.A., he constructed world maps in which he plotted the course of global warfare. The Goon had an excellent Webster dictionary with a gazetteer of cities and rivers which he had brought from California. John borrowed it from him to spot on his maps new islands and cities as they appeared in the Jap newspapers.

The news coverage was good. There were two prison camps in the vicinity which housed Chiang Kai-shek's captured Chinese troops. They worked on the same work projects as our men. Although forbidden to converse with them, it wasn't long before our men found a few English-speaking Chinese. Private First Class Ken Marshall, clarinet player par excellence from the Cabanatuan jazz band, arrived in Mitsushima. While in Shanghai with the Marines he had learned to speak Chinese fluently. It wasn't long before he was relaying news from his Chinese friends on the job. We got Jap newspapers from various sources. Stocky, forty-year-old Welsh Bob Jones stole some from the Nip headquarters. Carl

Wurtz and Jock Webster lifted them from the village near the freight yards. Blinky in the Oiwa machine shop saved them for us. Jack Bailey, a philosophy-reading Shanghai Marine, carried them in his shoes from Oiwa into Mitsushima.

In camp the newspapers were read by our medic, Corporal Bullock and "Hopalong" Hanson, a young Chinese lad captured in Singapore. He had fractured his thigh bone on the job two years ago. Treated by a Jap "bone specialist," his injured leg became two inches short. He and Private First Class Willie Myer of Baltimore were our camp cobblers. John Dunlop and "Pinky" Williams, both of whom read Kata Kana and Hira Gana (Japanese script), ground their brains into mush figuring out the news.

We also got news by messenger from Tokyo in this fashion.

We never had enough medicine. We could not buy any in the village drugstore. The Boy Scout took me frequently to the two tiny company hospitals in the village where I was able to scrounge only small amounts of medicine from a sad-faced overworked Jap civilian doctor and his two modest but ugly nurses, one of whom had a face full of freckles. To add to our medical supplies, Dick and I plotted to send patients to Shinagawa Hospital in Tokyo for diagnosis or treatment every month. The Boy Scout didn't object. We were able to get permission from the Jap C.O., Lieutenant Kubo, to do so. Returning from Shinagawa, these patients brought lifesaving medical supplies sewn into their clothes: sulfa drugs, amoebic dysentery pills, morphine, codeine, and surgical catgut—supplies worth their weight in gold. In addition they brought a transcript of the month's news, both global and local, from Lieutenant Jim Davis in Shinagawa.

At the end of May, 1945, when a hundred British prisoner officers arrived in camp, quiet, scholarly, pallid-faced Lieutenant Henderson came with them. During his captivity he learned to speak, read, and write Nippongo (Japanese picture writing) fluently. From his translations we got not only the war news but also the political speeches of the Nips printed in their newspapers. Through Henderson we first heard of the United Nations

Conference in San Francisco and the terms of the Potsdam Conference.

With the help of the Goon's Webster gazetteer, John laboriously plotted Allied advances on his homemade maps.

We learned of the capture of Warsaw by the Russians and their drive in January, 1945, to Frankfurt on the Oder, two hundred and seventy-five miles west of Warsaw. We cheered the "Russkies" when they took Budapest in February and Vienna in April. In the West we heard of the German attacks on London, using their V-1 and V-2 flying bombs. Late into the night in the barracks and in our quarters did arguments rage about the nature and construction of these instruments of death. The paltry descriptions given in the Nip papers were totally inadequate to give us much help. We sweated out the Battle of the Bulge, trying to discount the exaggerated reports of Allied disaster in the Nip papers. We prayed that action in the West would not settle down to a slow trench warfare as it did in World War I. When the Rhine was crossed in February, we were delirious with joy. The war against Germany would be over in weeks, we were sure.

We whooped when General Patton's Third Army made its wild dash across southern Germany. According to the Nip papers he remained stalled for weeks at a point north of the second 'd' in Darmstadt on our homemade maps.

Jokingly Dick said: "The boys have taken time off to relax in the company of convenient blondes in that city." As the weeks went by and Patton's army was still stalled in this sector, German blondes became actual, living personalities in our fevered imaginations. We cussed them; we described their ancestors in long, lurid oaths; we exhorted the G.I.'s that there were more attractive brunettes in Vienna.

In the Orient we heard of the opening of the Lido Road in northern Burma. We followed the great Allied offensive which terminated in the fall of Rangoon in March, 1945. We were hysterical when the news broke about the landing in Lingayen Bay, Luzon, in the Philippines in January, 1945. We were reborn when sketch maps of Bataan Peninsula appeared in the newspapers. Our forces were only seventeen hundred miles from Tokyo. We expected the next attack on the Japanese mainland. We were heartbroken when the Yanks stopped off to clean up Iwo Jima in February and Okinawa in April, 1945.

Shortly after my arrival in Mitsushima we made a pool, contributing one cigarette for each prediction on the capture of various cities and islands during 1945. Dick, the treasurer, paid off when the events took place. I lost all my predictions but won a twenty-five-dollar wager. In December, 1944, I bet him that the Japs would surrender within three to six months after the fall of Germany. Following the destruction of the Nip Navy, Air Force, and industrial centers, I hoped for the capitulation of a home-defense army made up of third-rate troops and high-school recruits. I felt that the cream of the Jap armies had already been destroyed or were isolated in China, Manchuria, Malaya, and in island outposts.

We prayed for a surrender. If an invasion of Japan took place, we all expected to be slaughtered. This thought preyed upon our minds day and night as we struggled to live on a constantly diminishing dietary.

In December, 1944, work on the dam had ceased. There was no more reinforcing steel and cement available. The prisoners continued to work dismantling, storing, and repairing equipment: cement mixers, blowers, dynamos, and cement chutes. About a hundred and fifty went into the mountains twice a day where trees were being felled. They returned after a round trip up and down hill toting logs weighing sixty to a hundred and fifty pounds. After several weeks of this backbreaking labor on starvation rations practically everybody in camp developed severe beriberi, swelling of the face, abdomen and legs, partial paralysis of the extremities, increasing blindness, and cardiac failure.

Dick and I had a series of conferences with Lieutenant Kubo. We pointed out the necessity of more food and medicine and less work if these men were to live. While these talks were going on, three men died of sudden heart failure due to beriberi. We made a beriberi survey of the camp. Of two hundred men and officers, a hundred and eighty-five had extensive clinical evidence of this disease. Forty of these, including myself, showed weakening of the heart. Lieutenant Kubo was impressed. In Tokyo he got permission to increase our food ration by a third, upping the caloric intake from fifteen hundred to two thousand calories daily. Although this diet was still grossly inadequate, quantitatively and qualitatively, for men doing heavy physical labor, this positive effort on his part saved many lives. He also got permission to employ the weaker men in weaving rope, hampers, boots, and raincoats out of straw. We put the forty beriberi cardiacs on this job.

Sitting on their butts in the fireless work barracks, these miserable men worked with their frozen fingers throughout the winter while they rested their weary hearts. Stronger men were employed salvaging equipment on the dam site. A squad of the strongest continued to tote logs, chop wood, and handle the trickle of freight that came into the railroad station. We pleaded with Lieutenant Kubo for more Red Cross medicine from Shinagawa. He arranged for the arrival of sacks of rice polishings which contained some vitamin B. We issued several ounces of this and a cup of brew made by fermenting rice flour and a little sugar with yeast to all our beriberi cases.

Dr. Fugi from Shinagawa came to camp on an inspection tour.

He greeted me cordially, laughing boisterously. "You remember the licking I gave you?"

"Yes, Dr. Fugi, I shall always remember you. So will these prisoners with beriberi remember you if you send them some vitamin capsules," I said smiling.

With soft soap and guile, Dick and I worked him over. He sent several thousand Red Cross vitamin B capsules.

We had one more beriberi death. Our cardiac patients in the straw shop were protected against physical labor by a small patch of red cloth sewn over their hearts. During Lieutenant Kubo's absence, feminine-acting Sergeant Aria pulled them all out of the straw shop. He lined them up ready to depart for the mountains to return with loads of wood. Dick and I got the word. We dashed out on the double.

"Sergeant Aria," Dick said smoothly, "these men, as you know, have beriberi heart disease."

"Yes, yes," the slopehead said, gesticulating gracefully, "I know. They have had a long rest. Now they can work."

"If they work, they die," I interrupted.

He became angry. "I am in charge of this camp. They do what I say."

Seeing that we were fighting a losing battle, Dick said soothingly: "Of course, you are in charge of this camp. These men work when you order them. They rest when you order them. Order the six weakest men back to work in the straw shop."

Pirouetting like a ballet dancer in a sulky mood, he said, "*Ush.*"

Dick and I went into a huddle and made our selections.

The rest of the cardiac cripples went out to labor. Soft-spoken Private B. E. Williams of Texas returned. He was carried back from the work detail in cardiac collapse, his face purple, his heart ticking faintly.

"Take it easy, Williams," I comforted, as he was laid on the hospital floor. "You'll be O.K."

"Don't kid me, Doc," he whispered, smiling wanly, "and don't waste any medicine on me. I'm cashing in my chips."

We gave him stimulants. We injected the last of our Red Cross vitamin B we had smuggled from Shinagawa. He died two hours later in the arms of our Limey medic, Hector Hart.

When Lieutenant Kubo returned to camp we reported the murder. Aria was scolded. He didn't pull the same Nip trick again. We also reported Buick for allegedly breaking a prisoner's eardrum. He had beaten a prisoner into insensibility but actually he hadn't broken his eardrum. I falsified the charge, however, by withdrawing some blood from the prisoner's arm and injecting it into his ear canal. When Lieutenant Kubo saw the blood trickling out of the prisoner's ear he was impressed. We reported the Snake for kicking a prisoner in the ribs. These two sadists were properly ticked off and warned by Kubo that they would be discharged if they were reported again for brutality. They behaved themselves for months thereafter.

Kubo, however, would not or could not exercise the same control over the "administrators" as he did over the guards. Little Glass Eye, in charge of quartermaster stores, was a vicious, easily excitable little devil who stole as much Red Cross clothing as he could lay his hands on. With their swollen feet, the prisoners found it was difficult to get shoes large enough to fit them properly. Little Glass Eye literally beat the prisoner into accepting small ones when they objected to the small sizes. The Punk, in charge of the kitchen, was almost as bad. Pig-faced, with squint, beady eyes, he stole our food supplies for the use of his family and friends. The only whipping I got in Mitsushima was from his fists—for "not saluting properly."

What troubled me more than hunger, homesickness, and whippings was the cold. Kubo unsuccessfully tried to get my winter clothes from the Bird in Camp Omori. He refused to send them. Little Glass Eye would not issue any new ones. I got a few clothes from Dick Whitfield and from the cooks: ex-pugilist, broken-nosed Private First Class Jim Bittner; Corporal George Piel of New Orleans, and the happy-go-lucky ex-hobo Lobe from all parts west of Chicago. I made a pair of little "booties" from some rags. Filipino Joe Diaz stole some paper cement bags which I wove into my "French whore" to break the breeze flowing through the shoddy blankets. At night I crawled into it on the floor, fully clothed, with a Red Cross lumberman's hat pulled over my ears. Dick and I put sawdust under the straw mats and sealed the cracks in the clapboard walls with strips of paper. I was still frozen. In the kitchen fire Lobe heated a round rock which I rolled between my blankets. That helped more than anything else. We got a load of straw to spread on the floor of our hospital. We got some old papers and made rice flour and water glue to cover the walls. Our convalescent patients who were on work details ate more of the glue than they used for the wallpaper. We papered the barracks. We were still cold.

Regardless of the weather, winter does not begin officially in Japanese military installations until January 4. Although it was well below freezing in December, we could not get them to issue winter clothing or permit fires until that date. Thereafter, we kept a wood fire burning in the hospital day and night. In our examining room we built an open wood fire on a concrete block during sick call. There was no stove, no chimney. In the barracks, a similar open fire was permitted for two hours before morning tenko and for two hours after supper. The buildings were filled with clouds of acrid smoke from the green wood. Men on the upper decks choked, spluttered, and cursed. Having clinical vitamin A deficiency, the smoke caused the formation of extensive ulcers of the cornea of the eye.

The only time we felt warm during the winter was when we got a hot bath every five days. A wooden tub, three feet deep and ten feet square, was filled with piping-hot water. Stripping hastily in the adjacent room, with the temperature twenty degrees below freezing, we hopped into the tub and thawed out the icicles in our marrow. Crowded together "butt to butt," we relaxed as the heat penetrated our frozen bodies. We laughed and giggled with the joy of coming to life again. We chatted gaily about the latest dope in the steam-filled Nu Yoku (bathroom). Two hundred men passed through the filthy pool, covered with the scum of our reeking bodies. We didn't care. It was hot! We were warm for the first time in five days.

There was a thick air of gloom in camp before the Christmas of 1944. Three men had died of beriberi in a week. It looked as if many more were going to kick the bucket. The rations were at their lowest with no prospects of improvement. The news was disturbing: the Germans were on the march in the Battle of the Bulge; the fighting in Leyte and Samar in the Philippines was dragging. Would the war ever end? Would we still be alive when it did end? These questions harried us constantly. To cut the gloom, Dick Whitfield and Pinky Williams decided to have a Christmas party. Pinky was a short, chunky, slightly cross-eyed Englishman. About thirty-five, governor of the Gilbert Islands, he had been

314 | Barbed-Wire Surgeon

captured at the very beginning of the war. The Japs asked him to write script and help broadcast prisoner news—letters from their propaganda radio station appropriately called "Bunka" in Tokyo. He refused. They threatened to kill him. He still refused. They sent him to Mitsushima to do hard labor as punishment. He lived, worked, and slept with the G.I.'s. They liked him. He cheerfully did his share of work and more.

Kubo consented to the Christmas party. For weeks after a hard day's labor, thirty British, American, Canadian, and Chinese prisoners practiced Christmas carols in the frozen dispensary. On Christmas Day we got permission to go out into the mountains for evergreens. We decorated the barracks and hospital with fir and pine boughs. Corporal Bullock decorated a Christmas tree with bits of white paper tied to its branches. He topped it with a tiny "Merry Christmas" sign. We exchanged pitiful gifts. In a little clearing, between the latrine and the dispensary, Dick and I read a Christmas service before the subdued, homesick, frosted prisoners. We joined with the glee club in "Holy Night" to commemorate the birth of Christ. The Japs issued a Red Cross food parcel to each man. We spent the day trading with each other and cooking up outlandish combinations of steamed barley and Stateside-canned food. Our starving prisoners contributed all their Klim cans of dried milk to a common pool to be used for the sick.

Some men, ravenous with hunger, ate their ten pounds of Red Cross food at one crack. They spent the night in the latrine.

Dick and I kept the food parcels of our hospital patients and the members of our "football teams." We had about eleven Englishmen and eleven Americans who qualified. They were a shiftless group of demoralized skeletons who were a never-ending source of trouble to us and to their fellow prisoners. They ate garbage, fell sick, and consumed our precious hoard of medicine. They traded their rice-barley rations for tobacco and developed beriberi. They stole Red Cross canned food and clothing from their bunkmates and traded it to Japanese civilians for more tobacco. They were constantly having accidents. By their failure to obey petty regulations they brought the wrath of the Japs down on themselves and the rest of the camp. Some had traded off their expected Red Cross parcels for rations of steamed rice-barley mix to the sharpsters in camp, of whom a poker-faced navy man was the worst. We declared these broken-down wrecks officially "bankrupt" to clear them of food debts. We forced them to eat their daily rice-barley rations at our "training table" in the hospital to prevent further trading of food for tobacco. Dick and I often discussed the wisdom of trying to keep this group of demoralized skeleton prisoners alive. We hoped one or two might snap out of it. A few did.

After New Year's, 1945, Paul de Bord, a Marine we had sent to Shinagawa Hospital for treatment, came back with news of Major Tom Hewlett, M.C., of Indiana. He was a thin, pale, haggard doctor when he left Cabanatuan in the summer of 1943. He landed at Fukuoka on Kyushu thirty miles from Nagasaki with five hundred prisoners from the Philippines. The camp rapidly grew in size until it housed eighteen hundred American, Dutch, British, and Canadian captives. These men worked twelve-hour shifts in the Mitsui coal mines. With the help of other doctors, he was able to keep six hundred sick men in camp doing light duty until the new Nip C.O., Second Lieutenant Uri, clamped down. Sick men were hustled out to be worked or beaten to death. Hewlett protested day after day. He was put in the guardhouse, stood at attention for hours, and was beaten. He was told he was to be shot. He received no food for four days; thereafter, a handful of rice daily. He developed pneumonia and almost died. After his recovery, he continued to fight the Japs and was able to get several cases of Red Cross medicine issued. Hewlett did a hundred and one major surgical operations in this camp with one death, a patient with peritonitis following a ruptured appendix.

Paul smuggled in a letter from Jim Davis in Shinagawa.

DEAR AL:

On Christmas Day a task force of carriers hit Tokyo. A thousand Grumman planes followed by three hundred

B-29's raided the city, flying through a howling snow-storm. They devastated the city, burning out ten square miles of its heart. Shinagawa was an island surrounded by a sea of flames. The Spider and his gang huddled in their air-raid shelters filled with trembling fear. With my group of fire fighters we prevented falling embers from burning down the camp. We are praying for a re-peat visit by the B-29's in the near future. We must de-stroy the Japanese industrial machine. And we will do it before many moons have passed.

Things have gone to pot in Shinagawa since you left, Al. The Spider is worse than ever, whipping patients and experimenting on them. All the docs, including the "quarterback" and medics, are now doing physical la-bor. We labor at freight terminals or farms doing pick and shovel work in addition to our professional duties. The chow has fallen off. We get a handful of barley three times a day. Everybody is losing weight.

Al, I've come to the toughest part of my letter. In De-cember the Nips evacuated practically all the prison-ers left in Cabanatuan. Colonel Duckworth and about three hundred permanently disabled persons were left behind. Seventeen hundred Americans were loaded on one prison ship. It had no markings to indicate its car-go. It was sunk by our submarines. There were only four survivors. I believe Colonel Beecher, C.O. of Cabanatu-an was one of them. On another prison ship there were eighteen hundred officers and G.I.'s. It was sunk by our dive bombers off the coast of the Philippines. The survi-vors were loaded on another Jap ship. Only three hun-dred reached Japan.

Al, a good many of your friends and mine were drowned or killed on these boats: Colonel Craig, who ran the med-ical department in Cabanatuan; Colonel Schock, who did the facial plastic surgery when you were in Bataan;

Father McDonnell, Chaplain Frank Tiffany, and Father Cummings, who saved so many lives smuggling food in from Manila; Ben Hessenberger, who ran the Carabao Clipper; Lieutenant Dale Henry and Lieutenant Abe Schwartz of the Carabao Wallow; Captain Jack LeMire, the adjutant of General Hospital No. 1; Captain Berkelheimer, the medic detachment commander; Captain Bennison and Bill Debacker, the doctors who were so sick in O'Donnell; Gus Laudicina, with whom you did so much foraging in Bataan; Charlie Keltz, and many more of the doctors you knew in the Philippines. Practically all the musicians and actors in Cabanatuan, including Lieutenant Ben Mossel, were lost.

I guess you and I were lucky to get to Japan earlier in the war.

Hugh Cleave and Al Mohnac join me in sending you our hopes for an early delivery from our body-breaking mind-crushing captivity.

JIM DAVIS

This letter with the news of the sinking of the prison ships and the bombing of Tokyo spread rapidly through the camp. We had read of the famous B-29 and seen pictures in the Nip papers of several of the huge monsters which had been shot down in the November raid on Tokyo. Nevertheless we had seen no B-29's over our camp. We saw and heard Nip planes overhead frequently. We called them "flying toros" (crates).

I was sitting huddled in my clothes, hands covered with a homemade pair of canvas mittens on January 3, 1945. To prevent frostbite I wore them when reading, sleeping, eating, playing bridge and acey-deucy. In the distance, I could hear the steady, faint drone of an airplane. The door flew open with a crash as stunted, toothless, twenty-two-year-old asthmatic Chinese Lim, our substitute medic, tumbled in.

"Captain!" he cried, baring his toothless gums in a hysterical grin, "Come out quick!"

"Pipe down, Lim," I said. "What's the matter?"

"Uncle Sam!" he blithered excitedly, "B-29's!"

I dashed out of my quarters into the compound. High in the translucent sun-blinding sky, moving slowly, were nine tiny white butterflies. Behind them they left a long thin white trail which plumed out gracefully like skywriting. It was the prettiest picture I have ever seen in my life; one that all prisoners of Japan will remember as long as they live. We watched them, hearts throbbing, until they disappeared over the horizon. Little Glass Eye came tearing down the company street, whaling the prisoners back into the barracks with a bamboo pole. We hastily ducked for cover. During the rest of our captivity these B-29's set the morale of the camp. If they appeared, which they did frequently, over our camp, we rejoiced at this miraculously tangible evidence of the war against Japan. If they didn't, we were in the dumps—forgotten men.

I paced the narrow flea-covered prison yard talking to myself:

"Forgotten men. Those words have an ugly sound. Of all the God damn dreary words in the English language they are the worst. Forgotten men. There ought to be a law against these horrible syllables."

"You'll be forgotten like thousands of others."

"The hell I will. I'll be remembered. I saw those B-29's. Uncle Sam remembers. My folks remember."

"You'll die in Japan. You'll be forgotten by everybody."

"No, I won't. Hanna will remember. She remembered in O'Donnell, Cabanatuan, and Bilibid. She is remembering this very minute."

"No she isn't. She has forgotten. She's young, attractive, vivacious. There are plenty of white men from neutral countries still free in Manila. She's out dancing and dining with them. She's probably married and in bed with one of them now. She's forgotten you."

"You're a damn liar. She remembers me. We couldn't see too much of each other before the war."

"Three years is a long time. Quit kidding yourself. She's forgotten. You will die in Japan. Your body will be cremated in a wood fire like thousands of other P.O.W.'s. They'll put your ashes in a little white box. Then the Japs will forget where they put it."

I paced up and down the compound feverishly muttering, "Forgotten men."

The sight of these planes and the newscasts were almost our only entertainment. The men were exhausted and frozen from their daily labors. After evening roll call and supper they crawled into their filthy blankets fully clothed and fell into a deathlike slumber. A few of the more active ones played poker, acey-deucy, carved pipes or read the dog-eared books we circulated throughout the camp. Pinky Williams put on a few variety shows. Most of the men were too tired to turn out for them.

Prisoners relied on their own ingenuity for oblivion. On Saturday nights, Ken Marshall played his clarinet and dark-faced Portuguese Cecil strummed his guitar. "Little Bull," an instructor in mathematics from Chicago, filled reams of cement paper with his complicated calculations. Jack Bailey, Shanghai Marine, and lanky, beriberi-swollen Nutthall, a Mormon missionary, argued philosophy. Cross-eyed "Big Bull" Sorenson, navy man, swapped tall sea stories with ex-hobo Lobe. Dick Whitfield wrote a book. The G.I.'s talked food, the war, and what they were going to do after it was over. They cussed and argued. They were too weak to scrap.

The camp was ridden with influenza and the grippe during the winter. We had fifteen pneumonia patients. Administering our Red Cross medicine sparingly and supplementing it with supplies smuggled in from Shinagawa, our medics—Bible-reading Hector Hart, stolid Corporal Bullock and gymnast Sergeant Maile—struggled to save these gasping skeletons. They lost one pneumonia patient.

With the coming of the spring of 1945, men took a new lease on life. I had suffered several severe beriberi heart attacks and had been bedridden a good part of the winter. It was good to get out of my room into the warm, life-giving sunshine again. Ice floes swept down the frozen river. The thick mantle of snow melted from the mountain slopes. The hardwood trees put out their first green buds which contrasted gaily with the dark of the evergreens. In May the hillsides were covered with purple azaleas and red-and-white cherry blossoms. On rare occasions I was sufficiently strong to stroll along the mountain paths after toting buckets of steamed barley out to the work details.

But the news of the surrender of Germany on May 7, 1945, was better than medicine. Men took their whippings with a grin. Starving prisoners buckled their belts another notch.

"Now these yellow bastards will see some action," we muttered to each other. We prayed for life to see Japan beaten to her knees.

A hundred British prisoner officers arrived from Zensuji, a camp on the island of Shikoku off the coast of Kobe. Enviously, we had read glowing reports in the Tokyo Times of the splendid treatment they were receiving—"No work, plenty of food, Red Cross boxes every week." Without exception, they all had beriberi. They were weak, haggard and emaciated. One major in the engineers had lost a hundred pounds since his capture in Singapore. Erect, blue-eyed Captain Gordon, Commanding Officer of H.M.S. Exeter, sunk in the Java Sea in 1942, resembled a bean pole. So did Commander Hudson. With the exception of three officers, they were an uncomplaining, well disciplined, Jap-hating group of men. Lieutenant Kubo rested them for a week. To these new arrivals our meager dietary was bountiful. They had been receiving one-third of what we were getting.

Lieutenant Kubo informed them that it was the order of the Japanese Military Headquarters that they be put to work. Dick and I spent weary hours arguing with him.

"These men will die if they do physical labor. They are all sick," we said.

Poker-faced, he answered gravely: "My hands are tied. My records must show they are all doing some form of work. Submit a list of the sickest men. We shall find lighter work for them."

He agreed to hospitalize ten officers. Six men were selected for administrative work, bookbinding, and tailoring.

A group of twenty whom we labeled the "Toothless and Ruthless" did gardening and chicken-farming inside the camp which was enlarged by moving its fence toward the river bank. Thirty labeled the "Old and Bold" climbed the mountains daily to tap pine trees for turpentine. The remainder, together with the fit G.I.'s in camp, labored on the mountain slopes and the riverbank, clearing small patches of land which they planted with soybeans, sweet and Irish potatoes and sweet corn. We never got a crop.

These officers did their work without bitching, much to the surprise of the G.I.'s. Because of their uncomplaining demeanor and by means of the variety skits deadpan Commander "Guns" Twist and his band of comedians put on, the morale of the camp rose slowly in spite of chronic starvation. They put their books into circulation in camp. These new prisoners were a godsend to Dick and me. They represented new faces to study, new stories to hear, and new personalities to enjoy for us and the three officers who had preceded these British officers to Mitsushima from Omori: hard-boiled B-17 pilot van Warmer, oily submarine engineer Lieutenant George Brown of New York, and comical Lieutenant "General" Magrath of London. These latter three messed with us in our tiny room.

One night in May, 1945, three weeks after the arrival of the new officers, we were sitting together eating our meager supper and happily discussing the news. The door slid open with a crash. A nauseatingly familiar voice growled, "Nanda (What the hell's going on here)?"

I looked up in horror, not believing my ears. I turned cold and faint as my heart stopped stock still, and then resumed its beat. The Bird was scowling at us. Lips dry and tongue paralyzed, I couldn't speak.

The General snapped out of his nightmare first. "Kyotski!" he bellowed. We all flew out of our seats and bowed.

"Good evening, Mr. Watanabi," he said smoothly, face as white as snow. "Won't you come in? We were talking about fishing."

The Bird relaxed and grinned. "Sit down. You did not expect to see me, I think."

"Yes. It was a pleasant surprise," the General carried on. "I hope you can pay us a long visit."

We waited breathlessly for the reply. He cocked his head with a leer smeared over his hard-bitten, handsome face. "Yes. A very long visit. I have been sent to discipline the new officers—and the old ones if necessary."

All night I tumbled and tossed, trying to drive the image of his sadistic face out of my brain. The next morning the General dashed in. "Al," he said quickly, "the Bird wants you. He's in a lousy mood."

I took off my shoes and slipped into my wooden clogs. It was easier to roll with the punch and go sprawling when wearing them. On the double I trotted to his office. He was waiting outside the compound.

"Yes, Watanabi San (Mr.), " I said, saluting.

"What?" he scowled.

I thought rapidly. He had been promoted from corporal to sergeant. Maybe he preferred his new title.

"Yes, Watanabi Gunso (Sergeant)."

"What?" he howled, clenching his fists.

Hold everything, I thought to myself feverishly, trying to figure out what the bastard wanted while I got ready to roll with the punch.

I got a brilliant flash: "Yes, Watanabi Gunso dono (most honorable Sergeant)."

He relaxed with a grin. "How do you like this camp?"

"Very good," I said warily. "It is very beautiful here, lovely mountains and beautiful river."

"Better than Omori?" he questioned.

"Omori had a fine jazz band and library," I countered side-stepping trouble like a broken-field runner.

"Why is there so much sickness in camp?" he asked.

I took a deep breath. "These Americans were sick when they came from the Philippines. The British were sick when they came from Singapore."

"You talk too much," he said, his eyes narrowing. "Why are they sick now?"

"They won't be sick if you give them as much food and medicine as you gave the prisoners in Omori. Omori was a very healthy camp." I finished rapidly.

He thought it over for a minute. Egotism got the best of him. He puffed his chest out and smiled.

"Finished," he barked.

I saluted and held the salute while he walked away. I'd fallen for this trick before. He turned suddenly and grinned when he saw me standing stiffly, still saluting.

"You remember the lessons I taught you very well," he said, returning the salute.

I left, dripping perspiration.

During June, 1945, the Bird managed to whip all the new officers on one pretext or another. Some of them were beaten many times. Captain Gordon and disease-ridden Commander Hudson were thrashed for attempting to protest to Lieutenant Kubo.

Colonel Sacaba, C.O. of all prisoners in the Tokyo area, inspected the camp several days later. He was a short, squat, powerfully built, middle-aged Jap with heavily hooded eyes. With him was his interpreter, black-faced Kuriama, a notorious slugger.

Mounted on a chair he addressed the new officers: "You have been sent here from your old camp to work. Japan is engaged in a life and death struggle. Everybody must work! You must not complain! You must be diligent! You must obey! All who are haughty, arrogant, disobedient or lazy will be punished on the spot! Finished!"

Encouraged by his boss's words, the Bird went to work again on the officer-prisoners.

They did pick and shovel work from seven A.M. to six P.M. They carried huge buckets of night soil slung over their shoulders to garden clearings in the mountains far away. He beat them unmercifully with and without pretext. Silent, faces bruised and swollen, they carried on, bodies broken but spirits unbeaten, cheered by the ever-increasing flights of B-29's overhead.

In the month of June, 1945, we were depressed by two more deaths in camp, both surgical, both avoidable. During my stay in Mitsushima, I had done many operations under local and spinal anesthesia, using a makeshift bench as an operating table and a few instruments borrowed from the local Jap hospital. Without gloves, gowns and an anesthetist, Dick Whitfield and I struggled through emergency procedures without any deaths. Late in March, 1945, Private First Class Skubina, a hard-headed American from Minnesota, slipped and fell on the ice, fracturing his skull. He hovered between life and death for a week. He gradually regained consciousness due primarily to the nursing of singing Hector Hart, our medic. Skubina then took a turn for the worse, developing weakness and incoordination of his arms, legs, and eye muscles. It was evident that he had a blood clot in the cerebellum, the part of the brain that houses the centers of muscular coordination at the base of the skull. Through Lieutenant Kubo we appealed repeatedly to Dr. Fugi at Omori for permission to send him to Shinagawa or a Tokyo military hospital for operation. We had no brain instruments and had no facilities to make them.

He wrote back: "It is impossible. There is no transportation available."

Skubina lingered on for months. When Dr. Fugi visited our camp on a tour of inspection we showed him this patient.

He smiled: "Nothing can be done. You cannot send him to Tokyo."

Skubina died. We did an autopsy. He had a liquified blood clot and abscess pressing on his cerebellum. This could have been drained if he had been operated on. He should have lived. Dr. Fugi murdered him by refusing to transfer him to Tokyo.

The second patient was a British officer with severe beriberi who had recurrent attacks of severe abdominal pain for months before his arrival in Mitsushima. This pain was associated with failure of the bowels to function. Dick and I went to see him one day during an attack. He was writhing in agony. His abdomen was spastic and painful. It was evident that an intraabdominal catastrophe had taken place which would require immediate surgical intervention. The Boy Scout and I got permission to borrow some instruments from the village hospital high up on the mountain slope. Exhausted by the trip, I struggled back, panting for air, crippled heart beating irregularly. We boiled some bed sheets, gave our patient a spinal anesthesia, iodinized and draped his abdomen. Ungowned, with hands scrubbed but ungloved, I opened the abdomen through a long rectus, an almost mid-line incision. It was filled with bloody fluid.

The right colon, the large bowel which is ordinarily bound tightly to the right side of the posterior abdominal wall, as a result of abnormal embryonic development was floating free, attached to a broad mesentery through which its blood vessels ran. This two-foot length of large bowel and half of the transverse colon was twisted on itself. Its walls were pitch black, dead, strangulated. It would have been necessary to resect it and connect up the end of the small bowel near the appendix with the viable large bowel near the stomach; a dangerous job under any circumstances with the best of tools and instruments. But it wasn't necessary to attempt it. After the abdomen was opened the patient's heart stopped beating. Intracardiac adrenalin and massage of the heart through the diaphragm was of no help. He was stone dead. I don't know why he died. Possible beriberi heart, surgical and anesthetic shock, or a combination of these factors. He was cremated and his ashes put in a little wooden box.

The Bird continued his slug-fest in the work areas during the day and in the barracks at night. Colonel Brigdon, a white-haired elderly British officer with a stiff knee, was beaten to the ground. Lanky, poker-faced Daniels, a member of our "football team," got himself into trouble. Every ten days, on our "rest day," the Japs sold us a half package (about one ounce) of "hair tobacco."

Daniels grumbled to our moon-faced interpreter, the Goon, "What about our tobacco issue, Mr. Machida? Aren't we getting any tobacco today?"

"What's the hurry?" the Goon replied maliciously. "If you don't get it this week you'll get it next."

"You can keep the God damn stuff," Daniels snarled. "Next week the Yanks and tanks will be here."

The Goon hotfooted it over to the Bird, with whom he curried favor, and reported the conversation. Daniels received a horrible beating. So did some innocent bystanders.

Under constant nervous tension, hard labor, and inadequate food, the health of the prisoners deteriorated during the summer of 1945. Officers and men lost weight steadily—about ten pounds a month. The average weight of the camp was one hundred and twenty pounds. Much of the weight was waterlogged beriberi tissue. Something had to be done. Several "murder squads" were formed among the officers. They impatiently waited their chance to throw the Bird over a cliff or drown him in the river. Armed with his two-handed sword and accompanied by guards bearing side arms, he was cagey. It was impossible to get at him alone on the work details.

"Al, we've got to do something," Dick said thoughtfully, his nose twitching. "The Bird is murdering his prisoners by inches. What do you say about trying to poison the bastard?"

"I'm all for it," I whispered quietly. "Of course, you know it means our necks if we get caught."

He nodded his head saying: "What should we use, Al?" I scratched my head: "We've got some digitalis, morphine, iodine, and atropine. Take your choice."

He thought for a while. "An overdose of digitalis causes nausea and vomiting. He might puke up what we gave him before he absorbed enough of it to stop his heart. And it would be impossible to conceal enough iodine in his food to do much damage."

"The trouble with using morphine and atropine," I said worried, "is that they might call in a Jap doctor to see him before he kicks off. The contracted pupils and slow respirations of morphine poisoning and the dilated pupils and restlessness of atropine poisoning are so God damn obvious."

"That's a chance we've got to take," Dick answered somberly.

It seemed almost as if the Bird had been listening outside our door. The next day he raised holy hell in the dispensary with the Boy Scout for having dangerous medications on the shelves of the pharmacy within reach of the prisoner doctors. He placed all medications which were poisonous under lock and key.

We trembled with apprehension for a few days. The row subsided. I still don't know whether this row was coincidental or whether somebody gave us away.

Dick slipped into the room quietly. "I've got an idea, Al. I want your advice on it."

"Shoot!" I said.

"What do you think of trying to kill the Bird with bacteria?"

"Sounds all right. We've got plenty of germs in camp. What kind were you thinking of using?"

"Amoebic or bacillary dysentery," he whispered.

A broad grin spread over my face. "Swell. If it doesn't kill the Bird, he'll know he's been sick."

Dick got some bloody diarrhea stools from two patients who we knew had amoebic and bacillary dysentery. Fishing out shreds of mucous and feces he deposited them carefully in a little brown bottle which contained saline and glucose as a culture medium. For good measure he dropped three fat juicy flies into the mixture. We had no incubator. We carried the bottle next to the skin for warmth. After a few days he made a warm saline suspension of the "gravy" as we called it. The next step in the procedure was to have it needled into the Bird's food. We approached Corporal George Piel, a survivor of St. Peter's ward in Cabanatuan. He was the cook for the Japs.

"What about it, George?" he was asked.

"I'll take care of it," he said, his black eyes glinting. "You'll get your head chopped off, if the Japs find out," he was warned.

"I'll take my chances," he growled stubbornly.

For five days Piel flavored the Bird's rice with the gravy. Nothing happened. We made a new gravy. This time we used contributions from a half-dozen stools. George again went into the flavoring business. Nobody else in camp was in on the murder attempt.

The General, who was liaison officer between the Japs and the prisoners, dashed into the dispensary two days later.

"Al," he said, "the Bird wants to see you. He's sick."

A wave of exultation spread over me. "What's the matter with my darling?"

"He said he emptied his guts out all night."

I trotted down to the Bird's quarters. The brave man was whimpering like a child.

"What is your trouble, Sergeant Watanabi?" I asked.

"I am very sick," he said, lifting his tear-stained face. "I have had diarrhea all night." He flung his bedclothes off and stumbled to the latrine. He stumbled back, his fists doubled in the pit of his belly.

"Why am I sick?" he asked suddenly.

"Many of the patients and Japanese in this camp have had diarrhea," I said, heart pounding hard. "There are too many flies in camp. They spread sickness. We get no fly spray to kill them."

He groaned: "You must give me some medicine. You must cure me."

I saw thousands of disarmed Americans herded up the road from Bataan. Begging for water, they were being driven from artesian wells and forced to drink from carabao wallows. I smelled the night-soil-perfumed air of O'Donnell through which long files of haggard prisoners were carrying corpses suspended from bamboo poles. The kogon-grass cemetery in Cabanatuan, with its three thousand Americans, stretched before my eyes. The blind and the lame of Bilibid stumbled by. Beetle-browed Dr. Tukuda howled for the death of French Canuck LeBell on the operating table at Shinagawa. White-

haired Captain James lay unconscious at the Bird's feet in Omori. Dr. Fugi grinned as he watched the dying Skubina in Mitsushima.

"Yes," I said slowly, "I'll cure you."

The Bird ran a "picket-fence" type of fever of 105° for ten days while the camp prayed for his death. Laughter could again be heard in camp. We almost became hysterically childish as the nervous tension fell away from us. Even the other Japanese in camp relaxed. They hated the Bird as much as we did. I went to see him at his order every day. Sick as he was, he was still suspicious. I had to swallow a sample of all medication before he took it. While I administered aspirin and sodium bicarbonate grooved to look like sulfadiazine pills, George continued to flavor his rice with gravy. The Bird lost fifteen pounds during the first week of his illness.

"You must eat your rice every day," I urged, "or you will lose more."

He was as tough as a bull. We couldn't kill him, but we kept the sadist under control. His dysentery took the starch out of him.

With scholarly Lieutenant Henderson doing the translating, we sweated out the arrival of papers in camp. He read us the terms of the Potsdam Conference late in July, 1945.

We call upon the government of Japan to proclaim now the unconditional surrender of all Japanese armed forces… Japanese sovereignty shall be limited to the Islands of Honshu, Hokkaido, Kyushu, Shikoku… Stern justice shall be meted out to all war criminals… Points in Japanese territory to be designated by the Allies shall be occupied… The Japanese Government shall remove all obstacles to the revival and strengthening of the democratic tendencies among the Japanese people. Freedom of speech and religion and of thought, as well as respect for the fundamental human rights, shall be established.

In the violent arguments that raged through the camp we split fifty-fifty in our views. Some thought that Japan was licked and would accept the terms. Others felt that they still had massive unbeaten armies in the Orient and would haggle for better terms. We all prayed an invasion of Japan itself would not be necessary to terminate the war. We all expected Russia to declare war or march without a declaration.

Japan refused to accept the terms.

On the evening of August 6, "Hendie" slipped into our quarters with a broad grin on his face. "The Japs are howling about the bombing of Hiroshima. They claim we killed one hundred and twenty-six thousand people. They say this bombing by the inhuman Americans is even worse than gas. I can't make out what we used."

We thought the Yanks were dropping four-ton block-busters in this raid.

On August 8, I saw stolid Hendie excited for the first time since we arrived in camp.

"Al," he exploded, "the Russians have declared war on Japan. They've invaded Manchuria at many points along the border. That's not the only thing the Japs are moaning about. We bombed Nagasaki and flattened it. I finally figured out the Kongi (picture writing) characters. We dropped an atomic bomb!"

During the next week the Japs in camp were subdued and preoccupied. Something was in the air. We could not find out what it was. We were unable to steal a newspaper. Rumor had it that a new Jap Cabinet was formed and issued a proclamation for the continuation of the war. All the school children in the village were formed into companies and trained with make-believe wooden rifles.

On August 15, several peculiar things took place in camp. The prisoners were not sent out to work. This had never happened before. It was not an official "rest" day. The Nip C.O. told the General that prisoners would not work until further notice. The siren on the mountain peak failed to sound off for the first time in months. We saw no B-29's or Jap planes.

In the evening I went to pay my professional call on the Bird. He was preoccupied. Turning toward me he asked suddenly: "What is democracy?"

Startled, I hemmed and hawed. "Why are you interested in democracy, Sergeant Watanabi?"

"I am a student of government. Tell me," he demanded. I quoted Lincoln's Gettysburg Address: "It is 'government of the people, by the people, for the people.'"

He blinked his eyes uncomprehendingly.

"In it, the government we elect tells the army what to do," I explained. "The army doesn't control the government. In it a factory worker can complain if his boss doesn't pay him enough to support his family. He can join a union and strike if he wants to. His boss can't shoot him. His boss can complain to the government if big companies like Mitsui and Mitsubishi are driving him out of business. If the politicians we elect don't help solve the problems of the people, we elect a new set. We don't kill them. That's democracy," I ended.

The Bird seemed to understand.

I took a deep breath. "I have told you something. Now I ask you to tell me something."

"What is it?" he asked suspiciously.

"I had a dream last night. I dreamed that the war had ended. It is true?"

He cocked his head, sucked wind between his teeth, and looked at me queerly. "I am not permitted to tell you what you already know."

CHAPTER 15.
Flight To Manila

FOR A WEEK WE LAY about the camp wondering if Japan had actually surrendered. The Nips wouldn't tell us. We weren't certain until several of the prisoners broke out of camp in the dead of night and visited Blinky at the Oiwa machine shop. Trembling with happiness, he assured them that Japan had surrendered. They brought back a newspaper which Hendie translated. It was true.

The Bird flew the coop. I never saw his ugly face again. The Snake and Buick left. Dignified Captain Gordon of the British Navy, our ranking prisoner, took over the Camp.

He spoke to the men: "The war is over. Japan has surrendered. Our forces haven't landed yet. I don't know when we shall leave this camp. Lieutenant Kubo will try to get us more food while we wait. We British and Americans don't believe in mob rule. These Japs who have starved and tortured us will eventually get their just deserts. I beg of you not to take the law into your own hands. Some of these Japs deserve to die. Be patient. After they are court-martialed many of them will be justly executed when our troops land. We must wait here for their arrival."

These G.I.'s who had been beaten and starved for three and a half years had their captors at their mercy; the Japs were no longer bearing arms. To their everlasting credit, the prisoners curbed their anger and their desire for revenge. I'm certain that no court-martial would have convicted them if they had slaughtered the Nips. They didn't.

A few hot heads grumbled and cussed. They were controlled by their bunkmates. The prisoners did something else which I shall always remember. Making up bundles of their old Red Cross shoes, blankets, and clothes, these starved men went into the village and out in the countryside to find the squalid huts in which lived the Jap foremen who had befriended them on their work details. They knew these small-timers hated the Jap military and monopolistic industrial machine. They knew their families were facing another hard winter. They gave these Jap civilians their pitifully shabby collection of clothes.

We took over the food supply in camp and issued a daily allowance to the Jap "administrators." Lieutenant Kubo rustled up some canned meat and seaweed from a neighboring army encampment. It helped. But we were ravenous for Stateside chow. We sent the Boy Scout to Shinagawa for more medicine. He came back with a load.

The men puttered around camp, played poker "on the cuff." They lay in the sunshine, soaking up health-giving rays. They and the officers argued interminably about what should be done to the Japanese.

"Cut off their nuts, and let the breed die out," one said.

"Let China and Russia occupy Japan. They'll know how to treat the slopeheads. The Americans will be too soft with them."

"Kill them all," one lantern-jawed officer said. "They're no good and never will be."

"It's not quite as simple as that," a middle-aged officer offered gently. "You can't kill off eighty million people. It just isn't done."

"What would you do?" he was challenged.

"I'd transform the military drive of the Japs for territorial expansion by raising their own standards of living in Japan so that they can consume products from their own factories."

"How?" the shout arose from many mouths.

"First, I'd strip Japan of its military and naval forces and restrict its industries to peacetime occupations. I'd execute those in the armed forces in government and in business who had planned the war," he said soberly.

"Then I'd force absentee landlords to sell their holdings at a reasonable price on long terms to the millions of peasants who are now sharecroppers. If they can make a living on the farm for themselves and their families, they won't have to send their sons to the army to get enough to eat.

"I'd break up the monopolistic groups in industry; the Mitsui, Mitsubishi, Sumitomo and Yasuda and other families that have crushed the small businessman in Japan. Before the war they controlled 62 per cent of the wealth of Japan. Through their governmental subsidies and 'Control Associations' the little fellow in this country has been driven out of business.

"I'd develop trade unionism throughout the country. The monopolistic group, backed by the army, has kept down the workers' share of national production. By doing so, they could devote the largest share of the national production to war materiel or to exports which made it possible to buy war supplies abroad."

"That sounds straight enough. But how are you going to reorganize the government so that the peasant, the industrial worker, and the small businessman will get a living wage; so that he can buy the products of the Jap industrial machine? Are you going to use the emperor?"

"I don't think so," he said slowly. "I'd prosecute him as a war criminal. He, the military and the monopolists have all planned Japanese domination of first the Orient and then the world. Any differences between them have been differences in timing and method rather than in basic policy. The emperor has used his 'divinity claims' as a means to an end—world domination. Emperor Hirohito has great financial interests which came before his love for his country. He must be destroyed."

"Who would you put in his place?"

"Not the old group of slick, double-faced, lying politicians who were front men of the emperor, the military and the monopolists. There are thousands of Japs who have been exiled for their democratic beliefs. There are thousands who are in the prison of the Kempei Tai now. I'd choose the future teachers of Japan from among these men and let them build a democracy with our help and under our supervision."

"How long would that take?"

"I'd occupy or supervise the country for the next fifty years until a new generation, trained in democracy, could take over."

Ten days went by. Officers and men were getting increasingly restless. We still lived in the lice- and flea-ridden barracks of Mitsushima. The singsongs and variety shows we put on did not help much. We were desperately anxious for the orders that would start us on the first leg of our trip home.

We had an officer-patient with a high, intermittent fever. I said to Dick: "It would be a hell of a break for Ed to kick off at this stage of the game. What about one of us taking him to Tokyo for diagnosis and treatment? At the same time, we could find out when we're getting out of this God-forsaken country."

We tossed a coin to see who would go. I lost.

Dick took off. That was the last time I saw him. The Boy Scout who went with Dick brought back a note.

I got Ed on board a hospital ship. He's O.K. The harbor is swarming with Allied ships of all classes. I saw the admiral. He says formal surrender ceremonies will take place on the battleship U.S.S. Missouri tomorrow, September 2. After that the Yanks will come after you. I had my first chocolate ice-cream soda. Oh, boy!

The next day I was sprawled out on the floor when our asthmatic Chinaman, Lim, chattered excitedly: "Captain, Captain, come quick!" He fled, with me on his tail.

Six tiny black specks appeared in the sky. Flying low over rugged mountain ranges, these planes wove back and forth in single file, following the course of the river. At a height of five thousand feet they roared over camp. They were six American Navy Grummans with black wings and square tips. Three hundred ragged prisoners ran up and down the little compound waving their arms hysterically and yelling themselves hoarse, trying to attract their attention. On the roofs of the barracks we had painted in huge orange letters "P.O.W.," on a black background.

We had laid out gray blankets forming the same letters on a strip of white sand outside the camp. The Nip papers had reported that American flyers were dropping food and medicine to prisoners-of-war camps isolated in the mountains. The flyers missed the signs, covered by the heavy ground mist which settled over the tiny valley in the early morning.

They disappeared over the horizon as we moaned and cussed. An hour later we heard the drone of motors in the west. They appeared again, lower this time, their black wings shining in the morning sun. Down through a cleft in the mountain range the flight leader dove straight for the camp, waggling his wings. We howled, cheered, and pounded each other. Tears of joy streamed down our faces. Hearts thumped with happiness as we saw the white star in its blue circle on the wings of the plane.

The planes followed one after another at a level of a thousand feet. They circled round and round the hidden valley, checking wind currents and trying various approaches to the little camp. Finally, the flight leader made his run, clearing the pine trees on the overhanging mountain range by feet. Down he dove steeply to a level of three hundred feet above camp. A black object hurtled down from the plane; an orange parachute fluttered open. A suspended fifty-five-gallon drum pendulumed back and forth three times and dropped with a thud in a clearing fifty feet square, between the Nip administration building and the galley—a bull's eye! The plane pulled out of its dive, clearing the barracks, and climbed rapidly to top the opposing hills. One after another the planes roared down and dropped their loads. One food packet landed in the doorway of the galley. The parachute of another failed to open. Its drum plummeted to the ground and buried itself deeply in the mud near the bank of the river. Something red fluttered down. The men high-tailed it. There was a note stuck in a sandbag which had a long, red cloth streamer. It read:

HELLO, FOLKS:

The crew of the U.S.S. Randolph send their best. Hope you enjoy the chow. Keep your chin up. We'll be back.

Our first contact with American forces in three and a half years!

The cooks went into action. There were gallon cans of preserved fruits, huge tinned hams, corned beef, meat and vegetable stew, dried milk, cigarettes, gum, chocolate, and candy.

The drum which had plummeted was filled with Baby Ruth candy bars. We dug them out of the muck and mud of the riverbed, dissolved and boiled them in our huge, shallow iron kawali (caldron). It made a delicious, hot, sweet soup. Chattering like kids at a Christmas party, we got our first bellyful of Stateside chow.

The next day we watched the air circus again as torpedo planes from the U.S.S. Lexington bombed the camp with food. Some of the containers tore away from their parachutes and smashed through the roof of a shack outside of camp.

Captain Gordon finally received instructions from Tokyo to entrain all P.O.W.'s for the coast.

On September 4, 1945, we packed our duds and prepared to leave camp. We gave five hundred yen to the Boy Scout and to One Arm who had done so much to protect the prisoners from beatings in and out of camp. We gave them blankets, shoes, clothes, and letters.

TO WHOM IT MAY CONCERN:

These Japs have helped American prisoners at the risk of their own physical comfort. They got us medicine when they could. They saved us from being whipped when they could. If they or their families need food during the winter, please help them. They deserve it. They're good Japs.

One Arm made a speech. Obviously moved by the unexpected gifts and letters, he said: "For your sake and for my sake, I am glad that this war has ended. I go back to my village to teach again. I hope I shall be permitted to teach the language of love and peace rather than hate and war."

Joking and laughing, we trudged up the gravel road cut in the side of the mountain overlooking the camp. The villagers were out en masse to witness our departure. While waiting for the train, the G.I.'s mingled with them, giving candy to the kids and presents of clothes to civilians with whom they had worked on the job. We loaded our six stretcher patients on the narrow-gauge electric train and pulled out of Mitsushima Valley forever.

For hours we crawled through mountains covered with huge pine trees. The railroad wheels beat out a message of freedom, "You're going home, You're going home, You're going home." Glum-faced, silent Nip guards without side arms accompanied us for protection against "enraged" civilians. The hills fell away as we descended toward the coast. We changed to a steam railroad in a bombed-out, coastal city and headed north toward Tokyo. Plenty of room, plenty of seats, no rush, no "Kura (Get along)."

At the fishing village of Aria, we left the train and walked to the beaches. Offshore was a hospital ship painted white with green trimmings and huge red crosses on its side. There were several LCT's near it. Eyes misty and with a lump lodged in my throat, I watched a "crash" boat pull away and head for us, the Stars and Stripes fluttering proudly in the breeze. The last time I had seen it was in April, 1942, at the surrender on Bataan. A squad of huge, powerfully built Marines piled out. They looked so fat and healthy! They were carrying Tommy guns and helmets we had never seen before.

"O.K., fellers," they said kindly, "it's all over but the shouting. Get your litter patients in first and then climb aboard."

Dazed by their sudden arrival, we stumbled into the craft. Off we went, spray flying high as we ploughed through the breakers.

The prisoners whispered among themselves as if afraid to dispel a magical dream.

"Wasn't that flag purty?"

"I want a gallon of milk."

"Just listen to that motor turn over."

"No more God damn Japs."

"No more benjo."

"I'm never going to be hungry again."

We clambered aboard the U.S.S. Rescue and were promptly told to strip and throw our lice-covered rags overboard. Into a steam-filled shower room we crowded. Oh, the first heavenly thrill of plenty of soap and piping-hot water squirting through the needle valves of the shower! We scrubbed and scrubbed our bodies, peeling off one layer of filth after another. We squirmed with pleasure under the jets. As we left the showers, medics with flit guns sprayed our heads and bodies with DDT while we pirouetted slowly, arms raised. In freshly washed pajamas sweet with cleanliness we walked through a line of docs who checked us over quickly. On the softest mattress, between the whitest sheets I have ever seen, I slipped into bed in the hundred-bed ward.

"How about some chow, Doc?" a navy medic asked. "What have you got?" I asked luxuriously.

"Anything you want."

"I'll have some poached eggs."

"How many?"

"Just keep 'em coming."

I put thirty-two down—then thirty-two came up. I fell asleep.

The next week was a delirious confusion of new sights, smells, and tastes! Smiling faces, gentle voices, the color of food, the whiteness of bread, the sharp tang of an orange, the juicy bite of a pear, the smooth cool richness of ice cream, the lift of an elevator, the feel of a chair against back and bottom, the muted violins of a concerto, the throbbing drums of boogie woogie over the radio. I gloated over a thick, tender steak and some delicious fried chicken. Everything was good, especially the firm, white bread. It tasted like angel cake.

Better than food was the God-sent feeling of safety. We had been living at the mercy of barbarous, hair-trigger personalities for so many years that the gentleness and kindness we were shown was enough to make us sob silently in our pillows. Terms like "freedom of speech," "trial by one's peers," "the right of redress," "habeas corpus," were no longer a series of glib words that rolled off the tongue. They had a flowing, vivid quality to the liberated prisoners who had existed for years without the protection of these monuments of civilization. They were music to our ears. We would never forget their significance.

When I was not eating and sleeping, I wallowed in magazines, books, and newspapers. By the light of the bedside lamp I read until my eyes burned and my brain was saturated: Ernie Pyle's books of the campaigns in Europe, treatises on a postwar world, discussions of the United Nations, the occupation of Germany, American-Russian-British power politics. After years of isolation from the stream of world events, this plunge into the minds of other people was exhilarating. There were so many blank spaces to fill between the bits of news we had been able to smuggle into prison camps.

I didn't understand what I was reading. There was too much to grasp. My brain was too confused. What I did grasp was that throughout the war the press and radio had retained a good measure of freedom of expression. I was not going back to an iron-bound dictatorship. Americans could read the New York Times, the Christian Science Monitor, PM or the Daily Worker, depending upon their individual tastes and their political views. Interpreted differently in these organs of fact and opinion, the news was still being printed for those who wanted to read. Criticism of industry, labor, and government was evident. The public still clung grimly to the old American custom of squawking if they didn't like what they saw. Because of, rather than in spite of, differences of opinion, the war had been pushed to a successful close.

Sufficiently certain of the public's basic love for the American way of life, the government had not attempted to throttle freedom of expression. Sufficiently certain of the loyalty of the G.I. and the gob, Yank and the Pacifican ran "bitching" columns in their sheets.

It was a good country, a self-critical country to which I was returning after years in Japan where a small group of power-loving, humanity-hating militarists and industrialists piped the tune and where millions of poverty-stricken, ignorant peasant farmers, laborers, and small businessmen danced and paid the piper with their lives. Because of their poverty, these millions were frustrated. Cleverly manipulated by the militarists and the monopolists, this frustration was transformed into a blind, searing hatred for the Americans who, they were told, were responsible for their poverty.

All democratic papers in Japan were suppressed, labor movements stifled, the stable middle-class businessmen driven into oblivion. The propagandists knew the broad streak of inferiority, the complex and emotional instability which is embedded in the substance of Japanese personality. They played on their vanity as "Sons of Heaven." They pointed toward the rich countries of the Orient where land was plentiful if they took it. By the millions their soldiers and officers were soaked in this trough of propaganda. They were great; other people of the Orient should be their slaves. Americans were soft and degenerate animals. When we were captured, they treated us as such.

When Japan surrendered, undefeated armies in China and on the Japanese mainland still retained this propagandist inculcation. Their leaders are ducking for cover. They have no sense of regret, other than the regret that they were defeated. They wait for another chance. They'll get it unless the Japanese press under our guidance debunks them; unless the next generation of Japs is taught the language of peace in their schools, magazines and books; unless the small businessman and worker develop an internal expanding economy which can supply food, shelter, and clothing to Japan's swarming millions.

Emotionally, I hated the Japanese. My brother prisoners and I had suffered too much at their hands. We had seen their cruelty and stupidity, their feeling of inferiority and vanity, their hatred for all white people, their inability to handle power without becoming sadistic. I didn't want to see another Jap as long as I live.

Intellectually, I sympathized with Mr. Moto, the peasant farmer, the factory worker, the civilian professional, the small-time businessman, and the intellectual. They might be able to build a democratic Japan with the help of a free press.

Maybe!

There were many nurses on board the U.S.S. Rescue, the first white women we had seen since 1942. I lay in bed and watched them for hours: the reflection of the light from their soft wavy hair, their long eyelashes, the poise of their heads, the play of their eyes, the swing of their carriage, the rustle of their stiffly starched skirts. It was music to hear the languid Southern drawl of blonde-haired "Ollie." I kept her talking at my bedside as long as I dared, just to hear a woman's voice. It was exciting to see gracefully built girls again, after the flat-chested, wide-hipped, trousered, pigeon-toed women of Japan. It was thrilling to hear them speak alertly in a self-respecting fashion after having studied the whipped, humble, whispering, kowtowing Jap female. We hadn't seen lipstick and make-up for a long time. We hadn't smelled perfume.

At night, lying drowsily in a half sleep, my nostrils flared up like a pointer flushing a partridge when one of the nurses whisked by my bed, leaving her trail of perfume. I spoke to a fellow prisoner about it.

"Johnny, do you get hot and bothered when you see the nurses?"

"Hell, no, Doc. No rise at all. But it's wonderful to see them."

Sex and passion had long dried into impotency. But the hunger and longing for femininity still persisted. We could appreciate the sweetness of womanhood all the more for having been deprived of it.

We sailed north along the coast, picking up batches of liberated prisoners. It was good to lie relaxed in my bed and watch them come to life under gentle handling, good food, and plenty of medicine. It was even better to be free of all responsibility for their health and their lives for the first time in years. No more battling the Japs for chow; no more stealing medicine; no more watching men die for the lack of it. I was just Joe Blow, liberated prisoner of war from Japan. I loved the feeling.

We sailed into Yokohama Bay under the shadow of towering Mount Fuji. The bay was filled with naval craft as far as the eye could see, the greatest armada of fighting ships the world has ever known. We trucked through the streets of Yokohama. The city was demolished, burned to the ground—a mass of rubble and tiny, hastily constructed, bent-sheet-metal shacks outside of which the inhabitants were grubbing little gardens. Here and there a steel bank safe stood, all that was left of a city block. We went to the Atsugi Airport which was crowded with huge B-29's and transport planes. A wave of exaltation flooded over me as we roared down the air strip. We were leaving the "quaint and picturesque" land of Japan for the last time.

In five hours we were circling the destroyed city of Naha in Okinawa. A typhoon blew up while we rested impatiently several days on that rain-swept island for the next leg of our trip. We finally got the go-ahead signal and took off in a four-motored transport plane. The weather was still rough. Rumor had it that a C-54 in our flight loaded with P.O.W.'s was lost at sea and that a B-24, buffeted by the tail end of a typhoon, had its bomb bay blown open, plummeting six prisoners on their way to freedom into the ocean.

As the land mass of northern Luzon loomed on the horizon, I trembled with happiness and fear of impending disaster. The mountain province with its heavily wooded slopes and deep gorges would not have made an ideal landing place. I felt better when we reached the flat plains north of Manila covered with the light green of young rice plants. Over the many tributaries of the Pampanga River, we flew toward the city of Manila. For our benefit the pilot circled it. In our smuggled Nip papers we had learned of the heavy fighting in this city. We weren't prepared for the scene of devastation that spread before us. The mile-square Walled City was a heap of rubble. All the new governmental buildings along Taft Avenue were a mass of ruins. Jai Alai was a hollow shell.

The suburb of Pasay, where I had left Hanna and her family, was completely burned out. I had had no news from them for a year and a half. The motors drummed: "Is she alive? Is she alive?"

In the hungry abyss of Shinagawa I had fed upon the vision of her radiant loveliness; in torture-ridden Omori I had clung to the memory of her sturdy mentality; and when the snow fell heavy on the slopes of Mitsushima I warmed my frost-bitten heart in the glow of her love. It may be that I survived because of that love. It would not have been possible to undergo the hunger, torture, and sadism of those years without it. The comforting embrace of death would have been irresistible. As the plane circled over the runways of Nichols Field, I whispered over and over again: "Please, God, let me see her, not her grave."

We landed at Nichols Field where a jazz band greeted us in the Red Cross hut with "Hail, Hail, the Gang's All Here." The gang was all here except the thousands who had died in prison camps in the Philippines and Japan. Through a Red Cross representative on the field I learned that most of the white civilians in Manila had been slaughtered during the fighting, even the Nazi Germans with their swastikas on their arms. I hitchhiked into the city to hunt for Hanna. I hurried to a Red Cross canteen in Plaza Goiti.

"Yes, the family is listed as living on Kitanlaad Street, Santa Mesa Heights, north of Manila," a Spanish woman dressed in mourning told me.

By foot and hitchhiking I traveled through the shattered city teeming with jeeps, trucks, staff cars, and thousands of smiling-faced Filipinos. I rode up Quezon Boulevard past Santo Tomas University, where four thousand American internees had been recaptured by the Yanks in February, 1945. Kitanlaad Street was a narrow dirt road off the beaten path. I ran down a road lined with banana trees and elephant plants to a frame building with large sliding windows made of carefully joined, ground sea shells. A long-haired, smiling Filipino answered the door quietly.

Hanna was bent over the dining-room table, her fingers picking up dishes listlessly.

Wavy brown hair tumbled over her shoulders, partially concealing the alabaster white of her face. There were deep vertical grooves in her forehead. The skin was tightly drawn over her finely chiseled nose and the curve of her jaw. The head on her stemlike neck drooped like a tulip bending forward. A kimono, carefully patched, swathed a shrunken, doll-like body.

She lifted her head. Her large brown eyes were covered with a dull glaze. A look of incredulity spread over her face. She wiped her eyes with the back of her hand and opened them again.

"They told me you were dead," she said slowly, enunciating each word like a child learning to speak. "Every day for a year and a half I went down to the Philippines Red Cross in Plaza Goiti. They said they didn't know where you were. Every day they said the same thing. They didn't know if you were alive. I didn't believe them. I knew you were alive but they wouldn't tell me. I knew! I knew! I knew!" she said fiercely.

"Then the American Red Cross came with the troops in February, 1945. I went to them. They said you were missing. They said your folks hadn't heard from you for years. They said they thought you were dead. I didn't believe them. They were liars. Everybody was lying to me," she said wildly, her eyes staring.

"Then Japan surrendered. The army here got lists of American prisoners in Japan. Your name was not on the lists. Many P.O.W.'s were brought back from Japan to Manila during the last three weeks. They hadn't seen you. They said you were dead. I believed them," she whispered dully, tears flooding her eyes. "I couldn't eat. I couldn't sleep. They said you were dead and I believed them. All I could see was your dead body," she sobbed hysterically.

I kissed the tears from her eyes, her lips, and her cheeks as she poured out her torrent of sorrow. Huddled in my arms, her wracking sobs ceased.

"Darling," I said, "the nights were long for me, too, in Japan. Sometimes I couldn't sleep. I thought about you and dreamed about you until my heart and head wanted to burst. I had all kinds of dreams. I didn't know if you had died or not. One night I dreamed I saw the Japs melting bells."

"Bells?" she said, raising her head.

"Yes, bells: all kinds of bells from India and China and the States, calesa pony bells and wedding bells."

She looked at me curiously.

"The Japs wanted to melt our wedding bell, Hanna. I tried to stop them but I couldn't. But a big American Marine stopped them."

"In Japan?"

"Yes, in Japan. Then I knew you were all right."

She looked at my gray head, bloodless lips, and starved body. "O.K., Al," she said, stroking my face soothingly, "we'll get the bells out of your brain." She had seen her share of liberated ex-P.O.W.'s in Manila, half cracked.

"No you won't Hanna," I said angrily. "I don't want to get rid of my wedding bell. I want it to ring. Will you marry this broken-down P.O.W. tomorrow?"

Her face flushed as she nodded.

We swapped stories of our experiences since my departure from the Philippines a year and a half ago. Her parents and brother Fred were all right. After his nightmarish experiences in Fort Santiago dungeon, he and Hanna continued their underground work with the guerrilla band the "Blue Eagles." They continued to send food and medicine into American prison camps until the last batch of prisoners was sent from Manila to Japan in December, 1944.

"When did you see your first American soldier?" I asked.

A mischievous grin spread over her taut features. "We were stuck in the middle of an artillery duel for ten days. Most of the houses around here were smashed. Ours was hit by shrapnel. We lived and slept in the air-raid shelter that Fred built in the cellar. On February 5 our Filipino neighbor came in wildly excited and said the Americans were coming. Sure enough, out in the fields we could see tall men coming toward our home. Fred grabbed a prewar bottle of whisky he had been saving for this occasion.

He tore out of the house with me on his heels. A tall young kid, face covered with mud, rifle held in readiness, was slowly coming across the rice paddy.

"We ran toward him, Fred whooping and waving his bottle of whisky. 'Here, Joe,' he said, 'this is for you, I've been saving it for a long time.'

"The soldier's eyes popped wide open. He looked at the bottle of liquor. He looked at me and said: 'Boy, oh boy! What a combination. A bottle of Johnny Walker and a white girl!'"

EPILOGUE

THE GREAT PROPELLERS OF THE Dutch ship Klipfontein throbbed steadily as she plowed through the vast expanse of the Pacific. Aboard were a thousand prisoners of war from Japan and a hundred civilians from the Santo Tomas internment camp. Hanna and I were having a curious honeymoon. She had a cozy cabin for two, but her cabinmate was Sister Vesalia, an American nun.

I slept below deck with the G.I.'s. I had found twenty-five survivors of the Carabao Wallow: Pappy Kiser, our ex-forager, was alive, his pixie face still grinning mischievously; so was half-blind Corporal Holliman, manager of the Carabao Country Club. Most of the other leading characters of the Carabao Wallow had died in snowbound Japan. We had a party. Pappy served ham sandwiches and Coca-Colas instead of unsweetened tea or soggy rice flakes flavored with Japanese tooth powder.

For three weeks we had waited in steaming, rain-soaked, wrecked Manila for passage home. Jai Alai was a shell. Santa Escolastica was burned down. The nuns were gone. Many of them were dead. Some were raped during the last bitter days of fighting in the city.

I searched for my Filipino surgical nurse, Benilda Castañeda, whom I had last seen in Capas when Dr. Takenoshita had driven me to that village in exchange for two pairs of silk stockings. Her sloe eyes glowed a welcome when I found her working at the Philippine Army Hospital at Camp Murphy. From her I learned that most of the nurses from our hospital in Limay had been recaptured alive in Santo Tomas in February, 1945; strapping Frances Nash of Atlanta; Easterling, who had protected Private Liebert after his brain operation with her own body during the bombing on Little Baguio; red-haired Frankie Lewey; and olive-skinned Cassiani, whose baggy trousers I had trimmed down for my own use. Captain Francis, our dentist who married his nurse Arline in a jungle hospital in Bataan, had been temporarily blinded by a bomb explosion. He and his wife were now on their way to the States.

Mr. Baugh, the elderly director of our glee club at Cabanatuan, had been killed by a stray shell after the Yanks had returned to Manila. Max Blouse, the civilian whose arm I had amputated, was back at work organizing a bus company. I couldn't find Sullivan, the engineer, and his mestiza Chinese wife whom Captain Osborne had delivered in Limay. Neither could I find the child, Victoria Bataan Sullivan. Captain Osborne and Andy Rader, our executive officer, were drowned in a "hell ship." Lieutenant Claude Fraley, dentist and forager par excellence of O'Donnell, was alive. Al Mohnac, the dentist with whom I had shared a bottle of pickles in Limay, and Al Poweleit, who had worked the underground with me in O'Donnell, were still in circulation. Ensign Jack Gordon of Atlanta, with whose help I had tried to make imitation Brunswick stew in Cabanatuan, had perished. Our fly-chasing X-ray doctor and Filipino Dr. Medina were still alive. So were the "Gold Dust" twins, Perilman and Gordon, and Private Liebert.

I hunted for Sergeant Moreno, my Filipino mess attendant who had refused to free himself in O'Donnell by signing a pledge of allegiance to Japan. I visited his barrio near burned-out Fort McKinley. The village street was lined with bamboo shacks covered with roofs of nipa palm. Supported on stilts, the dwellings leaned crazily. At the Moreno home I was told that Mrs. Moreno was at the village church.

I entered the darkened confines. At the altar an elderly lady knelt, lips moving silently. She finished her prayers, made the sign of the cross and turned toward me. I signaled to her. She sat on the hard wooden bench beside me, her dark face wrinkled questioningly.

I explained I had known her husband during the Bataan campaign. I had last seen him in Camp O'Donnell before the Christmas of 1942.

"I would like to see him before I leave Manila," I ended.

Her sad brown eyes dropped. "He died six months ago. The Japs worked him in the mines for two years. They tried to break his spirit. He was a very stubborn man. They broke his body."

"You know why he wasn't released?" I asked slowly. She nodded.

"He loved Uncle Sam more than his own life," I said. "And more than his wife and children," she whispered. Tears rolled down her face.

I was at a supper given for me by my friends in Boston. The room was filled with smartly clad young women and their husbands. I had a belly full of clam chowder, boiled lobster, and apple pie. I was warm, flushed, and slightly crocked. Hanna and I stood around talking. My friends wanted to hear some of my experiences. I told a few anecdotes that had a humorous twist.

A young matron with full lips and fuller bosom remarked brightly: "Of course, war and prison life must have been terrible, Al. But think of all the experience you men had. You must have learned a lot."

The room faded. I saw many pictures:

Doctors, dentists, and medics unloading supplies at Limay, sweating like stevedores.

Half a dozen surgeons doing crude, hasty surgery because there wasn't time to do their best work.

Out in the jungles of Bataan, specialist in internal medicine, Lieutenant Maw Kelly digging a latrine; lisping, expert chest surgeon Captain Barshop setting up a hospital tent; dental surgeon Lieutenant Al Mohnac loading litters into an ambulance.

Torn limbs flying through the air to lodge in the branches of the lonesome pine at Little Baguio as a bomb landed in the wards; Little

Lieutenant Willie Perilman coming out of his minor surgery shack to puke.

The gaunt Lang brothers trying to force a little rice down the throat of a dying soldier in St. Peter's Ward in O'Donnell. Haggard Father Budenbrook, silver-haired Tony Escota, his wife, and Spanish Mr. Mencarini marching off to die in Fort Santiago dungeon.

Prisoners dying of suffocation from diphtheria in the Zero Ward of Cabanatuan.

A blond aviator on a peg leg trading a ragged sweater for some peanuts in Bilibid.

The Spider in Shinagawa treating Seaman Fry's ulcer of the stomach by striking him in the belly with his fist.

In Omori, Captain Nelson Kaufman, with face bruised, standing rigidly at attention while the Bird wound up.

Skeleton-like wrecks huddling in their filthy rags in Mitsushima. The faces of dozens of doctors, dentists, nurses, and medics in their graves in the Philippines and Japan; the face of Captain Bulfamonte on Corregidor who was still missing when the Yanks returned.

Three doctors, former P.O.W.'s, permanently cracked-up, living their forlorn lives in an insane asylum.

Colonel Adamo, with his silver hair and wraithlike body, unable to return to active surgical practice.

Colonel Duckworth dying of a heart attack in Atlanta after his recapture by the Yanks.

"Yes," I whispered softly. "We learned a lot."

Near the Bobby Jones Golf Course in Atlanta we built a tiny white ranch house. It nestled in the shade of a giant lonesome pine similar to the one that had towered over the surgical pavilion at Little Baguio. A rustic sign swayed in the breeze on the freshly planted lawn. It read "Carabao Wallow."

A year in the States had done good things to me. From a low of one hundred and five pounds I was back to a hundred and seventy, which covered my five-foot-ten frame too amply. A beaten and battered and bomb-concussed brain was slowly coming to life. A fractured windpipe and ruptured eardrums, a stiff wrist and a partially paralyzed face had all responded to treatment after seven months at the Lowell General Hospital in Massachusetts. A heart weakened by chronic beriberi was beginning to beat normally. Even the fringe of gray hair above the ears showed signs of thickening.

My folks had met me at South Station in Boston. The little gray-haired lady I had seen in my mind's eye during the Yom Kippur service in Cabanatuan had turned snow white. My father's face had aged. Only his blue eyes retained a sparkle of vigor. They wept a little. I wept a little. They had heard rumors of my death: killed by bombs in Bataan; died of dysentery in O'Donnell; drowned in a "hell ship"; starved to death in Japan. They had clung blindly to their faith in my return.

I adjusted myself slowly to the American scene. I quit sitting tailor fashion on the floor. Badgered by my wife, I threw away my bamboo "butt shooter." In the lobbies of theaters and hotels I still edge up to the sand-covered "go-boons" and eye half-smoked cigarettes longingly. I still eye the bones and meat scraps in the garbage can at home.

Hanna came into the small library where I was writing. Life in the States had agreed with her. She had lost the haggard gray of her skin. The dormant animation of her face reawakened. Her five-foot-two frame was a constant series of eye-caressing moves. She was beginning to bulge ever so suspiciously about the middle.

"There's a letter from Greece," she said as her arms slipped around my neck.

It was from Dr. Dick Whitfield, British medical officer, who had been with me at Mitsushima. I read the letter aloud:

DEAR AL:

You will undoubtedly be surprised to receive this letter from Greece. Things are still so unsettled in England that I've taken a job in Athens working for UNRRA. I've heard from most of the British officers you knew in Mitsushima, including Captain Gordon, John Dunlop, and Pinky Williams. They're all right and send their best.

I imagine you've heard the news about the war-crime trials, but it's worth repeating even if you have. Your friend, General Homma, who was responsible for the death of 50,297 American and Filipino prisoners of war, has had his neck stretched. "Little Glass Eye" is doing a life sentence at hard labor. "Big Glass Eye," the "Punk," "Buick," Dr. Fugi and the "Spider" are in Sugamo Prison, Tokyo, awaiting trial for their lives. So is the "Goon." He asked Sergeant George Piel, who helped us put the "Bird" on "gravy train," to intercede for him. George wrote and told the "Goon" how "you used to keep me standing at attention from dawn until dusk trying to make me squeal on my fellow prisoners." George had a few suggestions he gave the "Goon" as to where he would get help—none of them printable.

As far as I can learn the "Bird" is still at large. Your cops haven't caught up with him yet.

Does your wife object to your wearing your hat and socks in bed on cold nights? Mine threatens to divorce me if I don't break the habit.

Let me hear from you soon.

Yours,

DICK

"Do you?" I asked Hanna.
She nodded. A mischievous smile played over her face.

EXTRAS

All photographs are part of the Alfred A. Weinstein papers, courtesy of Emory
University Manuscript, Archives, and Rare Book Library.

City of Atlanta Mayor, Ivan Allen, Jr., presents an award to Al.

Al at Fort McKinley in the Philippines,
December 8, 1941

Al in uniform

Hanna Kaunitz in the Philippines

Christmas 1944 at Mistsushima Prison Camp, Japan
(Al is third to the left)

Al at the Holmes Street apartments he developed for veterans in
Atlanta, 1949

Al at Holmes Street apartment party reminiscing about carrying
night soil, 1949

Al with actress Kim Novak

Hanna in front of **Barbed-Wire Surgeon** at bookstore

Ronnie, Al, Elsa, and Mack (left to right)

FROM THE FAMILY

MY FATHER DIED IN 1964 right after my 14th birthday, but I still have vivid memories of what a good dad and person he was. How he managed to fit in all he did every week is beyond me. He had his own private medical practice as a General Practitioner with a 5 1/2 day work week, was on call at night, wrote almost every evening--either working on his second book, The Scalpel's Edge, or one of the many articles published in papers and magazines, and was active in a variety of philanthropic and volunteer positions. He still made time every Saturday for date night with my mom, and Sunday he took out the kids.

I was blessed with a father who liked to discuss everything in the world and who never spoke down to me. Some of my best memories involve our after-dinner walks along Peachtree Creek and going on "night calls" with him to the hotels where he was a house doctor. He had an old Oldsmobile with a bench front seat where we would sit with our dog, Fluffy, between us and all eat Spanish peanuts together. Fluffy adored my dad and would lean against him during the drive, insuring that Dad would reach his patients with a liberal brushing of white fur on the right side of his suit.

Dad was involved in many traditional service and fundraising organizations in both the Jewish and secular Atlanta communities. He also gave talks at churches and other organizations about brotherhood. He won the Mayor's "Good Neighbor" award. However, the thing that gives me the most pride was his quiet service in the African American community in the 1950's, when this was rare. His medical office had one of the first (if not the first) integrated waiting rooms in the city and an integrated staff. This led the KKK to our phone for threatening calls. He gave financial awards to outstanding nurses at the then all-African American Hughes Spaulding Pavilion, one of the hospitals where he worked. But most important to me is the personal assistance he gave to members of his staff to allow them to advance.

The women who functioned as nurses, lab & X-ray techs, and administrators of ear and eye tests in his practice were

African American. These women all started out as his office cleaning ladies. When my dad saw that they had intelligence and attention to detail, he trained them for more professional positions. They were valuable and loyal employees and very kind to me on my regular visits to "help" at the office. If this epilogue finds its way into the hands of Catherine or Margaret or your families, I would so appreciate your contacting me through the publisher. I think of you often with great fondness.

I had only read Barbed-Wire Surgeon once before my dad died, and to me as a young teen, it was an adventure story with my dad as the hero (though he did not write about himself in this way). Now I read it with a deeper understanding of the sacrifices, torture, starvation, and especially the profound psychological toll he suffered. I marvel that my dad could have endured 3 1/2 years of this and come out of it as the loving father and sound individual that I remember. I'm sure there are ways that his experiences affected him that I didn't perceive, but there is no one left from his generation to ask.

I do know that one way he dealt with the POW trauma was to investigate post-war Japan. In 1962, my dad returned to Japan with my mother, Hanna, to make his peace with the Japanese nation and to seek out and give assistance to the families of guards who were decent to the POWs. He then published a magazine article about his journey.

There is always the danger of sanctifying someone in this kind of posthumous writing. My dad was far from a saint. He was a strong-willed and passionate man who was demanding of others as well as himself, had little tact, swore, and was prone to loud outbursts of temper. I was fortunate never to be the target of these, but I certainly heard the house reverberate with them!

As I write this epilogue and tribute, I am almost ten years older than my dad was when he died. I have two adult sons (the elder named for him) who remind me of him in various ways. I am thrilled for them and for my brothers, Mack and

Ron Weinstein, and their children, to see Barbed-Wire Surgeon re-published in print and eBook as a continuing tribute both to him and all the courageous POWs with whom he served.

He will always be my hero.

- Elsa Weinstein

I FEEL VERY PRIVILEGED AND honored to have been the son of Al Weinstein. My brother, Mack, and I were orphaned when we were very young and were adopted a few years later. Dad made me feel loved after many years of feeling abandoned.

I remember with great fondness my father's dedication to making other people's lives better regardless of their faith or skin color. That was very hard to do in Atlanta, Georgia, during the segregation years. He dedicated his life to healing people's lives both physically and mentally and was always concerned for people less fortunate than he was.

Dad always expressed the importance of a good education to all of his children. I didn't excel in academics; however, my forte was athletics. In high school, I lettered in three sports. I also played football in college. Even though my father was not a big sports fan, he attended all of my games possible. He respected my athletic ability and that was important to me.

I also remember when I was a young boy about 12 years old, I was at the swimming pool and got on the high dive and slipped backwards onto the cement. My father took me into the locker room and he got his doctors bag and fixed the gash in my head right on the spot. I had a full recovery.

As a very young child I had very bad asthma attacks almost on a daily basis. When that happened my father would come into my bedroom a give me a shot and the asthma would always clear up. I guess you could say he helped to save my life. I will always miss my father.

- Ron Weinstein

IN FEBRUARY OF 1964, I was in the U.S. army assigned to a communications battalion in Darmstadt, Germany. I will always remember the evening that I was assigned to operate a section that had several communication networks, one of which was a Red Cross network. Early in the morning, I received a teletype from a Red Cross office for the Company Commander. After transcribing the tape to printed form, I went to take it to the Commander's office. I glanced down at the message and the words seemed to jump off the page: "Inform Sergeant Weinstein that his father passed away yesterday afternoon."

As I searched for memories of my father, I remembered the family trip we took to the mountains. I remembered the trip we took as a family to Florida. I remembered the times that my brother and I went with Dad to baseball games to watch the Atlanta Crackers play. I remember going to 'help' at the office and how he loved to teach us.

I remembered how big we felt when we got to dress in surgical gowns and go into the operating room and watch him operate. I remembered attending with him when he was honored by groups such as the Jewish War Veterans for his work for them.

But these were just personal memories that were shared with my brother Ron and my sister Elsa.

It was not until later that I learned much more about my father from his many friends and admirers. After my father's death, I went on several book-signing events for his second book, The Scalpel's Edge. Everywhere I went, people were very eager to tell me of the many noble things that he had done. They told about his fight for civil rights when it was not so popular in Georgia. They told about how he helped to establish the first African American nursing school at the Hughes Spaulding Pavilion of Grady Hospital in Atlanta, and how he helped to build a housing community for veterans in Atlanta. They told of his work in the synagogue and the Jewish community. They told of his work for the returning veterans.

My dad did not talk too much about his imprisonment in POW camps and punishment camp. Once when I asked him about those times he replied that people could take away your freedom and they could take away your freedom to go anywhere you wanted, but they could never take away your integrity or your character.

Thanks, Dad.

- Mack Weinstein

Alfred Weinstein's "Somber Tapestry"

ALFRED ABRAHAM WEINSTEIN ENLISTED IN the US Army in response to Franklin Delano Roosevelt's declaration of a state of national emergency in 1940. According to his daughter Elsa Weinstein, a Harvard-educated doctor, he requested not to be posted to the European Theater because he did not want to be captured by the Nazis. Instead, he went to the Philippines and both suffered and witnessed horrors and atrocities equal in sadistic creativity under the Nazis' Axis ally, Imperial Japan. Despite his brilliant post-war medical career, Dr. Weinstein could not put his military past behind him, and so he felt compelled to write *Barbed-Wire Surgeon*.

It's easy to see why *Barbed-Wire Surgeon* was a bestseller and Book-of-the-Month Club selection. In his engaging, by turns humorous and grim writing style, Dr. Weinstein chronicled the horrifying and occasionally sublime details of the Philippine Campaign and its aftermath. There is another reason why *Barbed-Wire Surgeon* was such a huge hit: The families of hundreds of thousands of servicemen (and servicewomen!) endured agonizing years in which they waited for news of their loved one, MIA in the Philippines. A few escaped the Philippines in 1942— a submarine load of US military nurses escaped from Corregidor just before it was surrendered to the Japanese, and made it first to Australia, and then home to the US. They and a precious few others could report what life had been like on Bataan and Corregidor. But little news was available between the surrender of Corregidor in May 1942 and liberation of the Philippines in 1944-45. There must have been a large audience for those who wanted, even needed, to know what had happened to the "expendable" troops in the Philippines.

Published just three years after liberation, Dr. Weinstein's book was not only one of the best WWII memoirs, but one of the earliest to tell the entire campaign. As Weinstein says, *Barbed-*

Wire Surgeon is a "somber tapestry," but the darkness of his memoir is brightened by his love for Hanna, which, as he says in *Surgeon's* dedication, "kept a spark of life flickering in a dying body."

Hanna Kaunitz Weinstein's story is nearly as compelling as her husband's. Hanna, her brother Fritz; her mother, Elsa; and her father, Arpad, were *Manilaners*, European Jews who found sanctuary in the Philippines. Hanna's brother Hans, a highly respected doctor, had recognized early on the threat the Nazis posed for Jews and, after a world-wide search, found a job offer in Manila. During the Anschluss (Nazi forcible annexation of Austria in 1938), Hanna realized that her native Vienna, which she had loved as a place of gracious gentility, was a sinkhole of virulent anti-Semitism. Fortunately, Hans was able to sponsor the rest of the family to come to Manila, where they became four of 1,300+ *Manilaners* who found a home in Manila. Hanna had met Alfred in 1941 at Heacock's department store where she had worked as a sales girl, and they dated until the war separated them.

In one of WWII's many ironies, the Japanese, during their Occupation of the Philippines, categorized civilians strictly by consulting their passports. Thus Dutch, Polish, Americans, and the British were imprisoned in the internment camp on the University of Santo Tomas campus in Manila. Germans and Austrians, on the other hand, were designated allies, despite the large "J" for Jude stamped on many passports. Even German Jews who held expired passports (they had been denied passport renewal because were Jews) were often exempt from the cruelties the Japanese regularly wreaked upon Filipino and other civilians. Some of the *Manilaners* such as Hanna and Fritz Kaunitz took advantage of their Axis "allied" status to join the underground, risking their lives in the process.

In part to help Alfred, Hanna joined three different resistance groups, including the Blue Eagle guerrillas, and helped smuggle money, medicine, food, and clothing to Alfred and other POWs into the prison camps. After the war, he testified to the FBI that Hanna "risked her life to smuggle food and medicine into Camp

O'Donnell and Cabanatuan POW camps for me and for the use of sick and dying POWs whom I felt a deep responsibility as a physician and officer." He emphasized that Hanna continued her work for the resistance groups despite the arrest and execution of many of her fellow resistance workers. In a letter Alfred wrote to his brother, Dan, just after liberation, Alfred stated that Hanna and Fritz "saved hundreds of lives, including my own" by smuggling food and medicine to "Camp O'Donnell where 20,000 Americans and Filipinos died of starvation in six months." As Weinstein relates in *Barbed-Wire Surgeon*, Hanna was targeted by the Japanese during a Kempetai campaign to root out guerrillas, but she escaped arrest.

Fritz joined the Blue Eagles as well as Hanna, concentrating his efforts on aiding American and other Allied internees at the Santo Tomas internment camp. As with Hanna, Fritz had a personal reason for focusing his underground activities: his friend and business partner, Frank O'Brien, was imprisoned in Santo Tomas along with his wife and young son. Like many of the internees, Frank's weight dwindled to around 100 pounds during the Occupation, and it is likely that he, like many other internees, would have died of malnutrition.

In a 1946 letter to the Army's Recovered Personnel Division, Weinstein wrote that during the Occupation, Fritz "gave tens of thousands of pesos of his own money to these [Santo Tomas] internees to help them keep alive. Many of them were complete strangers to him." Fritz was not as lucky as Hanna; he was arrested by the dreaded Kempetai and imprisoned in Fort Santiago. There he was tortured but escaped through the help of a sympathetic Japanese guard who, of all things, had a fondness for the Viennese music Fritz would sing for him.

Fritz and Frank O'Brien both survived the war, and afterward moved to the US and renewed their business partnership. O'Brien served as Fritz's best man when Fritz married his wife, Jeanne, who said that for decades after the war Fritz carried a photograph (now lost) of the Kaunitz and O'Brien office building in Manila, destroyed by the Japanese.

Despite his almost cherubic appearance, Alfred Weinstein was, as the saying goes, one tough customer. He survived the Bataan Campaign, the Death March, three POW camps in the Philippines, transport aboard one of the "Hell Ships" to Japan, and three more POW camps in Japan before being liberated in September 1945.

Upon liberation, the Army sent liberated POWs home to recuperate. Like most of the liberated POWs, Weinstein was a very sick man: he weighed less than 100 pounds and had dysentery, near fatal malnutrition, and a severe case of beriberi, along with a windpipe broken by a sadistic Japanese guard. Instead of a quick flight home, Weinstein insisted on being returned to Manila, where, miraculously, he found Hanna alive and well (approximately 10% of Manila's residents died during the month-long Battle for Manila, February-March, 1945). They married immediately, and after Alfred had recuperated from the physical injuries of his POW years, Alfred and Hanna settled in Atlanta, Georgia, where Alfred became a prominent and highly respected doctor, maintaining a private practice while also teaching at Emory University's Grady Hospital.

Dr. Weinstein waged a long-term battle against Jim Crow (official and unofficial rules maintaining African-American subordination in the American South), having the first integrated waiting room in Atlanta; training African-American menial laborers in basic medical technology so that they could get better-paying jobs; and founding an award program for "colored" nurses in Grady Hospital.

Dr. Weinstein also took his war against Jim Crow outside Atlanta's medical community. Shortly after he returned from the war, Weinstein and a few other private investors, with some government funding, built the Holmes Street apartment complex to ease the post-war housing crunch. Because veterans often faced accusations of causing offensive noise levels due to playing musical instruments or having children, the Holmes Street apartments explicitly welcomed families and musical ex-GIs. Couples who had children were given birth bonuses, which were increased for twins.

A December 16, 1949, *Atlanta Constitution* advertisement for the Holmes Street Apartments encouraged children and musical instruments, but excluded members of "anti-American hate organizations like the Ku Klux Klan," stating, "Any tenant who joins one of these outfits must vacate his premises in 30 days and make room for somebody who believes in the brotherhood of men." Weinstein received threats for these advertisements. Refusing to be cowed, Weinstein said, "I gave them my office and my home address and I told them I still had the .45 I used to shoot carabao with."

Given his three plus years in Japanese POW camps, one may be skeptical that Alfred really did have a gun he had used in the Philippines (or that he had ever shot carabao with it, as carabao were essential farming livestock), but one has to admire Weinstein's stand against the late 1940s KKK. The Holmes Street Apartment complex received wide media attention, including an article in the January 2, 1950 edition of *Time* magazine.

In addition to his private practice and his teaching at Grady Hospital, Weinstein was very active in charitable work through various organizations, especially the Jewish War Veterans of Atlanta. In addition to *Barbed-Wire Surgeon*, he wrote a fictional novel, *The Scalpel's Edge* (published posthumously, in 1967) about racial politics in Atlanta's medical community, as well as dozens of articles for magazines and newspapers such as the *Southern Israelite,* the *Atlanta Journal and Constitution,* the *Harvard Medical Alumni Bulletin,* and the "Commander's Column" for the Atlanta Jewish War Veterans (Post #112).

Despite the many horrors Alfred Weinstein had seen and suffered personally during the war, he maintained a lifelong commitment to basic human decency and fairness. In particular, he remembered the kindnesses shown him by various Japanese guards during his POW years. In September 1945, as Alfred and his fellow prisoners prepared to leave the Mitsushima POW camp in Japan, they gave two of the camp's kind officers, "Boy

Scout" (Nishi Gaki) and "One Arm" (Yokichi Nishino), money, clothes, and a letter stating that they were "good Japs" who had helped the prisoners. Alfred corresponded with "Nishino San" until the end of Nishino's life, and with his family thereafter, and sent the Nishino family money as late as 1960. Alfred also corresponded with and sent medicine to "Boy Scout" (Nishigaki) until Nishigaki's death in 1952.

In some ways, Alfred Weinstein spent the rest of his life moving ahead: his life-long campaign to overturn Jim Crow in Georgia and his repeated publications urging all Americans to renounce all forms of prejudice and bigotry are examples of his commitment to forward thinking rooted in concrete action. In some ways, however, Alfred Weinstein spent the rest of his life coming to terms with the past. On his honeymoon cruise from Manila to the States aboard a medical transport ship, Dr. Weinstein treated the desperately ill veterans of the Philippine campaign, many of them friends and comrades from the Bataan and POW days. While his bride shared a cabin with a nun (it was in this way that the new Mrs. Weinstein was able to travel to the US aboard a military transport ship—one wonders how the nun secured passage), Alfred treated the USAFFE veterans. Between almost obsessive bouts of eating and marveling at the creature comforts of clean sheets, real beds, and smiling nurses, the frail but recuperating survivors of Bataan and Corregidor shared their stories with Dr. Weinstein. This is how Weinstein collected the staggering amount of detail he would compile into *Barbed-Wire Surgeon*. He had kept several diaries during the war, but they all had been destroyed or lost during the harrowing war years. On the trip home, Weinstein and his USAFFE comrades engaged in what we would now call group therapy, rehashing their trials, sorrows, huge losses, and precious victories throughout the three and a half POW years.

The Weinsteins' modest house in Atlanta was nicknamed "Carabao Wallow," the name of the Cabanatuan POW camp "country club" Weinstein and other doctors had established to lift the men's morale. Carabao Wallow in Atlanta became a mecca for USAFFE veterans, and the Weinsteins maintained an active correspondence with veterans who planned trips across the nation to visit and rendezvous with other veterans.

Perhaps the most poignant example of Weinstein's coming to terms with his past was in returning to Japan. Although he chose not to testify at the war crimes trials against Japanese officials, in 1962, just two years before he died, Weinstein published an article in the *Atlanta Journal and Constitution Magazine* about how "I Made My Peace with Japanese War Criminals."

By then both "Nishigaki San" and "Nishino San" (San being a Japanese term of respect) had died, and Weinstein visited their widows, who are pictured with Alfred in the magazine article with gifts they gave him for his family. Answering his own rhetorical question of why it had taken him 18 years to visit Japan, Alfred gave not the expected answer (i.e., that it had taken him that long to be psychologically able to visit the country where he had suffered so greatly, and so many comrades had died needlessly) but instead that "I'd wanted to see another generation of Japanese young folks grow up so that I could meet them and say 'I cannot hate you because of the sins committed by your fathers.'"

Weinstein ended the article not just with the observation that, having visited Japan in person, he was laying his own inner demons to rest, but with the lessons Nishino San and other kindhearted Japanese taught him: "that man can remain compassionate, if he wills it, even when surrounded by a mass of evil men."

While *Barbed-Wire Surgeon* remains, in my opinion, one of the best and most engaging of the Philippine WWII memoirs—and thus illuminates a chapter of history that has fallen into obscurity—its lasting lesson, just as vital today as it was during the war, is that humans of every race, creed, and nationality are capable of the extremes of savagery and heroism, and that malevolence and benevolence are choices we make.

By Sharon Delmendo

Alfred, Hanna, and *An Open Door: Holocaust Haven in the Philippines*

BARBED-WIRE SURGEON IS A FASCINATING story, and one of the best WWII memoirs. Alfred Weinstein and Hanna Kaunitz Weinstein are part of a larger story, and one even less well known: that of the at least 1,300 European Jews who found shelter from the Holocaust in the Philippines. Following the Spanish-American and Philippine-American Wars, the Philippines was an American colony. In 1935, the US established the Philippine Commonwealth, a ten year transitional period during which Filipinos would restructure the government and economy for full independence, slated for July 4, 1946. During the Commonwealth period, the US retained power over key governmental elements, including foreign affairs, the granting of visas, and national defense. During the Philippine Commonwealth era, there were loopholes and grey areas that provided the potential for the admittance of European refugees.

As the Nazi's control over Europe expanded and tightened, hundreds of thousands of Jews made the agonizing decision to leave their homelands, only to find doors all over the world shut to them. The Philippines was one of the few willing to take large numbers of Jewish refugees. Commonwealth President Manuel Quezon was willing to take tens of thousands of Jewish refugees into the Philippines—up to one million, by one report—but the US State Department, which had the power to grant visas to US territories, including the Philippines, was quietly but firmly opposed to admitting significant numbers of Jewish immigrants.

President Quezon, working with US High Commissioner Paul McNutt, Manila's Jewish Refugee Committee, and American and European Jewish relief organizations and benefactors, worked diligently to exploit the loopholes in the Commonwealth political structure and fund the immigration and resettlement of thousands of Jewish refugees. Hanna Kaunitz and her family (brothers Hans and Fritz and parents Elsa and Arpad) were five of the over 1,300 "Manilaners" (Jewish refugees who found shelter in the Philippines).

Some of the Manilaners, like Hanna and Fritz Kaunitz, joined resistance organizations during the Japanese Occupation of the Philippines. Other Manilaners such as Ben Hessenberger, who appears briefly in *Barbed-Wire Surgeon,* enlisted in the USAFFE (United States Armed Forces of the Far East), and suffered many of the same travails Alfred Weinstein so eloquently portrayed in *Barbed-Wire Surgeon.*

I read *Barbed-Wire Surgeon* in the course of researching my second book, *Pacific Theater,* a study of WWII films set in the Philippines and filmed in Hollywood while the war was in progress. When independent filmmaker Noel "Sonny" Izon asked me to partner with him on a documentary film on the Manilaners, I shelved *Pacific Theater* to work on the documentary and to write the companion book, *In Time of Need, An Open Door: Holocaust Haven in the Philippines.*

For more information about *An Open Door,* please visit our website, www.anopendoormovie.com.

Sharon Delmendo
Professor of English
St. John Fisher College
Rochester, NY 14618
sdelmendo@sjfc.edu

CPSIA information can be obtained
at www.ICGtesting.com
Printed in the USA
BVHW032322240223
659219BV00006B/363